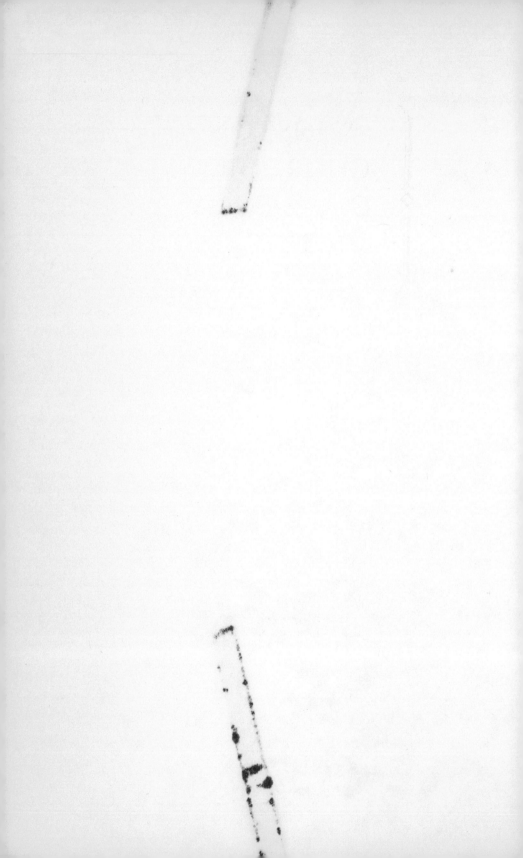

WINSTON CHURCHILL On AMERICA And BRITAIN

WINSTON CHURCHILL

on AMERICA and BRITAIN

A SELECTION OF HIS THOUGHTS ON ANGLO-AMERICAN RELATIONS

Foreword by LADY CHURCHILL
Preface by W. AVERELL HARRIMAN

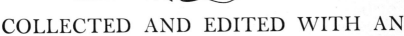

COLLECTED AND EDITED WITH AN
INTRODUCTION BY KAY HALLE

WALKER AND COMPANY
New York

First published in the United States of America in 1970 by the Walker Publishing Company, Inc.
Published simultaneously in Canada by The Ryerson Press, Toronto.

ISBN: 0-8027-0323-2

Library of Congress Catalog Card Number: 71-126111

Printed in the United States of America.

Designed by Carl Weiss.

ACKNOWLEDGMENTS

My profound thanks to Elizabeth Beverly for her invaluable help with the arrangement and typing of this Collection.

I am grateful to the publishers and others in this list that follows for their gracious permission for the use of extracts and illustrations that appear in this Jubilee Volume.

ATHENEUM PUBLISHERS:

HAROLD NICOLSON, DIARIES AND LETTERS 1930–1939, edited by Nigel Nicolson. Harold Nicolson's Diaries and Letters copyright © 1966 by William Collins Sons & Co., Ltd. Reprinted by permission of Atheneum Publishers.

CASSELL AND COMPANY LTD.

WINSTON S. CHURCHILL WAR SPEECHES, 1939–45, Compiled by Charles Eade, Vol. III. Copyright in this edition Cassell and Company Ltd. 1951.

EUROPE UNITE, Speeches 1947 and 1948 by Winston S. Churchill. Edited by Randolph S. Churchill, Cassell and Company Ltd. 1950.

THE UNWRITTEN ALLIANCE, Speeches 1953–1959 by Winston S. Churchill, edited by Randolph S. Churchill. © in this collection, Cassell and Company Ltd. 1961.

THE CONDE NAST PUBLICATIONS INC.:

VANITY FAIR, 1931.

Acknowledgments   [v]

COWARD-MC'CANN, INC.:

Reprinted by permission of Coward-McCann, Inc. from MY 21 YEARS IN
THE WHITE HOUSE by Alonzo Fields. Copyright © 1961 by Alonzo Fields.

DUELL, SLOAN AND PEARCE, INC.:

F.D.R.: HIS PERSONAL LETTERS, edited by Elliott Roosevelt. Copyright
© 1948 by Duell, Sloan and Pearce. Reprinted by permission of Hawthorn
Books.

LESLIE FREWIN PUBLISHERS LIMITED:

The extract from THE WIT OF SIR WINSTON is reproduced by kind permission of the authors, Adam Sykes and Iain Sproat, and the publishers, Leslie
Frewin Publishers Limited. Copyright © 1965 by Adam Sykes and Iain Sproat.

FUNK & WAGNALLS CO., INC.:

I WAS WINSTON CHURCHILL'S PRIVATE SECRETARY by Phyllis Moir.
Copyright 1941 by Wilfred Funk, Inc.

THE HAMLYN PUBLISHING GROUP LIMITED:

Reproduced by permission of the Hamlyn Publishing Group Limited from
THE RIVER WAR by Winston Churchill.

HARCOURT BRACE JAVONOVICH, INC.:

Reprinted by permission of Harcourt, Brace & World, Inc. from a BIOGRA-
PHY OF EDWARD MARSH by Christopher Hassell; copyright 1959, by
the author.

HARPER & ROW, PUBLISHERS, INC.:

THE CHURCHILLS, FROM THE DEATH OF MARLBOROUGH TO THE
PRESENT by A. L. Rowse; copyright © 1958 by A. L. Rowse.

ROOSEVELT AND HOPKINS, AN INTIMATE DIARY by Robert E.
Sherwood; copyright 1949, 1950 by Robert E. Sherwood.

HOUGHTON MIFFLIN COMPANY

THE SECOND WORLD WAR by Winston S. Churchill; the following vol-
umes copyrighted by Houghton Mifflin: III. THE GRAND ALLIANCE, 1950;
IV. THE HINGE OF FATE, 1950; V. CLOSING THE RING, 1951; VI.
TRIUMPH AND TRAGEDY, 1953.

THE SINEWS OF PEACE by Winston S. Churchill, edited by Randolph S.
Churchill, 1949.

IN THE BALANCE by Winston S. Churchill, edited by Randolph S. Churchill, 1952.

STEMMING THE TIDE by Winston S. Churchill, edited by Randolph S.
Churchill, 1954.

ALFRED A. KNOPF, INC.:

THE WAR AND COLONEL WARDEN by Gerald Pawle; copyright © 1963 by the author.

LITTLE, BROWN & COMPANY:

THE UNRELENTING STRUGGLE, War Speeches by the Rt. Hon. Winston S. Churchill, C.H., M.P., Compiled by Charles Eade. Copyright 1942 by Winston S. Churchill.

THE END OF THE BEGINNING, War Speeches by the Rt. Hon. Winston S. Churchill, C.H., M.P., Compiled by Charles Eade. Copyright 1943 by Winston S. Churchill.

ONWARDS TO VICTORY, War Speeches by the Rt. Hon. Winston S. Churchill, C.H., M.P., Compiled by Charles Eade. Copyright 1944 by Winston S. Churchill.

THE DAWN OF LIBERATION, War Speeches by the Rt. Hon. Winston S. Churchill, C.H., M.P., Compiled by Charles Eade. Copyright 1945 by Winston S. Churchill.

G. P. PUTNAM'S SONS:

STEP BY STEP by the Rt. Hon. Winston S. Churchill, C.H., M.P. Copyright 1939 by Winston S. Churchill.

WHILE ENGLAND SLEPT by the Rt. Hon. Winston S. Churchill, C.H., M.P., with a Preface and Notes by Randolph S. Churchill. Copyright 1938 by Winston S. Churchill.

BLOOD, SWEAT, AND TEARS by the Rt. Hon. Winston S. Churchill, C.H., M.P., with a Preface and Notes by Randolph S. Churchill, M.P. Copyright 1941 by Winston S. Churchill.

CHARLES SCRIBNER'S SONS:

Reprinted with the permission of Charles Scribner's Sons from AMID THESE STORMS by Winston Churchill. Copyright 1932 Charles Scribner's Sons; renewal copyright © 1960 Winston S. Churchill.

Reprinted with the permission of Charles Scribner's Sons from A ROVING COMMISSION: My Early Life by Winston S. Churchill. Copyright 1930 Charles Scribner's Sons; renewal copyright © 1958 Winston Churchill.

Reprinted with the permission of Charles Scribner's Sons from THE AFTER-MATH, 1918–1928 by Winston Churchill. Copyright 1929 Charles Scribner's Sons; renewal copyright © 1957 Winston S. Churchill.

Reprinted with the permission of Charles Scribner's Sons from Volume I, THE WORLD CRISIS by Winston Churchill. Copyright 1923, 1927 Charles Scribner's Sons; renewal copyright 1951, 1955 Winston S. Churchill.

SIMON & SCHUSTER, INC.:

WINSTON CHURCHILL'S SECRET SESSION SPEECHES, Compiled and with introductory notes by Charles Eade, editor of *The Sunday Dispatch*. Copyright 1946 by Simon & Schuster, Inc.

Acknowledgments [vii]

THE VIKING PRESS, INC.:

IF, OR HISTORY REWRITTEN by Winston Churchill. Copyright 1931 by The Viking Press, Inc.

A. P. WATT & SON:

AN AMBASSADOR OF PEACE by Viscount D'Abernon, originally published by Hodder and Stoughton. Reprinted by permission of A. P. Watt & Son for the Estate of Lord D'Abernon.

THE WORLD PUBLISHING COMPANY:

IRREPRESSIBLE CHURCHILL, A Treasury of Winston Churchill's Wit, selected and compiled with historical commentary by Kay Halle. Copyright © 1966 by Kay Halle.

MAGAZINES:

BBC—*The Listener.* An extract from the BBC Television broadcast 'As I Remember'—Baroness Asquith in conversation with Kenneth Harris, April 30th, 1967, and subsequently published in *The Listener.*

Collier's. "The Shattered Cause of Temperance," August 13, 1932; "Land of Corn and Lobsters," August 5, 1933; "While the World Watches President Franklin D. Roosevelt," December 29, 1934; "What Good's a Constitution?" August 22, 1936.

Saturday Review, London. "American Intervention in Cuba," March 7, 1896.

Strand Magazine. "The American Mind and Ours," August, 1931.

NEWSPAPERS:

Cleveland Press. February 4, 1932.

Daily Mail, London. "My New York Misadventure," Part I, January 4, 1932; "I Was Conscious Through It All," Part II, January 5, 1932.

Daily Telegraph and *Morning Post,* London. "What I Saw and Heard in America," November 18, 1929; "What I Saw in America of Prohibition," December 2, 1929; "Fever of Speculation in America," December 9, 1929; "Vastness of America's Industry," January 27, 1930.

News of the World, London. "The Union of the English-Speaking Peoples," May 15, 1938.

WINSTON S. CHURCHILL SERVED AS
DEPUTY PRESIDENT OF THE
ENGLISH-SPEAKING UNION
OF BRITAIN AND THE COMMONWEALTH
FROM 1954 UNTIL HIS DEATH.
AT A DINNER
HELD BY THE ENGLISH-SPEAKING UNION
ON JUNE 8, 1954, HE SAID:

*"The English-Speaking Union
plays an active and vital part in the whole
vast process of bringing the English-speaking
nations of the world into unity and keeping
them in effective harmony."*

THIS VOLUME IS DEDICATED
TO THE GOLDEN JUBILEE OF
THE ENGLISH-SPEAKING UNION
IN HONOR OF
WINSTON S. CHURCHILL
THE FIRST ATLANTIC CITIZEN
WHO, BY AN ACT OF THE CONGRESS
OF THE UNITED STATES
AND A PROCLAMATION BY
PRESIDENT JOHN F. KENNEDY
WAS CREATED
AN HONORARY AMERICAN CITIZEN
ON APRIL 9, 1963

CONTENTS

SIGNIFICANT SPEECHES BY
WINSTON CHURCHILL IN AMERICA

SPEECHES TO AND ABOUT AMERICA BY
WINSTON CHURCHILL FROM LONDON

AMERICAN HISTORY RETOLD BY
WINSTON CHURCHILL

WINSTON CHURCHILL, JOURNALIST—
ON AMERICA

FOREWORD

Nothing engaged the heart and mind of my Husband throughout his life more than his deeply held belief that only good could come to the world through a strong and close English-Speaking Union. He thought of himself as "a child of both worlds," and indeed he was, and would say of that Special Relationship, "If we are together nothing is impossible. If we are divided all will fail."

May I say that I speak for us both on this memorable Golden 50th Anniversary of the English-Speaking Union with high hopes that this milestone along the way will unite even more closely those who believe in the strongest bonds between the English-Speaking peoples and are honouring those ties in this year of 1970.

*Clementine
Spencer-Churchill*

PREFACE

As we hail the Fiftieth Jubilee Anniversary of the English-Speaking Union, I am moved by stirring memories. It was my good fortune to be sent to London by President Roosevelt at a time, unparalleled in history when Britain stood alone as the defender of Western civilization against the full fury of the Axis onslaught. For an American to be in England at that time was a thrilling experience. Never in history has a people stood together more solidly. The moral strength of the British people was incomparable and the focus of that strength was, of course, Churchill.

The Battle of the Atlantic was on at that time and taking its deadly toll. The outlook was grim, but Prime Minister Churchill had implicit confidence in the British people's determination to hold out; and they, in turn, had full trust in him. But he knew that victory could not be won without American help. He understood our problems, especially the isolationist tradition that was delaying our action. Yet he had complete confidence that, in time, we would stand at Britain's side.

I was with him the night he received the news of the Japanese attack on Pearl Harbor. We were dining at Chequers, the official country house of British prime ministers. He seemed rather tired that evening and a bit less buoyant than usual. Suddenly the announcement of the attack came over the small radio he had turned on to hear the BBC nine o'clock news. Almost immediately the

Admiralty rang up to confirm the report. At once the Prime Minister went to the telephone to call President Roosevelt and pledged to him, without hesitation, Britain's full support in the war against Japan. "We are all in the same boat now," came the President's reply. From that moment on, never did the leaders of two nations work together in such intimacy and so successfully as President Roosevelt and Prime Minister Churchill.

Later at Fulton, Missouri, after his defeat in 1945, the ever indomitable Mr. Churchill told us, "We must never cease to proclaim in fearless tones the great principles of freedom and the rights of man which are the joint inheritance of the English-speaking world and which through Magna Carta, the Bill of Rights, the Habeas Corpus, trial by jury and the English common law find their most famous expression in the American Declaration of Independence." He also thought that the basic principles of our Declaration of Independence, our Constitution with its Bill of Rights, derived from the British tradition. As he put it, "The Declaration, was in the main a restatement of the principles which had animated the Whig struggle against the later Stuart and the English Revolution of 1688."

It is significant that he should have spoken of the closeness of our relationships on so many occasions, knowing so well that America was composed of millions of peoples from other lands whose cultures, naturally, had influenced our national life. But he loved to remind us, with a twinkle, that the British had come here first and that, perhaps, the others had been drawn to America because of our British heritage, which they accepted.

Again, he once said that "We must stand together, conscious of our common heritage and our common obligations."

To me, this Fiftieth Anniversary of Anglo-American unity is another monument, not only to that intimacy I watched hold fast between America and Britain in war, but to our special relationship that flows on undiminished—based as it is on the indestructible foundation of our commonly held ideals.

W. Averell Harriman

INTRODUCTION

 # SIR WINSTON S. CHURCHILL

HALF AMERICAN — WHOLLY BRITISH
THE FIRST ATLANTIC CITIZEN

In the midst of a heavy air raid on London during World War II, Prime Minister Winston Churchill's Parliamentary Private Secretary, Harvie Watt, directed his cab driver to take him to the Prime Minister's residence, at 10 Downing Street. Between the shattering blasts, Mr. Watt heard his cabbie praying, "I hope nothing happens to him until we can show our gratitude."

Twenty years later that same sentiment moved the 88th Congress of the United States to break a precedent by voting Aye on the Resolution that, "The President of the United States is hereby authorized and directed to declare by proclamation that Sir Winston Churchill shall be an honorary citizen of the United States."

Not even the Marquis de Lafayette, who joined the rebel cause in the American War of Independence, enjoyed the unprecedented honor bestowed on Sir Winston. When the Federal Constitution was ratified in 1789, Lafayette, who had been made an Honorary American Citizen of the states of Maryland and Virginia, was graciously declared to be a citizen of the United States by virtue of his state citizenships. Sir Winston, on the other hand, is the only foreigner to be made an Honorary American Citizen by Act of the Congress of the United States.

But in Sir Winston's life much was unprecedented. "A young

man in a hurry," he was born two months prematurely on November 30, 1874, at Blenheim Palace, the country seat of his paternal grandfather, the 7th Duke of Marlborough. His parents, Lord Randolph Churchill and the American beauty, Jennie Jerome, had met in August of 1873 at a ball on the cruiser *Ariadne,* which was docked at Cowes. Though Lord Randolph was barely twenty-four and Miss Jerome was nineteen, they overcame parental opposition and were married on April 15, 1874 in the British Embassy in Paris.

At the time of Winston Churchill's birth, Queen Victoria was on the throne, General Grant was President, and the Civil War had ended ten years earlier. Horses and railroads were the only means of travel and there were no planes, telephones, radio, or television.

Both the Churchill and Jerome families were actively concerned with new ideas and scientific advancements. Winston Churchill was later to recall that his parents' house at 2 Connaught Place was the first to be electrified in London. People came to stare not only at Lady Randolph's sensational beauty but also at her daring.

Among Winston Churchill's American ancestors of whom he was proudest were his Iroquois Indian forebearers, especially his half-Indian great-grandmother, "brown and lithe" Clarissa Wilcox of Palmyra, New York. Samuel Jerome, a great-grandfather, though of British descent, fought with the colonists in the War of Independence, while another great-grandfather, Major Libbeus Ball of the 4th Massachusetts Regiment, fought with General Washington. But it was his descent from Lt. Reuben Murray, his maternal great-grandfather who served in the Connecticut and New York regiments for three years in General Washington's Continental Army, that qualified Mr. Churchill for membership in the Society of the Cincinnati. In 1947 he was informed of his election to the Society. In 1952 during his installation speech in Washington he assured his audience that, "History unfolds itself by strange and unpredictable paths. . . . Therefore it seems to me that I may say that when the events took place which this Society commemorates, I was on both sides then in the war [Revolutionary] between Us and We."

Tall and darkly handsome Leonard Jerome, Churchill's American grandfather, was born in Syracuse in 1818, the son of Isaac Jerome. The most restless and enterprising of his father's seven sons, he undoubtedly set the mold for his grandson Winston's adventurous nature. Of pioneer Huguenot stock, he worked his way through Princeton and a law degree. At twenty-seven, with his brother Lawrence, he bought the Rochester *Daily American*. Both were great admirers of President Lincoln and filled the pages of their paper with anti-slavery articles. Soon they were well on their way to a fortune and Leonard married shy Clara Hall, daughter of the lovely half-Iroquois Clarissa, and they moved to Rochester, New York. Though she loved her husband devotedly, Clara could not match his vitality nor appetite, as he put it, for "the jungle where men tear and claw." The lure of Wall Street was so strong upon him that he finally moved his family to New York and into a splendid mansion on Madison Square at the corner of Twenty-sixth Street. There, among other innovations, Winston Churchill's grandfather put in fountains that gushed champagne for his grand parties and was one of the first to install indoor water closets, which were attacked by the newspapers of the day as not only "insanitary but immoral."

Indulging his passion for opera, he added a private theater as well as stables to his mansion. Delighting in the company of such songbirds as Adelina Patti and Jenny Lind, he named his second daughter Jennie, after the opera star.

Though there were only nineteen New York millionaires in that era of creative men, Jerome had soon become one of them. As a friend of Commodore Cornelius Vanderbilt, he often vacationed on the Commodore's private railroad car that took him West to hunt buffalo.

Jerome's eldest daughter, Clara, later married a grand eccentric, the English rider and crack shot, Moreton Frewen. After heeding the "Call of the Wild," he bought vast tracts of land and represented investors in Colorado and Wyoming, where he raised cattle, campaigned to save game herds of the Big Horn Mountains, and anticipated our Marines and New Frontiersmen by many fifty-mile hikes. Some of his backers lost their shirts as a result of Frewen's investments, which earned him the sobriquet "Mortal Ruin."

Among his many adventures, Mr. Jerome joined the journalist-publisher of the *New York Herald,* James Gordon Bennett, and his son in financing polar expeditions and the circulation boosting Stanley's mission to find Livingstone in Africa. With his friend, the banker August Belmont, he formed the Academy of Music, precursor of the Metropolitan Opera Company. Loving racing, he founded the American Jockey Club, started flat racing, and built a track in the Bronx, which became Jerome Park, and was inaugurated with General Grant, hero of Appomatox, sitting with the co-founders in the box of honor. "Kentucky," Jerome's race horse which he bought for $40,000, bore his blue and white racing colors and never lost a race. Jerome became so captivated by the four-in-hands he saw in London, that he equipped and drove one of his own down Fifth Avenue—the first ever seen in the streets of New York.

Yachting became a popular sport with the New York plutocrats of that period. So, in 1866 Leonard Jerome sailed in the first Atlantic race on the *Henrietta,* from Sandy Hook, New York to Needle's Point in the Isle of Wight. His own grandly fitted out steam yacht *Clara Clarita* took him to Newport for whale fishing and on one occasion to the middle of the Atlantic, where he went to the rescue and recovery of the first transatlantic cable that had broken down.

The high adventure of making millions and sometimes losing them continued to fascinate Jerome, who was also a man of enormous physical strength. Some time later at the age of seventy while he was attending a weight lifting contest he challenged the winner and won! Among his multiple interests he became part owner and consulting Director of *The New York Daily Times,* which became *The New York Times,* and employed his powers against corrupt Boss Tweed, then dominating the Democratic machine in New York. As a reward he was made Consul to Trieste and sailed to his post in Italy with his wife and small daughter, Clara.

After two years the sporting and artistic pleasures of Trieste palled. Jerome was glad to return to New York but his wife remained enthralled by Europe. On January 4, 1854, their second daughter Jennie was born in Brooklyn and five years later in

August, 1859, their last child Leonie arrived while they were in Paris. Jerome then returned to Wall Street to make and lose a few more fortunes and became an important figure in railroads, and a gambler in "the Street."

When their daughters were in their teens Mrs. Jerome wished to educate them intensively in the French manner. Her husband generously allowed her to take a house in Paris and live in splendor while he labored from his New York Club and visited them occasionally. A strict disciplinarian, Mrs. Jerome groomed the girls to take cold baths every day, learn to speak three languages fluently, and play the piano. The Empress Eugenie was so charmed by Mrs. Jerome that she invited her—the first American—to the great balls at the Tuileries. On learning of this honor, Mr. Jerome sent his wife a beautiful diamond rivière to wear at Court. Their eldest daughter Clara made her debut at a palace ball and was invited to houseparties at Compiegne until the Franco-Prussian War broke out in 1870. Then, with her three daughters, Mrs. Jerome caught the last train out of Paris before the Siege, following the Empress into her exile in England, while Mr. Jerome sailed from New York to install his family in Browns Hotel in London.

When it became possible to return to Paris the Jeromes discovered that a shell had landed in the celler of their house. Happily their art collection remained intact. The three girls resumed their studies and took piano lessons with Chopin's pupil, Stephan Heller. Later Jennie would be playing duets with Paderewski.

After marrying Lord Randolph Churchill, Jennie became the most sought-after hostess in London and was equally witty in French and German. Brilliant rather than intellectual, and at a time when few ladies attended the Gallery of the House of Commons, Lady Randolph could be found there sitting beside elderly Mrs. Gladstone, listening intently to the cut and thrust of Lord Randolph's eloquent speeches. If New York was in awe of Leonard Jerome's drive, London was captivated by his daughter Jennie's creative energy, beauty, and charm.

At Winston Churchill's birth a racing friend of his father put it most prophetically. "Interesting breeding! Stamina goes through the dam and pace through the sire." As the second son of the

7th Duke of Marlborough, Lord Randolph served as secretary to his father, who had been appointed Viceroy of Ireland by Disraeli in 1876. Typical of the healthy rebellion that proved to be a built-in characteristic of all Churchills, Lord Randolph, though a Conservative, campaigned to convert his party to a more popular movement which he christened the Tory Democrats. Rising fast in the House by his superhuman capacity for work and biting wit, he became Secretary for India, Chancellor of the Exchequer, and Leader of the House of Commons. In Parliamentary skill he was unmatched. These same talents were to reappear later in an even more effective form in his son Winston, who gloried in the fact that he was "a child of both worlds."

As a young man he first visited his Motherland in November of 1895 before his twenty-first birthday. Passionately in search of adventure, he and Reggie Barnes, a fellow subaltern in the 4th Hussars, sailed for Cuba, stopping en route in New York with Lady Randolph's friend Bourke Cockran, a brilliant orator and Democratic Congressman. After their New York visit the two young soldiers then proceeded on to Cuba and the uprising there against the Spanish colonial administration. Young Churchill managed to be made a courtesy member, military observer, and reporter on the staff of General Valdes, who was directing operations against the insurgents. He preceded another adventurous youth, Teddy Roosevelt, who two years later appeared in Cuba with the Rough Riders.

Always in need of money to support his ambitions, young Winston returned to America for a lecture tour in December of 1900, five years after his Cuban adventure. During those five years between his American visits he had fought in India's Northwest Frontier and in Africa's Sudan at Omdurman against a Moslem sect of 60,000 Dervishes, to avenge the death of General Gordon, in the last great cavalry charge in which lances were used. Forty-seven years later he was to be jointly responsible with President Truman for the consent in principle to unleash the atomic bomb on Japan in World War II.

As a reporter he had covered the Boer War, was captured, and became famous for his dramatic escape. At twenty-six he had seen more battles than all Europe's generals and had five books and a novel, *Savrola,* to his credit. Brimful of experiences, he literally talked and wrote his way across America, lecturing every day but Sunday for five months. Later he was to say of that period in his life, "I lived from mouth to hand!" Before his first audience in New York he was introduced by Mark Twain:

"Mr. Churchill by his father is an Englishman, by his mother he is an American, no doubt a blend that makes the perfect man. England and America; we are kin. And now that we are kin in sin there is nothing more to be desired. The harmony is perfect—like Mr. Churchill himself whom I now have the honour to present to you."

On his return to England he plunged into a career in politics, culminating on May 10, 1940, when, having held almost every Cabinet post, he was to realize his life-long ambition. Summoned by King George VI, he was asked to form the Government as Prime Minister. With most of Europe lost, the United States neutral, Russia then joined with Nazi Germany, France occupied, and the Luftwaffe poised to strike his "Island Kingdom," he immediately summoned his War Cabinet. Unflinchingly he listed each catastrophe. Then, in the words of one who was present, "When our chins were lowered to table level after his cumulative recital of doom, the Anglo-American bulldog lifted us with his growl, 'But I must say, Gentlemen, the moment invigorates ME remarkably.'" Each seat in the War Cabinet Room had a name card, excepting Churchill's. His bore a silver plate with the engraving, "Please understand that there is no depression in this house and we are not interested in the possibilities of defeat. They do not exist—Victoria R.I."

Analyzing Mr. Churchill's personality, the British historian A. L. Rowse noted, "The strength of the two natures mixed in him —the self-willed English aristocrat and the equally self-willed primitive American each with a hundred horsepower capacity for getting his way . . . he lacked some ordinariness which ordinary people ordinarily have."

And in 1931, Harold Nicolson wrote that 'He will live in English history long after those who have made it are forgotten, for he is an Anglo-American freak, and England loves her freaks devotedly (once they are safely dead)."

But that was written in 1931. Happily the "Anglo-American freak" lived not only to make history but to receive the gratitude and love of Great Britain and the United States, as well, long before his death.

"Half American and wholly British," he was, but his American imprintation revealed itself in his restless energy and flamboyant optimism, and, above all, in his peculiarly American way of attacking problems by the throat with a determination to solve them. Whatever errors of judgment he may have made in his long and crowded lives, certain of his British foes and colleagues sought to attribute them to "his impetuous American blood" and independent, outspoken judgments. Therefore, "Winston isn't to be trusted" was the rationale for relegating him to the wilderness. They actually meant that he was too American. They were to discover, to their salvation, that these very American characteristics were to sustain them and their Allies in their deadliest and "finest hour."

Ten American cities and four states gave Winston Churchill the keys to their hearts. Though he had not gone to college he held over twenty honorary degrees from American universities and institutions. The Distinguished Service Medal was bestowed upon him by General Pershing in 1919 for his services to the United States as British Minister of Munitions in World War I. On one of his sixteen visits to his Motherland he won the honor of wearing the United States Air Force pilot's wings.

In 1966, President Lyndon B. Johnson, at a special ceremony in the private apartments of the White House, accepted from Ambassador W. Averell Harriman a bronze head of Sir Winston by the sculptor, Sir Jacob Epstein, as a gift to the White House from his wartime associates. On accepting it in the presence of a small gathering of Sir Winston's friends and grandson Winston, President Johnson waved off a secretary standing by with a prepared speech. Then, with emotion, he declared, "When I was a young Congressman, I had occasion, during World War II, to come to this very room to see President Roosevelt. And there was this *great American* [here President Johnson placed his hand lovingly and firmly on the bronze head of Sir Winston]—not fully clad, with a cigar in one hand and a glass of brandy in the other. And, I dare say—if it had not been for this *great American*—none of us would be here today!"

Shortly before his death, Sir Winston was informed that the Washington Branch of the English-Speaking Union was placing a nine-foot bronze statue of him by William McVey before the British Embassy, with one foot on British, the other on American soil, to commemorate the Proclamation and Act that made him an Honorary American Citizen. It was the first statue of its kind to straddle the soil of two nations. On learning of this honor, Sir Winston wrote the English-Speaking Union in Washington:

"It gives me the greatest pleasure that the statue should stand on both American and British soil, and I feel that it will rest happily and securely on both feet."

Of the many national and international concerns that crowded the ninety years of Sir Winston's vibrant life, none was more unswerving than his passion to maintain and encourage the closest Anglo-American unity.

He believed it fundamental to an evolution toward world unity. Throughout his long life endless variations on his cherished theme fell from his lips and pen.

From the rich vein of all that Sir Winston Churchill wrote and said about America and Britain, I have tried to pan out some of that gold, for this volume, to illuminate the timelessness of his views. They include lesser known speeches and writings on what he called our Special Relationship that have not appeared before between covers and therefore I have excluded the speeches at Fulton, Missouri and to the United States Congress that are so well known. This volume was collected in the hope of encouraging Sir Winston's dream of the United States and Great Britain "standing side by side and shoulder to shoulder. . . . I cannot believe there is any other fact in the whole world which can compare with that. That is what I have dreamed of, aimed at, worked for."

KAY HALLE
Washington, D. C.

WINSTON CHURCHILL
On AMERICA
And BRITAIN

VIEWS

ON

ANGLO-
AMERICAN
LIFE

AND

HISTORY

IMPACT OF AMERICA
ON YOUNG CHURCHILL

ON BOURKE COCKRAN

When I first went to the U.S. in 1895, I was a subaltern of cavalry.
I was met on the quay by Mr. Bourke Cockran,* a great friend of

---

* In a letter to her cousin, Randolph Churchill, Anita Leslie recalled a conversation
with Adlai Stevenson in 1965 when he described his visit to Prime Minister Chur-

my American relations, who had most kindly undertaken to look after me during my stay in the city. I must record the strong impression which this remarkable man made upon my untutored mind. I have never seen his like, or in some respects his equal. With his enormous head, gleaming eyes and flexible countenance, he looked uncommonly like the portraits of Charles James Fox. It was not my fortune to hear any of his orations, but his conversation, in point, in pith, in rotundity, in antithesis, and in comprehension, exceeded anything I have ever heard.

AMID THESE STORMS

※※※

WINSTON CHURCHILL TO LADY RANDOLPH
November 10, 1895

My dearest Mamma,

I am sorry to say that the letter which I wrote two days ago missed the *'Lucania'* and so this will get to you almost as soon. I & Barnes are staying with Mr. Bourke Cockran in a charming and very comfortable flat at the address on this paper.

Everybody is very civil and we have engagements for every meal for the next few days about three deep. It is very pleasant staying here as the rooms are beautifully furnished and fitted with every convenience & also as Mr. Cockran is one of the most charming hosts and interesting men I have met. Last night we had a big dinner here to 10 or 12 persons all of whom were on the Judiciary. Very interesting men—one particularly—a Supreme Court Judge —is trying a *"cause célèbre"* here now—and so we are going to hear the charge to the Jury on Wednesday and in all probability the capital sentence.

---

chill in 1953 and asked Mr. Churchill whose oratory had influenced him most. The reply was immediate. "It was an American [W. Bourke Cochran, New York lawyer and politician] who inspired me when I was nineteen and taught me how to use every note of the human voice like an organ. He was my model. I learned from him how to hold thousands in thrall." [K.H.]

Eva [Purdy] is in great form and talks unceasingly—but has arranged things very well. She has engaged an excellent valet and—as I told you—made every sort of engagement for us.

Tomorrow we are going to see the Headquarters of the Atlantic Military district and do the harbour in a tugboat & Tuesday we go to West Point where I believe they will show us everything there is to see. The Horse Show begins tomorrow and Kitty Mott has a box to which we are both invited.

A Mr. Purdy took us round New York last night to Koster and Bial's & supper at the Waldorf. The Entertainment was good and the supper excellent. Today I snatch a quiet hour to pen you a line —but I lunch with Eva at 1—call on the Hitts at 3—the Cornelius Vanderbilts at 5 & dine with Kitty at 8—so you see that there is not much chance of the time hanging heavily. They really make rather a fuss over us here and extend the most lavish hospitality. We are members of all the Clubs and one person seems to vie with another in trying to make our time pleasant.

I have been civil and vague to the reporters and so far I can only find one misstatement in the papers.

What an extraordinary people the Americans are! Their hospitality is a revelation to me and they make you feel at home and at ease in a way that I have never before experienced. On the other hand their press and their currency impress me very unfavorably.

I have great discussions with Mr. Cockran on every conceivable subject from Economics to yacht racing. He is a clever man and one from whose conversation much is to be learned.

I think we shall go by rail to Tampa as there is

[letter incomplete]

WINSTON S. CHURCHILL,

COMPANION VOL. I, PART I

❀❀❀

WINSTON CHURCHILL TO HIS AUNT,
MRS. JOHN LESLIE
November 12, 1895

My dear Aunt Leonie,

I was very glad to get your letter at Queenstown and have been meaning to write you an answer for the last day or two. We are staying with a friend of yours Mr. Bourke Cockran in his charming flat in Fifth Avenue and so are very comfortable. He is such a nice man and we have made great friends.

I have been industriously seeing American institutions of all kinds, and have been impressed by many things—but I feel that I should like to think over and digest what I have seen for a few weeks before forming an opinion on it.

So far I think the means of communication in New York have struck me the most. The comfort and convenience of elevated railways—tramways—cable cars & ferries, harmoniously fitted into a perfect system accessible alike to the richest and the poorest—is extraordinary. And when one reflects that such benefits have been secured to the people not by confiscation of the property of the rich or by arbitrary taxation but simply by business enterprise—out of which the promoters themselves have made colossal fortunes, one cannot fail to be impressed with the excellence of the active system.

But New York is full of contradictions and contrasts. I paid my fare across Brooklyn Bridge with a paper dollar. I should think the most disreputable "coin" the world has ever seen. I wondered how to reconcile the magnificent system of communication with the abominable currency—for a considerable time and at length I have found what may be a solution. The communication of New York is due to private enterprise while the state is responsible for the currency: and hence I come to the conclusion that the first class men of America are in the counting houses and the less brilliant ones in the government.

✄✄✄

Yesterday we went round all the forts and barracks and in the evening we went over the ironclad cruiser *New York*. I was much struck by the sailors: their intelligence, their good looks and civility and their generally businesslike appearance. These interested me more than [the] ship itself, for while any nation can build a battle-ship—it is the monopoly of the Anglo-Saxon race to breed good seamen.

Altogether, my dear Aunt Leonie, my mind is full of irreconcilable and conflicting facts. The comfort of their cars and the disgraceful currency—the hospitality of American Society and the vulgarity of their Press—present to me a problem of great complexity. I am going to prolong my stay here a few more days on purpose to see more.

Everyone is very civil and we have been shewn everything. Today I go to the Court to hear a *cause célèbre*. I met the judge at dinner two nights ago and he suggested my coming. Tomorrow I am going over West Point and have the fire department alarmed—so you see I am not likely to find time hang heavily.

Well *au revoir*, my dearest Auntie, Hoping this letter will not seem *too* ponderous.

Yours ever
WINSTON S. CHURCHILL,

WINSTON S. CHURCHILL,
COMPANION VOL. I, PART I*

❊❊❊

WINSTON CHURCHILL TO HIS BROTHER, JACK
November 15, 1895

My dearest Jack,

I daresay Mamma showed you my letter of the 10th, which gave

---

* These letters of young Churchill on his first visit to America are from Vol. I of the six-volume biography commenced by his son Randolph Churchill who, after his untimely death in 1968, has been succeeded by Oxford historian Martin Gilbert who was appointed to complete the remaining three volumes. [K.H.]

an account of the voyage and such news as was to hand at that time. I am still staying with Mr. Bourke Cockran, whom you met in Paris, in his very comfortable and convenient flat in 5th Avenue. We have postponed our departure from New York for three days as there was lots to see and do. On Sunday we start for Havana by the route of Philadelphia—Washington—Savannah—Tampa Bay and Key West—arriving there on Wednesday morning, all being well.

Mr. Cockran, who has great influence over here, procured us orders to visit the Forts of the Harbour and West Point—which is the American Sandhurst.

I am sure you will be horrified by some of the Regulations of the Military Academy. The cadets enter from 19–22 & stay 4 years. This means that they are most of them 24 years of age. They are not allowed to smoke or have any money in their possession nor are they given any leave except 2 months after the 1st two years. In fact they have far less liberty than any *private* school boys in our country. I think such a state of things is positively disgraceful and young men of 24 or 25 who would resign their personal liberty to such an extent can never make good citizens or fine soldiers. A child who rebels against that sort of control should be whipped— so should a man who does not rebel.

The other night Mr. Cockran got the Fire Commissioner to come with us and we alarmed four or five fire stations. This would have interested you very much. On the alarm bell sounding the horses at once rushed into the shafts—the harness fell on to them— the men slid half dressed down a pole from their sleeping room and in 5½ seconds the engine was galloping down the street to the scene of the fire. An interesting feat which seems incredible unless you have seen it.

There is a great criminal trial going on now—a man who shot a fellow who had seduced his sister. I met the judge at dinner the other night and he suggested my coming to hear the case. I went and sat on the bench by his side. Quite a strange experience and one which would be impossible in England. The Judge discussing the evidence as it was given with me and generally making him- self socially agreeable—& all the while a pale miserable man was fighting for his life. This is a very great country my dear Jack. Not pretty or romantic but great and utilitarian. There seems to no such thing as reverence or tradition. Everything is eminently practical and things are judged from a matter of fact standpoint. Take for instance the Court house. No robes or wigs or uniformed ushers. Nothing but a lot of men in black coats & tweed suits. Judge prisoner jury counsel & warders all indiscriminately mixed. But they manage to hang a man all the same, and that after all is a great thing.

I saw Sunny last night & am dining with the Vanderbilts this evening. He is very pleased with himself and seems very fit. The newspapers have abused him scurrilously. But the essence of American journalism is vulgarity divested of truth. Their best papers write for a class of snotty housemaids and footmen & even the nicest people here have so much vitiated their taste as to appreciate the style.

I think mind you that vulgarity is a sign of strength. A great, crude, strong, young people are the Americans—like a boisterous healthy boy among enervated but well bred ladies and gentlemen. Some day Jack when you are older you must come out here and I think you will feel as I feel—and think as I think today.

Picture to yourself the American people as a great lusty youth— who treads on all your sensibilities perpetrates every possible horror of ill manners—whom neither age not just tradition inspire with reverence—but who moves about his affairs with a good hearted freshness which may well be the envy of older nations of the earth. Of course there are here charming people who are just as refined and cultured as the best in any country in the world—but I believe my impressions of the nation are broadly speaking correct. I have written you quite a long letter & cannot write again today so send this to Mamma after reading.

With best love Ever your loving brother
WINSTON S. CHURCHILL

WINSTON S. CHURCHILL,
COMPANION VOL. I, PART I

❈❈❈

WSC TO W. BOURKE COCKRAN

February 29, 1896

(Extract)

Bachelor's Club W.

. . . I hope the United States will not force Spain to give up Cuba —unless you are prepared to accept responsibility for the results of such action. If the States care to take Cuba—though this would be very hard on Spain—it would be the best and most expedient course for both the island and the world in general. But I hold it a monstrous thing if you are going to merely procure the establishment of another South American Republic—which however degraded and irresponsible is to be backed in its action by the American people—without their maintaining any sort of control over its behaviour.

I do hope that you will not be in agreement with those wild, and I must say, most irresponsible people who talk of Spain as "beyond the pale" etc etc. Do write and tell me what you do think . . . .

I commend rather a good book to your notice, *The Red Badge of Courage,** a story of the Civil War. Believe me it is worth reading.

WINSTON S. CHURCHILL,

VOL. I

F.D.R. TO WINSTON CHURCHILL IN LONDON

The White House
March 19, 1943

Dear Winston,

I did not know you came to the United States when you were at

* By Stephen Crane, American writer.

the baby carriage age, nor did I know you had visited Amenia. It is in Duchess County about 20 miles back of Hyde Park.

My best to you
LETTER IN F.D.R. LIBRARY

F.D.R. enclosed a letter he had received stating that Winston Churchill and his mother had visited America many years before. Churchill in reply said that his first visit to America had been in December, 1895, when he was already too big for any baby carriage. F.D.R.'s reply follows:

F . D . R . TO WINSTON CHURCHILL

The White House
March 30, 1943

For Former Naval Person
SOME BABY!

Roosevelt
F.D.R.: HIS PERSONAL PAPERS

⌘⌘⌘

ON AMERICA

AT SCHOOL AT BRIGHTON, YOUNG WINSTON,
AGED SEVEN, REACTED TO A *PUNCH*
CARTOON OF THE AMERICAN
CIVIL WAR.

1882

Here, too, I gained my first great interest in the American Civil War. First of all Mr. Punch was against the South, and we had a picture of a fierce young woman, Miss Carolina, about to whip a naked slave, a sort of Uncle Tom, with a kind of scourge which, not being yet myself removed out of the zone of such possibilities, I regarded as undoubtedly severe. I was all for the slave. Then later on the Yankees came on the scene. There was a whole regiment of them running away from a place called Bull Run; their muskets, with bayonets fixed, were on their shoulders as they doubled in fours, and their noses were long and red. They ran very fast, and the signpost pointed to Canada. The legend was "I'se gwine to take Canada." So Mr. Punch had turned against the North; and apparently there was a row between the North and England too. However, the war went on, and there was a picture of North and South, two savage, haggard men in shirts and breeches, grappling and stabbing each other with knives as they reeled into an abyss called Bankruptcy. Finally, I seem to remember a picture of Lincoln's tomb, and Britania, very sad, laying a wreath upon the cold marble, rather like the one we used to see on Mr. Gladstone-Caesar's brow.

AMID THESE STORMS

※※※

American historians will perhaps be somewhat lengthy in explaining to posterity exactly why the United States entered the Great War on 6 April, 1917, and why they did not enter at any earlier moment. American ships had been sunk before the German submarines; as many American lives were lost in the *Lusitania* as in all the five American ships whose sinking immediately preceded the declaration of war. As for the general cause of the Allies, if it was good in 1917 was it not equally good in 1914? There were plenty of reasons of high policy for staying out in 1917 after waiting so long.

It was natural that the Allies, burning with indignation against Germany, breathless and bleeding in the struggle, face to face with mortal dangers, should stand amazed at the cool, critical, detached attitude of the great Power across the Atlantic. In England particularly, where laws and language seemed to make a bridge of mutual comprehension between the two nations, the American abstention was hard to understand. But this was to do less than justice to important factors in the case. The United States did not feel in any immediate danger. Time and distance interposed their minimizing perspectives. The mass of the people engaged in peaceful industry, grappling with the undeveloped resources of the continent which was their inheritance, absorbed in domestic life and politics, taught by long constitutional tradition to shun foreign entanglements, had an entirely different field of mental interest from that of Europe. World Justice makes its appeal to all men. But what share, it was asked, had Americans taken in bringing about the situation which had raised the issue of World Justice? Was even this issue so simple as it appeared to the Allies? Was it not a frightful responsibility to launch a vast, unarmed, remote community into the raging centre of such a quarrel? That all this was overcome is the real wonder. All honour to those who never doubted, and who from the first discerned the inevitable path.

THE WORLD CRISIS

꘎꘎꘎

ON THE VERSAILLES PEACE CONFERENCE
AFTER GERMANY'S DEFEAT

On the one hand, one hundred million strong, stood the young American democracy. On the other cowered furtively, but at the same time obstinately, and even truculently, the old European diplomacy. Here young, healthy, hearty, ardent millions, advancing so hopefully to reform mankind. There, shrinking from the lime-lights, cameras and cinemas, huddled the crafty, cunning, intriguing, high-collared, gold-laced diplomats. Tableau! Curtain! Slow music! Sobs; and afterwards chocolates!

THE AFTERMATH,

1918–1928

꘎꘎꘎

1932

Responding to questions after a speech in New York City, Winston Churchill was asked: "Would you become an American citizen if we could make you President of the United States? I know our Constitution disqualifies you but we can amend that, as we did in the case of Prohibition."

There are various little difficulties in the way. However, I have been treated so splendidly in the United States that I should be disposed, if you can amend the Constitution, seriously to consider the matter.

PRESS CONFERENCE, N. Y. CITY

August 4, 1938

How heavily do the destinies of this generation hang upon the government and people of the United States! From many lands in Europe and in Asia eyes are turned towards this large, strong English-speaking community, which lies doubly shielded by its oceans, and yet is responsive to the surge of world causes. Will the United States throw their weight into the scales of peace and law and freedom while time remains, or will they remain spectators until the disaster has occurred; and then, with infinite cost and labour, build up what need not have been cast down? This is the riddle of a Sphinx who under the mask of loquacity, affability, sentimentality, hard business, machine-made politics, wrong-feeling, right-feeling, vigor and weakness, efficiency and muddle, still preserves the power to pronounce a solemn and formidable word.

In what position, physical, moral or psychological, do the United States stand today? The fierce struggle which is proceeding between the anti-capitalist or anti-rich-men forces of that vast country on the one side, and the anxieties of its practical economic well-being on the other, has reached a kind of equipoise. It is good politics to hunt the millionaires, to break up the monopolies, to tax and discipline the vested interests. But these have great powers of resistance. They fight, they will keep on fighting; and until the quarrel is settled, properity stands a-tiptoe outside the door. Yet there never was a time when it was more important to the whole world for the United States to be prosperous as well as militarily strong. The European democracies have a real advantage over the Dictator States in wealth, credit and sea-borne trade; but their strength and energy at any given moment are intimately related to the prosperity or adversity of the United States.

When things are going well in America, the more solid pedestrian forces in the free countries of Europe are conscious of a new draught of strength. When things go ill, they are weakened through a hundred channels in those very elements of strength which ought to reward law-respecting, peace-interested, civilized States. Economic and financial disorder in the United States not only depresses all sister countries, but weakens them in those very forces which might either mitigate the hatreds of races or provide the means to resist tyranny. The first service which the United States can render to world causes is to be prosperous and well-armed.

The arming part is being achieved on a very large scale. Enormous supplies have been voted by Congress for the expansion of the armed forces, particularly the Navy, to levels far above what any immediate direct danger would seem to require. No American party resists the President's desire to make the United States one of the most heavily armed, scientifically prepared countries in the world. Pacifism and the cult of defencelessness have been discarded by all parties. There never was in peace a time when the American armaments by land, air and sea, reached so imposing a height, or were sustained by so much national conviction.

In the meanwhile, the movement of American opinion upon world affairs is remarkable. Side by side with the loudest reiterations of "Never again will we be drawn in," there is a ceaselessly growing interest in the great issues which are at stake both in Europe and the Far East. There never was a peace-time when the newspapers of the United States carried more foreign news to their readers, or when those readers showed themselves more anxious to be informed about affairs taking place thousands of miles away, or more inclined to develop strong intellectual and moral convictions about them. There are literally scores of millions of men and women in the United States who feel as much opposed to the tyrannies of Totalitarian Governments, Communist or Nazi, as their grandfathers were to the continuance of slavery.

STEP BY STEP

September 30, 1941

Nothing is more dangerous in wartime than to live in the temperamental atmosphere of a Gallup Poll, always feeling one's pulse and taking one's temperature. I see that a speaker at the weekend said that this was a time when leaders should keep their ears to the ground. All I can say is that the British nation will find it very hard to look up to leaders who are detected in that somewhat ungainly posture.

SPEECH—HOUSE OF COMMONS

December, 1941

Silly people and there were many, not only in enemy countries, might discount the force of the United States. Some said they were soft, others that they would never be united. They would fool around at a distance. They would never come to grips. They would never stand blood letting. Their democracy and system of recurrent elections would paralyse their war effort. They would be just a vague blur on the horizon to friend or foe. Now we should see the weakness of this numerous but remote, wealthy and talkative people. But I had studied the American Civil War, fought out to the last desperate inch. American blood flowed in my veins. I thought of a remark which Edward Grey had made to me more than thirty years before—that the United States is like a "gigantic boiler. Once the fire is lighted under it there is no limit to the power it can generate."

THE SECOND WORLD WAR,

VOL. III

⌘⌘⌘

1946

On March 4, traveling by train with President Truman to the Fulton, Missouri speech, Mr. Churchill noted the Presidential seal on the wall of the Presidential Club Car. Mr. Truman explained that, before he took office, the eagle on the seal carried a quiver of war-like arrows in one talon and the ivy or olive branch of peace in the other, with its head turned toward the warlike quiver of arrows. As President he had requested that the Seal be changed so the eagle faced the olive branch. Mr. Clark Clifford had been charged with carrying it out, which meant changing all the existing seals of the office of President.

MR. CHURCHILL: *(to President Truman)*:
Why not put the eagle's neck on a swivel so that it could turn to the right or left as the occasion presented itself?

IRREPRESSIBLE CHURCHILL

⌘⌘⌘

May 7, 1946

For at least two generations we were, as the American writer Walter Lippmann has reminded us, a guardian, and almost a guarantor of the Monroe doctrine upon which, as Canning's eye foresaw, the free development of South America was founded. We and the civilised world owe many blessings to the United States, but have also in later generations made our contribution to their security and splendour.

SPEECH—WESTMINSTER

⌘⌘⌘

June 5, 1946

It cannot be in the interest of Russia to go on irritating the United States. There are no people in the world who are so slow to develop hostile feelings against a foreign country as the Americans, and there are no people who, once estranged, are more difficult to win back. The American eagle sits on his perch, a large, strong bird with formidable beak and claws. There he sits motionless, and M. Gromyko is sent day after day to prod him with a sharp pointed stick—now his neck, now under his wings, now his tail feathers. All the time the eagle keeps quite still. But it would be a great mistake to suppose that nothing is going on inside the breast of the eagle.

SPEECH—HOUSE OF COMMONS

❌❌❌

October 28, 1947

At this point I must turn to the United States, with whom our fortunes and interests are intertwined. I was sorry that the Hon. Member for Nelson and Colne (Mr. Sidney Silverman), whom I see in his place, said some weeks ago that they were "shabby moneylenders." That is no service to our country nor is it true. The Americans took little when they emigrated from Europe except what they stood up in and what they had in their souls. They came through, they tamed the wilderness, they became what old John Bright called, "A refuge for the oppressed from every land and clime." They have become today the greatest state and power in the world, speaking our own language, cherishing our common law, and pursuing, like our great Dominions, in broad principle, the same ideals.

SPEECH—HOUSE OF COMMONS

❌❌❌

My wife was forced to rest in the Citadel, but next day Mary [daughter] and I travelled to Hyde Park. We visited the Niagara Falls on the way. The reporters asked me what I thought of them, and gave the following account of our talk: " 'I saw them before you were born. I came here first in 1900.' 'Do they look the same?' 'Well,' he replied, 'the principle seems the same. The water still keeps falling over.' "

THE SECOND WORLD WAR,

VOL. V

⌘⌘⌘

No people respond more spontaneously to fair play. If you treat Americans well they always want to treat you better.

THE SECOND WORLD WAR,

VOL. IV

⌘⌘⌘

June 28, 1954

REPORTER: Sir Winston, do you think larger Conservative and Republican majorities in Congress—in Parliament and Congress—would improve U.S.-British relations?

PRIME MINISTER CHURCHILL: I am all for a Conservative majority. . . . I am not going to choose between Republicans and Democrats; I want the lot. Any British Government, Conservative or Socialist—I disagree with the Socialists—but Conservative or Socialist, will try hard to work with the United States. When they are in opposition they can't control their tail. It is hard enough to control your tail when you are in office!

PRESS CONFERENCE AT THE STATLER HOTEL,
WASHINGTON, D.C.

⌘⌘⌘

ON AMERICANS

AT A LORD MAYOR'S BANQUET
November 9, 1953

I remember a saying I heard in my youth: Every word of Daniel Webster weighs a pound. But that was before television!

❉❉❉

OF PRESIDENT WOODROW WILSON

President Wilson reached at the Armistice the zenith of his power and fame. Since the United States had entered the war in its thirty-second month he had proclaimed more vehemently and, upon occasion, more powerfully than anyone else, the righteousness of the Allied cause. Coming into the struggle fresh and cool, he had seemed to pronounce the conclusions of an impartial judge upon the terrible and frantic disputation. High above the swaying conflict, speaking in tones of majesty and simplicity, deeply instructed in all the arts of popular appeal, clad with power unmeasured and certainly unexhausted, he had appeared to the tortured and toiling combatants like a messenger from another planet sent to the rescue of freedom and justice here below. His words had carried comfort to every Allied people, and had been most helpful in silencing subversive peace propaganda in all its forms.

THE AFTERMATH,
1918–1928

❉❉❉

If Wilson had been either simply an idealist or a caucus politician, he might have succeeded. His attempt to run the two in

double harness was the cause of his undoing. The spacious philan-
thropy which he exhaled upon Europe stopped quite sharply at the
coasts of his own country. There he was in every main decision a
party politician, calculating and brazen. A tithe of the fine principles and generous sentiments he lavished upon Europe, applied
during 1918 to his Republican opponents in the United States,
would have made him in truth the leader of a nation. His sense of
proportion operated in separate water-tight compartments. The
difference in Europe between France and Germany seemed trivial,
petty, easy to be adjusted by a little good sense and charity. But
the differences between Democrat and Republican in the United
States! Here were really grave quarrels. He could not understand
why the French should not be more forgiving to their beaten enemy;
nor why the American Republicans should not expect cold comfort
from a Democratic Administration. His gaze was fixed with equal
earnestness upon the destiny of mankind and the fortunes of his
party candidates. Peace and goodwill among all nations abroad,
but no truck with the Republican Party at home. That was his
ticket and that was his ruin, and the ruin of much else as well.
It is difficult for a man to do great things if he tries to combine a
lambent charity embracing the whole world with the sharper forms
of populist party strife.

THE AFTERMATH,
1918–1928

✳✳✳

OF AMERICAN-BORN LADY NANCY ASTOR, THE FIRST FEMALE MEMBER OF PARLIAMENT AND A PROHIBITIONIST
1927

I have a great regard and respect for the noble lady, but I do not
think we are likely to learn much from the liquor legislation of
the United States.

SPEECH—HOUSE OF COMMONS

✳✳✳

1941

On Prime Minister Churchill's arrival in the U.S. the press came aboard for interviews.

After he had expressed his relief that Russia was driving Hitler back in the East, Edward Folliard, a Southern-born reporter for the *Washington Post* asked one of the first questions.

EDWARD FOLLIARD: Does the Prime Minister feel that America's entry into the war was another great climacteric?
PRIME MINISTER CHURCHILL: I sho' do.

IRREPRESSIBLE CHURCHILL

✶✶✶

OF PRESIDENT FRANKLIN D. ROOSEVELT
December 30, 1941

I have been all this week with the President of the United States, that great man whom destiny has marked for this climax of human fortune. We have been concerting the united pacts and resolves of more than thirty States and nations to fight on in unity together and in fidelity one to another, without any thought except the total and final extirpation of the Hitler tyranny, the Japanese frenzy, and the Mussolini flop.

✶✶✶

OF PRESIDENT FRANKLIN D. ROOSEVELT
January 27, 1942

During those three weeks which I spent in Mr. Roosevelt's home and family, I established with him relations not only of comradeship, but, I think I may say, of friendship. We can say anything to each other, however painful. When we parted he wrung my hand, saying, 'We will fight this through to the bitter end, whatever the cost may be.' Behind him rises the gigantic and hitherto unmobilized power of the people of the United States, carrying with them in their life and death struggle the entire, or almost the entire, Western hemisphere.

At Washington, we and our combined staffs surveyed the whole scene of the war, and we reached a number of important practical decisions. Some of them affect future operations and cannot, of course, be mentioned, but others have been made public by declaration or by events. The vanguard of an American army has already arrived in the United Kingdom. Very considerable forces are following as opportunity may serve. These forces will take their station in the British Isles and face with us whatever is coming our way. They impart a freedom of movement to all forces in the British Isles greater than we could otherwise have possessed. Numerous United States fighter and bomber squadrons will also take part in the defence of Britain and in the ever-increasing bombing offensive against Germany. The United States Navy is linked in the most intimate union with the Admiralty, both in the Atlantic and the Pacific. We shall plan our naval moves together as if we were literally one people.

SPEECH—HOUSE OF COMMONS

⚘⚘⚘

OF W. AVERELL HARRIMAN
September 8, 1942

The main purpose of my journey was, however, to visit Premier Stalin in Moscow. This was accomplished in two long flights with a break at Teheran. We flew across the two mountain systems, each about 300 miles wide, which lie south of the Caspian Sea and between which spread the plains and plateaus of Persia. Some of these peaks go up to 18,000 or 19,000 feet, but as we flew by day we had no need to go higher than 13,000 feet. We flew across long stretches of the Caspian Sea and up the Ural River towards Kuibishev (formerly Samara), and reached Moscow in the afternoon.

In this part of my mission I was accompanied by Mr. Averell Harriman, President Roosevelt's personal representative. The House will see that it was a great advantage to me to have the support of this most able and forceful man, who spoke with the august authority of the President of the United States. We spent four days in conferences with Premier Stalin and M. Molotov, sitting sometimes for five and six hours at a time, and we went into everything with the utmost candour and thoroughness. At the same time, the Chief of the Imperial General Staff and General Wavell, who accompanied me, had further conferences with Marshals Voroshilov and Shaposhnikov, and dealt with the more technical aspects of our joint affairs. Naturally I should not give any account of the subjects we discussed or still less of the conclusions which we reached. I have reported all these to the War Cabinet, and Mr. Harriman has reported them to President Roosevelt, but all must remain secret.

SPEECH—HOUSE OF COMMONS

❊❊❊

ON FOREIGN AFFAIRS (MIDDLE EAST)
July 30, 1951

The situation in Asia is indeterminate. It follows from what I have already said that I attach great importance to the announcement that the President [Truman] was sending Mr. Averell Harriman to Persia. He is a man who has a complete grasp of the whole world scene and a man of the highest personal capacity.

SPEECH—HOUSE OF COMMONS

❊❊❊

ON MacARTHUR'S GENERALSHIP
February 11, 1943

We must also express our admiration for the hard-won successes of the Australian and American Forces, who, under their brilliant commander General MacArthur, have taken Buna in New Guinea and slaughtered the last of its defenders.

The ingenious use of aircraft to solve the intricate tactical problems, by the transport of reinforcements, supplies, and munitions, including field guns, is a prominent feature of MacArthur's generalship, and should be carefully studied in detail by all concerned in the technical conduct of the war.

SPEECH—HOUSE OF COMMONS

⌘⌘⌘

OF HARRY HOPKINS
PRESIDENT FRANKLIN D. ROOSEVELT'S
SPECIAL ASSISTANT

Harry Hopkins, that extraordinary man, . . . played, and was to play, a sometimes decisive part in the whole movement of the war. His was a soul that flamed out of a frail and failing body. He was a crumbling lighthouse from which there shone the beams that led great fleets to harbour. He had also a gift of sardonic humour. I always enjoyed his company, especially when things went ill. He could also be very disagreeable and say hard and sour things. My experiences were teaching me to be able to do this too, if need be.

THE SECOND WORLD WAR,

VOL. III

⌘⌘⌘

OF GENERAL DWIGHT D. EISENHOWER
August 2, 1944

General Eisenhower assumed the command of the Expeditionary Force gathered in Britain. No man has ever labored more skillfully or intensely for the unification and goodwill of the great forces under his command than General Eisenhower. He has a genius for bringing all the allies together, and is proud to consider himself an allied as well as a United States commander.

SPEECH—HOUSE OF COMMONS

⌘⌘⌘

FROM A MESSAGE FROM PRIME MINISTER
CHURCHILL TO PRESIDENT TRUMAN
May 9, 1945

Let me tell you what General Eisenhower has meant to us. In
him we have had a man who set the unity of the Allied Armies
above all nationalistic thoughts. In his headquarters unity and
strategy were the only reigning spirits. The unity reached such a
point that British and American troops could be mixed in the line
of battle and large masses could be transferred from one command
to the other without the slightest difficulty. At no time has the principle of alliance between noble races been carried and maintained
at so high a pitch. In the name of the British Empire and Commonwealth I express to you our admiration of the firm, far-sighted, and
illuminating character and qualities of General of the Army
Eisenhower.

THE SECOND WORLD WAR,

VOL. VI

❈❈❈

FROM WINSTON CHURCHILL'S SPEECH TO
MRS. ROOSEVELT AT THE PILGRIM'S DINNER
April 12, 1948

Here tonight we do more than honour to his [President Roosevelt's] memory. We have the good fortune to have among us Mrs.
Roosevelt. Many of us know what we owe to our wives in life's
varied journeys. Mrs. Roosevelt has made her own distinctive contribution to the generous thought of modern society. In her speech
tonight she has given us a measure of the individual bearing and
influence and comprehension which she brought into the field of
world affairs. But at this moment when we are celebrating the
setting-up of the Roosevelt monument and fine statue in London,
which recalls to me the figure which I loved and honoured, we must
ascribe to Mrs. Roosevelt the marvellous fact that a crippled man,

victim of a cruel affliction, was able for more than ten years to ride the storms of peace and war at the summit of the United States. The debt we owe to President Roosevelt is owed also to her. I am sure she feels around her tonight, in this old parent land, and in this great company, the esteem and affection of the whole British people.

The ancients spoke of personages who were happy in the occasion of their death. Certainly President Roosevelt died in full career and undisputed control at the moment when certain victory was in view. He did not live to endure the quarrels of allies, hitherto united by common perils; nor to endure the exhaustion of the spiritual forces which, during a life-and-death struggle for a noble cause, had lifted men and whole nations far above their normal level. He did not have to face the grave economic aftermath of splendid sacrifices and deeds. He was spared all this. In my sombre moments, when I have them, as I sometimes do, I remember the lines of Lindsay Gordon—

> "We tarry on; we are toiling still.
> He is gone and he fares the best.
> He fought against odds; he struggled uphill.
> He has fairly earned his season of rest."

But I do not think that could be the epitaph of the famous man whose memory we honour tonight. First because the troubles we now encounter are less than those he overcame. Next because the United States which sustained him has risen, as the result of his direction and Presidency, to the foremost place among the nations. And above all that, having this solemn and awful responsibility and burden cast upon her, the Great Republic has neither bowed nor flinched before her task and her duty. She has found from her free democracy and federal system a wealth of gifted men and a unity of national purpose equal to all the tasks which may be set. These tasks will be hard, the burdens heavy, the decisions difficult and grave. But they will not be too much for us to bear; and in the championship of all the world causes with which the name of Franklin Roosevelt is bound up, the British Empire and Commonwealth of nations will prove itself a valiant and faithful friend and ally of the United States, in peace as it was in war, in the future as in the past. Thus, as Mrs. Roosevelt has bade us believe, thus all will come right.

⊠⊠⊠

OF GENERAL GEORGE MARSHALL

Hitherto I had thought of Marshall as a rugged soldier and a magnificent organiser and builder of armies—the American Carnot. But now I saw that he was a statesman with a penetrating and commanding view of the whole scene.

THE SECOND WORLD WAR,

VOL. IV

⊠⊠⊠

As a guest of Mr. John D. Rockefeller III on March 8, 1946, Mr. Churchill accompanied General Eisenhower to Williamsburg, Virginia, where he was to speak to the Virginia General Assembly. One of the General's historic-minded young aides asked if he might brief Mr. Churchill for the occasion with a two-page profile on Mr. Rockefeller.

MR. CHURCHILL   (*after perusing it*) :
Hmmm! You number your Rockefellers. We number our Georges!

(*and in the same speech*)

MR. CHURCHILL: I read the other day that an English nobleman, whose name is new to me, has stated that England would have to become the 49th state of the American Union. I read yesterday that an able American editor had written that the U.S. ought not to be asked to re-enter the British Empire. It seems to me and I dare say it seems to you, that the path of wisdom lies somewhere between these scarecrow extremes.

IRREPRESSIBLE CHURCHILL

ON APRIL 21, ON THE AMERICAN LOAN, AT THE ROYAL ALBERT HALL
1948

Nor should it be supposed as you would imagine, to read some of the left wing newspapers, that all Americans are multimillionaires of Wall Street. If they were all multimillionaires that would be no reason for condemning a system which has produced such material results.

SPEECH

✻✻✻

AMERICA AND BRITAIN CONTRASTED

COMPARING AMERICAN AND BRITISH RAILWAY ENGINES IN THE SUDAN

The American engines were sooner delivered and £1,000 cheaper. They broke down rarely. . . . The fact that they were considerably faster soon won them a good reputation on the railway, and the soldier who travelled to the front was as anxious to avoid his country's locomotives as to preserve his honour.

THE RIVER WAR

✻✻✻

WINSTON CHURCHILL TO BOURKE COCKRAN
November 5, 1896

My dear Bourke,

I was very glad to get your letter last mail and to hear of your campaign. I congratulate you upon the issue. A telegram received here last night informed us of McKinley's election—which, as you say vindicates the common sense of an Anglo-Saxon democracy. You have passed through a great struggle and have won a glorious victory—but I suppose like all great triumphs it has been expensive. I wonder if you would care to calculate how much this year's Presidential election has cost you—in dollars—considering for the purpose not only the actual electoral expenses, but also the disturbance of business & the fluctuations of capital. Of course I know you maintain that the contest is of great value as an educating institution, & I am prepared to willingly admit that no price was too much to pay to smash Bryan and display to the world on what firm foundation American credit and honour repose. But I am inclined to think if you consider one election with another—you will agree with me that your system of government costs you more than ours. You may rejoice, that it is better to be free than wealthy. That itself is a question about which discussion is possible: but I assert that the English labourer enjoys an equal freedom with the American workman & in addition derives numerous advantages from the possession of those appurtenances of monarchy—which make government dignified and easy—& the intercourse with foreign states more cordial.

I know what a stalwart democrat you are. But look at the questions philosophically—cynically if you like. Calculate the profit and the loss. Consider the respect human beings instinctively and involuntarily feel for that which is invested with pomp and circumstance. As a legislator discard unbending principles & ethics and avail yourself of the weaknesses of humanity. Yours may be the government for gods—ours at least is suitable to men.

Your tour of political meetings must indeed have been interesting and I regret so much that I had not the opportunity of accompanying you and listening to your speeches. From what I have seen—I know that there are few more fascinating experiences than to watch a great mass of people under the wand of the magician. There is no gift—so rare or so precious as the gift of oratory—so difficult to define or impossible to acquire.

My Indian experiences have now lasted for over a month. Our voyage out was pleasant and prosperous—though of course in the Red Sea the heat was excessive. Bangalore—which is my permanent address while in this country—possesses a beautiful climate and is for many other reasons an agreeable place to live in.

This country would fascinate you. Indeed I imagine no more interesting experience than for an American to visit India. A more amazing contrast than that between the United States and this country—passes the wit of man to devise. I give you an invitation to come. My house is large and there is ample room for visitors. I need not say how delighted Barnes and I would be if you could. The expense of the trip & the time consumed would be well repaid by the value of the experience. You can't think how interesting this country is. I am staying here for a polo tournament which we now stand a good chance of winning. Ten miles away is the independent city of Hyderabad containing nearly 300,000 inhabitants and all the scoundrels in Asia. Alone among Indian Princes the Nizam has preserved by his loyalty in former days his internal independence and the consequence is that the natives assume a truculent air and all carry arms. Hence the presence of the 19th Hussars—whose guest I am—and who with nearly 14,000 European and native soldiers are assembled here in the great camp of Secunderabad to overcome the turbulent city. The spectacle is at least instructive. You must come out here—if only for a flying visit.

Yours very sincerely

WINSTON S. CHURCHILL,

PS I cannot tell you how much letters are appreciated out here—so do write.   WSC

WINSTON S. CHURCHILL,

COMPANION VOL. I, PART II

✖✖✖

In England the political opinion of men and parties grows like a tree shading its trunk with its branches, shaped or twisted by the winds, rooted according to its strains, stunted by drought or maimed by storm. In America opinions are taken from the standard textbooks and platforms are made by machinery according to the exigencies of party without concern for individuals. We produce few of their clear-cut political types or clear-cut party programmes. In our affairs as in those of Nature there are always frayed edges, borderlands, compromises, anomalies. Few lines are drawn that are not smudged. Across the ocean it is all crisp and sharp.

AMID THESE STORMS

❦❦❦

On a June weekend in 1942 at Hyde Park, a discussion with President and Mrs. Franklin Roosevelt centered on what small but significant gestures might be made to strengthen Anglo-American understanding. Prime Minister Churchill, the traditionalist, listened gravely to a suggestion from Richard Miles of the British Embassy staff in Washington that the British might make a start by changing from their right hand to the American custom of left-hand driving as a small gesture of international goodwill.

PRIME MINISTER CHURCHILL: No! No!—It *won't* do. If a band of ruffians should set upon you, your sword arm wouldn't be free!

IRREPRESSIBLE CHURCHILL

❦❦❦

September 8, 1942

We are sea animals, and the United States are to a large extent ocean animals. The Russians are land animals. Happily, we are all three air animals.

SPEECH—HOUSE OF COMMONS

❦❦❦

April 30, 1967

After the Teheran Conference, Lady Violet Bonham Carter, noting Prime Minister Churchill's downcast expression, asked him how he felt.

THE PRIME MINISTER: I realized at Teheran for the first time what a small nation we are. There I sat with the great Russian bear on one side of me, with paws outstretched and on the other side the great American buffalo, and between the two sat the poor little British donkey, who was the only one of the three who knew the right way home.

> BRITISH BROADCASTING CORPORATION
> *The Listener*

※※※

1944

In Washington after the Second Quebec Conference in September Prime Minister Churchill was asked to comment on an announcement by Colonel Robert McCormick, anti-British owner of the Chicago *Tribune,* that if Britain behaved she might be eligible to become one of the United States.

PRIME MINISTER CHURCHILL: What do you mean? Great Britain and the United States all one? Yes, I'm all for that, and you mean me to run for President?
(*and*)

PRIME MINISTER CHURCHILL: I read some of the papers when I am over here, these great big papers about an inch thick— very different from the little sheets with which we get on in Great Britain.

On a visit to the White House following the Quebec Conference a young lady is said to have asked the P. M. what he thought of the United States.

PRIME MINISTER CHURCHILL: Toilet paper too thin, newspapers
too fat!

IRREPRESSIBLE CHURCHILL

❊❊❊

In the military as in the commercial or production spheres the
American mind runs naturally to broad, sweeping, logical conclusions on the largest scale. It is on these that they build their
practical thought and action. They feel that once the foundation
has been planned on true and comprehensive lines all other stages
will follow naturally and almost inevitably. The British mind does
not work quite in this way. We do not think that logic and clear
cut principles are necessarily the sole keys to what ought to be done
in swiftly changing and indefinable situations. In war particularly
we assign a large importance to opportunism and improvisation,
seeking rather to live and conquer in accordance with the unfolding
event than to aspire to dominate it often by fundamental decisions.
There is room for much argument about both views. The difference
is one of emphasis, but it is deep seated.

THE SECOND WORLD WAR,

VOL. III

❊❊❊

On the train to Fulton, Missouri, on March 4, President Truman,
his Secretary, Charlie Ross, Clark Clifford and Mr. Churchill were
playing poker at 2:30 A.M.

MR. CHURCHILL: If I were to be born again, there is one country
of which I would want to be a citizen. There is one country
where a man knows he has an unbounded future.

Q.:   Which?

MR. CHURCHILL: The U.S.A., even though I deplore some of
your customs.

Q.: Which, for instance?

MR. CHURCHILL: You stop drinking with your meals.

IRREPRESSIBLE CHURCHILL

❈❈❈

May 9, 1946

And had not Europe's children of earlier times come back across the Atlantic Ocean with strong and rescuing arms, all the peoples of Europe might have fallen into the long night of Nazi totalitarian despotism. Upon Britain fell the proud but awful responsibility of keeping the Flag of Freedom flying in the old world till the forces of the new world could arrive.

SPEECH—STATES-GENERAL OF THE NETHERLANDS

❈❈❈

October 9, 1951

I have never accepted a position of subservience to the United States. They have welcomed me as the champion of the British point of view. They are a fair-minded people.

SPEECH—WOODFORD GREEN

❈❈❈

DISCUSSING AMERICA'S CONTRIBUTION TO
THE ALLIED VICTORY OF WORLD WAR I
WITH HIS SECRETARY EDWARD MARSH

EDWARD MARSH: I'm in favour of kissing him [Uncle Sam] on both cheeks.

WINSTON CHURCHILL: But not on all four.

A BIOGRAPHY OF EDWARD MARSH

❈❈❈

In January 1952 on his first visit to Washington after becoming Prime Minister a second time, the European Defence Force was under discussion and exploration by all sides, especially the proposal that national uniforms should be scrapped in favor of a new European one.

PRIME MINISTER CHURCHILL: (*to Secretary of Defense Robert Lovett*):   Oh, No! That would be a sludgy amalgam.

At another of these Potomac conferences, arguments arose over failure to agree about a standard rifle for the NATO forces. One meeting took place at the British Embassy.

FIELD MARSHAL LORD SLIM: Well, I suppose we could experiment with a bastard rifle—partly American—partly British.

PRIME MINISTER CHURCHILL: Kindly moderate your language, Field Marshal, it may be recalled that I am myself partly British, partly American.

During the same talks on various NATO Army and Navy Commands, the Prime Minister noticed Secretary of Defense Robert Lovett fixing him with his banker's eye.

MR. LOVETT: Mr. Churchill, who is going to command in the English Channel? I am told it was determined in Rome.

PRIME MINISTER CHURCHILL: Thank you for that crumb, Mr. Lovett. I suppose the President and I should issue a joint communiqué that naval traffic in the Potomac will be under the supervision of the U.S. Navy?

IRREPRESSIBLE CHURCHILL

⚘⚘⚘

October 9, 1951

Dining on the Presidential Yacht "The Williamsburg" with President Truman during the 1952 Potomac Conference in Washington, D.C., the Prime Minister sat between Secretary of State Dean Acheson and Mutual Security Administrator W. Averell Harriman.

All through the meal ice water was drunk, and the wine glasses remained empty. Not until the end of the meal were the goblets filled for toasts to King George VI.

PRIME MINISTER CHURCHILL: (*to Ambassador Sir Oliver Franks*):
I could have respected the ancient tradition of a dry Navy, but this tantalising business of the empty wine glass—and then this matter of too little and too late—I hope you don't follow such barbarous practices in *your* house [the British Embassy], Franks!

On his trip to Washington, D.C., January 1952, he was offered a second drink at a dinner at the British Embassy.

PRIME MINISTER CHURCHILL: I accept it for many reasons. One, because I am thirsty, and another, because I have gotten more out of alcohol in the course of my life—than alcohol has gotten out of me!

IRREPRESSIBLE CHURCHILL

⌘⌘⌘

May 27, 1953

You (America) may be larger and we (Britain) may be the older. You may be the stronger, sometimes we may be the wiser.

SPEECH—WESTMINSTER HALL

⌘⌘⌘

Prime Minister Churchill, "half American and all British," an expert on the Revolution of 1776 and the Civil War, was once asked to address a patriotic gathering at Yorktown, Virginia, honoring the part that city played in the Revolution.

PRIME MINISTER CHURCHILL: I would be glad to oblige but not to celebrate!

IRREPRESSIBLE CHURCHILL

ON DUAL NATIONALITY

INDEPENDENCE DAY DINNER
July 4, 1950

Among Englishmen I have a special qualification for such an occasion, I am directly descended through my mother from an officer who served in Washington's Army. And as such I have been made a member of your strictly selected Society of Cincinnati. I have my pedigree supported by affidavits at every stage if it is challenged. . . . The drawing together in fraternal association of the British and American people, and of all the people of the English-speaking world may well be regarded as the best of the few things that have happened to us and to the world in this century of tragedy and storm.

SPEECH—LONDON

✳✳✳

FROM A SPEECH TO THE SOCIETY OF CINCINNATI, ON BECOMING A MEMBER
January 16, 1952

I regard this as the most memorable day in my crowded life. You have conferred upon me an honor which I deeply value. I shall frame and treasure this document and keep it for my own descendants in the coming years.

History unfolds itself by strange and unpredictable paths. We have little control over the future and none at all over the past. Therefore it seems to me that I may say that when the events took place which this society commemorates, I was on both sides then in the war between us and we.

You will remember that some of the most famous English statesmen proclaimed the justice of the American cause; and I was reading again only this morning to refresh my memory the words of the elder Pitt, the famous Lord Chatham:

"If I were an American, as I am an Englishman, and foreign troops landed in my country, I would never lay down my arms—never, never, never."

Those are the kind of words which roll along the centuries and play their part in wiping out the bitterness from former quarrels and in effacing tragedies that have occurred, so that we remember battles only to celebrate the military virtues of those who took part in them on both sides.

I am deeply grateful and proud of my American ancestry and think it is a wonderful thing that I have the honor to rejoice in that fact, while at the same time I have never failed in the proper observance of correct constitutional duties to my own country.

I deeply value the honor, and may it be a help to all those forces —they are in my opinion irresistible—which gather our nations together, not for unworthy purposes or combinations of strength, but in order to defend the freedom of the world . . . I hope this gathering may portend events from which nothing but good can come for both our nations.

THE SOCIETY OF THE CINCINNATI,
WASHINGTON, D.C.

✠✠✠

DOCUMENTS CONCERNING SIR WINSTON CHURCHILL'S HONORARY AMERICAN CITIZENSHIP

⌘⌘⌘

AN ACT OF THE 88TH CONGRESS OF THE UNITED STATES OF AMERICA
January 9, 1963

⌘⌘⌘

REMARKS BY PRESIDENT JOHN F. KENNEDY AT THE WHITE HOUSE CEREMONIES
April 9, 1963

THE PROCLAMATION OF PRESIDENT JOHN F. KENNEDY CONFERRING UPON SIR WINSTON CHURCHILL THE HONORARY CITIZENSHIP *and*

SIR WINSTON CHURCHILL'S LETTER OF REPLY TO PRESIDENT KENNEDY READ BY HIS SON, RANDOLPH S. CHURCHILL

AN ACT OF THE 88TH CONGRESS OF THE UNITED STATES OF AMERICA

BE IT ENACTED BY THE SENATE AND HOUSE OF REPRESENTATIVES OF THE UNITED STATES OF AMERICA IN CONGRESS ASSEMBLED, That the President of the United States is hereby authorized and directed to declare by proclamation that Sir Winston Churchill shall be an honorary citizen of the United States of America.

APPROVED APRIL 9, 1963.

✻✻✻✻

REMARKS OF PRESIDENT JOHN F. KENNEDY AT THE WHITE HOUSE CEREMONY
April 9, 1963

Members of the Congress, members of the Cabinet, His Excellency the British Ambassador,* Ambassadors of the Commonwealth, old friends of Sir Winston led by Mr. Baruch, ladies and gentlemen:

We gather today at a moment unique in the history of the United States. This is the first time that the United States Congress has solemnly resolved that the President of the United States shall proclaim an honorary citizenship for the citizen of another country

* Sir David Ormsby-Gore, later Lord Harlech.

and in joining me to perform this happy duty the Congress gives Sir Winston Churchill a distinction shared only with the Marquis de Lafayette.

In proclaiming him an honorary citizen, I only propose a formal recognition of the place he has long since won in the history of freedom and in the affections of my—and now his—fellow countrymen.

Whenever and wherever tryranny threatened, he has always championed liberty. Facing firmly toward the future, he has never forgotten the past. Serving six monarchs of his native Great Britain, he has served all men's freedom and dignity.

In the dark days and darker nights when Britain stood alone— and most men save Englishmen despaired of England's life—he mobilized the English language and sent it into battle. The incandescent quality of his words illuminated the courage of his countrymen.

Indifferent himself to danger, he wept over the sorrows of others. A child of the House of Commons, he became in time its father. Accustomed to the hardships of battle, he has no distaste for pleasure.

Now his stately ship of life, having weathered the severest storms of a troubled century, is anchored in tranquil water, proof that courage and faith and the zest for freedom are truly indestructible. The record of his triumphant passage will inspire free hearts all over the globe.

By adding his name to our rolls, we mean to honor him—but his acceptance honors us far more. For no statement or proclamation can enrich his name now—the name Sir Wintson Churchill is already legend.

THE PROCLAMATION
OF
THE PRESIDENT OF THE UNITED STATES
OF AMERICA

Whereas Sir Winston Churchill, a son of America though a subject of Britain, has been throughout his life a firm and steadfast friend of the American people and the American nation; and

Whereas he has freely offered his hand and his faith in days of adversity as well as triumph; and

Whereas his bravery, charity and valor, both in war and in peace, have been a flame of inspiration in freedom's darkest hour; and

Whereas his life has shown that no adversity can overcome, and no fear can deter, free men in the defense of their freedom; and

Whereas he has expressed with unsurpassed power and splendor the aspirations of peoples everywhere for dignity and freedom; and

Whereas he has by his art as an historian and his judgment as a statesman made the past the servant of the future;

Now, therefore, I, John F. Kennedy, President of the United States of America, under the authority contained in an Act of the 88th Congress, do hereby declare Sir Winston Churchill an honorary citizen of the United States of America.

In witness whereof, I have hereunto set my hand and caused the Seal of the United States of America to be affixed.

Done at the City of Washington this ninth day of April, in the year of our Lord nineteen hundred and sixty-three, and of the Independence of the United States of America the one hundred and eighty-seventh.

JOHN F. KENNEDY

✳✳✳

28 HYDE PARK GATE

LONDON, S.W. 7

April 6, 1963

Mr. President,

I have been informed by Mr. David Bruce that it is your intention to sign a Bill conferring upon me Honorary Citizenship of the United States.

I have received many kindnesses from the United States of America, but the honour which you now accord me is without parallel. I accept it with deep gratitude and affection.

I am also most sensible of the warm-hearted action of the individual States who accorded me the great compliment of their own honorary citizenships as a prelude to this Act of Congress.

It is a remarkable comment on our affairs that the former Prime Minister of a great sovereign state should thus be received as an honorary citizen of another. I say "great sovereign state" with design and emphasis, for I reject the view that Britain and the Commonwealth should now be relegated to a tame and minor role in the world. Our past is the key to our future, which I firmly trust and believe will be no less fertile and glorious. Let no man underrate our energies, our potentialities and our abiding power for good.

I am, as you know, half American by blood, and the story of my association with that mighty and benevolent nation goes back nearly ninety years to the day of my Father's marriage. In this century of storm and tragedy I contemplate with high satisfaction the constant factor of the interwoven and upward progress of our peoples. Our comradeship and our brotherhood in war were unexampled. We stood together, and because of that fact the free world now stands. Nor has our partnership any exclusive nature: the Atlantic community is a dream that can well be fulfilled to the detriment of none and to the enduring benefit and honour of the great democracies.

Mr. President, your action illuminates the theme of unity of the English-speaking peoples, to which I have devoted a large part of my life. I would ask you to accept yourself, and to convey to both Houses of Congress, and through them to the American people, my solemn and heartfelt thanks for this unique distinction, which will always be proudly remembered by my descendants.

(sig. cut) WINSTON S. CHURCHILL

❊❊❊

A comment on Sir Winston Churchill receiving an Honorary American Citizenship.

VINCENT SHEEAN IN A CABLE TO
LADY CHURCHILL

"Sir Winston has saved England by annexing America!"

ON THE ENGLISH
LANGUAGE

January, 1942

President [Roosevelt] has chosen the title "United Nations" for all the Powers now working together. This is much better than "Alliance," which places him in constitutional difficulties, or "Associated Powers," which is flat.

THE SECOND WORLD WAR,

VOL. III

❋❋❋

July 11, 1943

I am very much interested in the question of Basic English. The widespread use of this would be a gain to us far more durable and fruitful than the annexation of great provinces. It would also fit in with my ideas of closer union with the United States by making it even more worth while to belong to the English-speaking club.

THE SECOND WORLD WAR,

VOL. V

❋❋❋

November 4, 1944

Prime Minister Churchill discussed the possibilities of Basic English with F.D.R. at the Quebec Conference. They agreed that "it has tremendous merit in it." President Roosevelt, on June 5, 1944, wrote Cordell Hull "If Stalin, Chiang Kai-shek and I had had . . . Basic English our conferences would have been . . . easier . . . than having . . . interpreters and . . . would soon take the place of French as the 'so-called' language of diplomacy." But in a letter to the Prime Minister which he never sent he concluded: "I wonder what the course of history would have been if, in May 1940, you had been able to offer the British people only blood, work, eye water and face water; which I understand is the best that Basic English can do with five famous words."

PRIME MINISTER CHURCHILL: Basic English is not intended for use among English-speaking people, but to enable a much larger body of people who do not have the good fortune to know the English language to participate more easily in our society.

IRREPRESSIBLE CHURCHILL

✠✠✠

ON RECEIVING A DEGREE AT THE
UNIVERSITY OF MIAMI
February 26, 1946

The great Bismarck—there were great Germans in those days—said at the close of his life, that the most important fact in the world was that the British and American peoples spoke the same language. Certainly we have a noble inheritance in literature. It would be an enormous waste and loss to us all if we did not respect, cherish, enjoy and develop this magnificent estate, which has come down to us from the past and which not only unites us as no such great communities have ever been united before, but is also a powerful instrument whereby our conception of justice, of freedom, and of fair play and good humor may make their invaluable contribution to the future progress of mankind.

SPEECH—MIAMI, FLA.

⌘⌘⌘

FROM ''A REVIEW OF THE WAR''
September 28, 1944

The United States is a land of free speech; nowhere is speech freer, not even here where we sedulously cultivate it even in its most repulsive forms. But when I see some of the accounts given of conversations that I am supposed to have had with the President of the United States, I can only recall a Balfourian phrase. . . . when he said that the accounts which were given bore no more relations to the actual facts than the wildest tales of the Arabian Nights do to the ordinary incidents of domestic life in the east.''

SPEECH—HOUSE OF COMMONS

⌘⌘⌘

AMERICA AND BRITAIN TOGETHER

April 4, 1925

We are often told that the gold standard will shackle us to the United States. I will deal with that in a moment. I will tell you what it will shackle us to. It will shackle us to reality. For good or for ill, it will shackle us to reality.

SPEECH—HOUSE OF COMMONS

⌘⌘⌘

November 23, 1932

These are not the days when you can order the British nation or the British Empire about as if it were a pawn on the chessboard of Europe. You cannot do it. Of course, if the United States were willing to come into the European scene as a prime factor, if they were willing to guarantee to those countries who take their advice that they would not suffer for it, then an incomparably wider and happier prospect would open to the whole world. If they were willing not only to sign, but to ratify, treaties of that kind, it would be an enormous advantage. It is quite safe for the British Empire to go as far in any guarantees in Europe as the United States is willing to go, and hardly any difficulty in the world could not be solved by the faithful co-operation of the English-speaking peoples. But that is not going to happen tomorrow.

SPEECH—HOUSE OF COMMONS

※※※

On a visit to Chartwell on October 8, 1933, James Roosevelt, the President's eldest son, was among the guests. It was not long after his father's first inaugural. Mr. Churchill and Mr. Roosevelt had not yet become "the good companions" they later became as they had met only fleetingly at a dinner at Gray's Inn in London long years before, during World War I when President Roosevelt was Assistant Secretary of the Navy and Mr. Churchill was Minister of Munitions.

After dinner on this particular weekend Mr. Churchill initiated a guessing game, drawing from each of us a confession of our fondest wish. His guests fumbled and qualified their answers. But when the question was put to him, he shot back without a flicker of hesitation, "I wish to be Prime Minister and in close and daily communication by telephone with the President of the United States. There is nothing we could not do if we were together." Then, turning to a secretary, he called for a piece of paper on which he inscribed the insignias of a pound and a dollar sign intertwined. "Pray, bear this to your father from me," he said to James.

Roosevelt: "Tell him this must be the currency of the future."

"What will you call this new currency, Sir?" asked young Roosevelt.

"The sterling dollar," said Mr. Churchill.

"What, Sir, if my father should wish to call it the dollar sterling?" grinned Roosevelt.

"It's all the same, we are together," beamed Mr. Churchill. [K.H.]

UNION OF THE POUND AND THE DOLLAR

This union of the pound and the dollar was originated by the Hon. Winston Churchill and presented to me during a visit to Chartwell. He requested me to transmit it to my Father as a token of the currency of the future.

James Roosevelt, Oct. 8th, 1933

✹✹✹

June 14, 1939

At a dinner in London Walter Lippmann related to Mr. Churchill that Joseph P. Kennedy, U.S. Ambassador to Great Britain, had informed him that war with German was inevitable and that Britain would be defeated.

Mr. Churchill's reply: "It may be true, it may well be true, that this country will, at the outset of this coming and to my mind almost inevitable war, be exposed to dire peril and fierce ordeals. It may be true that steel and fire will rain down upon us day and night scattering death and destruction far and wide. It may be true that our sea-communications will be imperiled and our food-supplies placed in jeopardy. Yet these trials and disasters, I ask you to believe me, Mr. Lippmann, will but serve to steel the resolution of the British people and to enhance our will for victory. No, the Ambassador should not have spoken so, Mr. Lippmann; he should not have said that dreadful word. Yet supposing (as I do not for one moment suppose) that Mr. Kennedy were correct in his tragic utterance, then I for one would willingly lay down my life in combat, rather than, in fear of defeat, surrender to the menaces of these most sinister men. It will then be for you, for the Americans, to preserve and to maintain the great heritage of the English-speaking peoples. It will be for you to think imperially, which means to think always of something higher and more vast than one's own national interests. Nor should I die happy in the great struggle which I see before me, were I not convinced that if we in this dear, dear island succumb to the ferocity and might of our enemies, over there in your distant and immune continent the torch of liberty will burn untarnished and (I trust and hope) undismayed."

HAROLD NICOLSON, DIARIES & LETTERS, 1930–1939

⚙⚙⚙

FROM A BROADCAST ADDRESS
February 9, 1941

In order to win the war Hitler must destroy Great Britain. He may carry havoc into the Balkan States; he may tear great provinces out of Russia; he may march to the Caspian; he may march to the gates of India. All this will avail him nothing. It may spread his curse more widely throughout Europe and Asia, but it will not avert his doom. With every month that passes the many proud and once happy countries he is now holding down by brute force and vile intrigue are learning to hate the Prussian yoke and the Nazi name as nothing has ever been hated so fiercely and so widely among men before. And all the time, masters of the sea and air, the British Empire—nay, in a certain sense, the whole English-speaking world—will be on his track, bearing with them the swords of justice.

The other day, President Roosevelt gave his opponent in the late Presidential Election a letter of introduction to me, and in it he wrote out a verse, in his own handwriting, from Longfellow which, he said, 'applies to you people as it does to us.' Here is the verse:

> . . . Sail on, O Ship of State!
> 　Sail on, O Union, strong and great!
> Humanity with all its fears,
> With all the hopes of future years,
> 　Is hanging breathless on thy fate!

What is the answer that I shall give, in your name, to this great man, the thrice-chosen head of a nation of 130,000,000? Here is the answer which I will give to President Roosevelt: Put your confidence in us. Give us your faith and your blessing, and, under Providence, all will be well.

We shall not fail or falter; we shall not weaken or tire. Neither the sudden shock of battle, nor the long-drawn trials of vigilance and exertion will wear us down. Give us the tools, and we will finish the job.

WORLD BROADCAST

✖✖✖

AT THE LORD MAYOR'S DAY LUNCHEON
AT THE MANSION HOUSE
November 10, 1941

To return for a moment before I sit down to the contrast between our position now and a year ago, I must remind you, I do not need to remind you here in the City, that this time last year we did not know where to turn for a dollar across the American exchange. By very severe measures we had been able to gather and spend in America about £500,000,000 sterling, but the end of our financial resources was in sight—nay, had actually been reached. All we could do at that time a year ago was to place orders in the United States without being able to see our way through, but on a tide of hope and not without important encouragement.

Then came the majestic policy of the President and Congress of the United States in passing the Lend and Lease Bill, under which in two successive enactments about £3,000,000,000 sterling were dedicated to the cause of world freedom without—mark this, for it is unique—the setting up of any account in money. Never again let us hear the taunt that money is the ruling thought or power in the hearts of the American democracy. The Lend and Lease Bill must be regarded without question as the most unsordid act in the whole of recorded history.

SPEECH—LONDON

※※※

FROM A BROADCAST ADDRESS
February 15, 1942

The other day I crossed the Atlantic again to see President Roosevelt. This time we met not only as friends, but as comrades, standing side by side and shoulder to shoulder, in a battle for dear life and dearer honor, in the common cause, and against a common foe. When I survey and compute the power of the United States and its vast resources and feel that they are now in with us, with the British Commonwealth of Nations all together, however long it lasts, till death or victory, I cannot believe there is any other fact in the whole world which can compare with that. That is what I have dreamed of, aimed at and worked for, and now it has come to pass.

SPEECH—LONDON

※※※

AT A LUNCHEON AT THE BRITISH EMBASSY IN WASHINGTON

Winston Churchill addressed his British and American wartime associates including Vice President Henry Wallace, Secretary of

War Henry Stimson, Secretary of the Interior Harold Ickes, Chairman of the Foreign Relations Committee Senator Tom Connally, and the Undersecretary of State Sumner Welles.

I could see small hope for the world unless the United States and the British Commonwealth worked together in fraternal association. I believed that this could take a form which would confer on each advantages without sacrifice. I should like the citizens of each, without losing their present nationality, to be able to come and settle and trade with freedom and equal rights in the territory of the other. There might be a common passport or a special form of passport or visa. There might even be some form of common citizenship, under which citizens of the United States and of the British Commonwealth might enjoy voting privileges after residential qualification and be eligible for public office in the territories of the other, subject of course, to the laws and institutions there prevailing.

THE SECOND WORLD WAR,

VOL. IV

※※※※

FOREIGN POLICY
November 7, 1945

Those same deep, uncontrollable anxieties which some of us felt in the years before the war recur, but we have also a hope that we had not got then. That hope is the strength and resolve of the United States to play a leading part in world affairs. There is this mighty State and nation, which offers power and sacrifice in order to bring mankind out of the dark valley through which we have been travelling. The valley is indeed dark, and the dangers most menacing, but we know that not so far away are the broad uplands of assured peace. Can we reach them? We must reach them. This is our sole duty.

I am sure we should now make it clear to the United States that we will march at their side in the cause that President Truman has devised, that we add our strength to their strength, and that their stern sober effort shall be matched by our own. After all, if everything else fails—which we must not assume—here is the best chance of survival. Personally I feel that it is more than survival. It may even be safety, and, with safety, a vast expansion of prosperity. Having regard to all these facts of which many of us here are aware at the present time, we may confidently believe that with the British Empire and Commonwealth standing at the side of the United States we shall together, be strong enough to prevent another world catastrophe. As long as our peoples act in absolute faith and honour to each other, and to all other nations, they need fear none and they need fear nothing. The British and American peoples come together naturally, and without the need of policy or design. That is because they speak the same language, were brought up on the same common law, and have similar institutions and an equal love of individual liberty. There is often no need for policy of statecraft to make British and Americans agree together at an international council table. They can hardly help agreeing on three out of four things. They look at things in the same way. No policies, no pacts, no secret understandings are needed between them. On many of the main issues affecting our conduct and our existence, the English-speaking peoples of the world and in general agreement.

It would be a mistake to suppose that increasingly close and friendly relations between Great Britain and the United States imply an adverse outlook towards any other Power. Our friendship may be special, but it is not exclusive. On the contrary, every problem dealing with other Powers is simplified by Anglo-American agreement and harmony.

SPEECH—HOUSE OF COMMONS

❊❊❊

FROM A SPEECH AT A RECEPTION IN NEW YORK
March 15, 1946

The only question which in my opinion is open is whether the necessary harmony of thought and action between the American and British peoples will be reached in a sufficiently plain and clear manner and in good time to prevent a new world struggle or whether it will come about, as it has done before, only in the course of that struggle. . . .

Now I turn to the other part of my message—the relations between Great Britain and the United States. On these the life and freedom of the world depend. Unless they work together, in full loyalty to the Charter, the organization of the United Nations will cease to have any reality. No one will be able to put his trust in it and the world will be left to the clash of nationalisms which have led us to two frightful wars. I have never asked for an Anglo-American military alliance or a treaty. I asked for something different and in a sense I asked for something more. I asked for fraternal association, free, voluntary, fraternal association. I have no doubt that it will come to pass, as surely as the sun will rise tomorrow. But you do not need a treaty to express the natural affinities and friendships which arise in a fraternal association. On the other hand, it would be wrong that the fact should be concealed or ignored. Nothing can prevent our nations drawing ever closer to one another and nothing can obscure the fact that, in their harmonious companionship, lies the main hope of a world instrument for maintaining peace on earth and goodwill to all men.

I thank you all profoundly for all your gracious kindness and hospitality to me during this visit I have paid to your shores. Mine is not the first voice raised within your spacious bounds in the cause of freedom and of peace. Nor will it be the last that will be encouraged by the broad tolerance of the American people. I come to you at a time when the United States stands at the highest point of majesty and power ever attained by any community since the fall of the Roman Empire. This imposes upon the American people a duty which cannot be rejected. With opportunities comes responsibility. Strength is granted to us all when we are needed to serve great causes. We in the British Commonwealth will stand at your side in powerful and faithful friendship, and in accordance with the World Charter, and together I am sure we shall succeed in lifting from the face of man the curse of war and the darker curse of tyranny. Thus will be opened ever more broadly to the anxious toiling millions the gateways of happiness and freedom.

SPEECH—NEW YORK

✻✻✻

FROM A SPEECH
May 10, 1951

It is not a matter of whether there is a war with China or not, but whether there is a rift between Britain and the United States or not. That is the thought that haunts me . . . on every ground, national, European, and international, we should allow no minor matters— even if we feel keenly about them—to stand in the way of the fullest, closest intimacy, accord and association with the United States.

SPEECH—HOUSE OF COMMONS

✻✻✻

FROM A SPEECH
January 14, 1952

The two world wars of the terrible twentieth century have turned the economic balance of power from the Old World to the New. It is certain that Europe could not have survived without the moral and material help which has flowed across the ocean from Canada and the United States.

SPEECH—OTTAWA, CANADA

✻✻✻

FROM A SPEECH
November 9, 1953

Let us stick to our heroes John Bull and Uncle Sam.

SPEECH—MANSION HOUSE, LONDON

❈❈❈

ALLIES IN WAR

WRITING THE HISTORY OF WORLD WAR I
April 6, 1917

Of all the grand miscalculations of the German High Command none is more remarkable than their inability to comprehend the meaning of war with the American Union. It is perhaps the crowning example of the unwisdom of basing a war policy upon the computation of material factors alone. The war effort of 120,000,-000 educated people, equipped with science, and possessed of the resources of an unattackable continent, nay, of a New World, could not be measured by the number of drilled soldiers, of trained officers, of forged cannon, of ships of war they happened to have at their disposal. It betokens ignorance of the elemental forces resident in such a community to suppose they could be permanently frustrated by a mechanical instrument called the U-boat. How rash to balance the hostile exertions of the largest, if not the leading, civilized nation in the world against the chance that they would not arrive in time upon the field of battle! How hard to condemn the war-worn, wearied, already out-numbered heroic German people to mortal conflict with this fresh, mighty, and, once aroused, implacable antagonist!

There is no need to exaggerate the material assistance given by the United States to the Allies. All that could be sent was given as fast and as freely as possible, whether in manhood, in ships or in money. But the war ended long before the material power of the United States could be brought to bear as a decisive or even as a principal factor. It ended with over 2,000,000 American soldiers on the soil of France. A campaign in 1919 would have seen very large American armies continually engaged, and these by 1920 might well have amounted to 5,000,000 of men. Compared to potentialities of this kind, what would have been the value of, let us say, the capture of Paris? As for the 200 U-boats, the mechanical hope, there was still the British Navy, which at this period, under the aegis of an overwhelming battle-fleet, maintained upwards of 3,000 armed vessels on the seas.

But if the physical power of the United States was not in fact applied in any serious degree to the beating down of Germany; if for instance only a few score thousand Germans fell by American hands; the moral consequences of the United States joining the Allies was indeed the deciding cause in the conflict.

WORLD CRISIS,

VOL. I

⚹⚹⚹

Mr. Churchill was the only Englishman to receive the American Distinguished Service Cross, presented to him by General John J. Pershing in 1918.

The award designates, . . . for distinguished service and gallantry in the face of the enemy. The latter qualification was waived in my case.

IRREPRESSIBLE CHURCHILL

⚹⚹⚹

Mr. Churchill expressed irritation with what he deemed to be the United States' small commitment to White Russian intervention against the Bolsheviks.

They also proposed to send a detachment of the Young Men's Christian Association to offer moral guidance to the Russian people.

THE AFTERMATH,
1918–1928

❅❅❅

ON THE NEW ARMY
May 19, 1939

I have always thought that the union of these two great forces [the British and American navies], not for purposes of aggression or narrow selfish interests, but in an honorable cause constitutes what I may call the sheet-anchor of human freedom and progress.

SPEECH—CORN EXCHANGE, CAMBRIDGE

❅❅❅

THEIR FINEST HOUR
June 18, 1940

If we can stand up to him [Hitler], all Europe may be free and the life of the world may move forward into broad, sunlit uplands. But if we fail, then the whole world, including the United States, including all that we have known and cared for, will sink into the abyss of a new Dark Age made more sinister, and perhaps more protracted, by the lights of perverted science. Let us therefore brace ourselves to our duties, and so bear ourselves that, if the British Empire and its Commonwealth last for a thousand years, men will say: "This was their finest hour."

SPEECH—HOUSE OF COMMONS

❅❅❅

ON THE WAR SITUATION
August 20, 1940

His Majesty's Government are entirely willing to accord defence facilities to the United States on a 99 years' lease-hold basis, and we feel sure that our interests no less than theirs, and the interests of the Colonies themselves, and of Canada and Newfoundland, will be served thereby. . . .

Undoubtedly, this process means that these two great organizations of the English-speaking democracies—the British Empire and the United States—will have to be somewhat mixed up together in some of their affairs for mutual and general advantages. For my own part, looking out upon the future, I do not view the process with any misgivings. I could not stop it if I wished—no one can stop it. Like the Mississippi, it just keeps rolling along. Let it roll! Let it roll on in full flood, inexorable, irresistible, benignant, to broader lands and better days.

SPEECH—HOUSE OF COMMONS

❈❈❈

A STATEMENT TO THE HOUSE OF COMMONS ON THE PASSING OF THE UNITED STATES LEASE-LEND BILL
March 12, 1941

The Lease-Lend Bill became law yesterday, when it received the signature of the President. I am sure the House would wish me to express on their behalf, and on behalf of the nation, our deep and respectful appreciation of this monument of generous and far-seeing statesmanship.

The most powerful democracy has, in effect, declared in solemn Statute that they will devote their overwhelming industrial and financial strength to ensuring the defeat of Nazism in order that nations, great and small, may live in security, tolerance and freedom. By so doing, the Government and people of the United States have in fact written a new Magna Carta, which not only has regard to the rights and laws upon which a healthy and advancing civilization can alone be erected, but also proclaims by precept and example the duty of free men and free nations, wherever they may be, to share the responsibility and burden of enforcing them.

In the name of His Majesty's Government and speaking, I am sure, for Parliament and for the whole country, and indeed, in the name of all freedom-loving peoples, I offer to the United States our gratitude for her inspiring act of faith.

SPEECH—HOUSE OF COMMONS

✳✳✳

SPEECH—LONDON

On the battleship *Prince of Wales* in Placentia Bay, Newfoundland, the first wartime meeting of President Roosevelt and Prime Minister Churchill took place, in 1941.

This service was felt by us all to be a deeply moving expression of the unity of faith of our two peoples, and none who took part in it will forget the spectacle presented that sunlit morning on the crowded quarter-deck—the symbolism of the Union Jack and the Stars and Stripes draped side by side on the pulpit; the American and British chaplains sharing in the reading of the prayers; the highest naval, military, and air officers of Britain and the United States grouped in one body behind the President and me; the close-packed ranks of British and American sailors, completely intermingled, sharing the same books and joining fervently together in the prayers and hymns familiar to both.

THE SECOND WORLD WAR,

VOL. III

✳✳✳

A WARNING TO JAPAN
November 10, 1941

Should the United States become involved in war with Japan, the British declaration will follow within the hour.

SPEECH—MANSION HOUSE, LONDON

❊❊❊

To create great Armies is one thing; to lead them and to handle them is another. It remains to me a mystery as yet unexplained how the very small staffs which the United States kept during the years of peace were able to not only build up the armies and Air Force units, but also to find the leaders and vast staffs capable of handling enormous masses and of moving them faster and farther than masses have ever been moved in war before.

THE SECOND WORLD WAR,

VOL. IV

❊❊❊

1941

The day after Pearl Harbor at a British Chiefs of Staff meeting one of the Chiefs still advocated a cautious approach to the United States.

PRIME MINISTER CHURCHILL: Oh! that is the way we talked to her [the U.S.] while we were still wooing her; now that she is in the harem, we woo her quite differently.

IRREPRESSIBLE CHURCHILL

❊❊❊

WRITING ON AMERICAN NAVAL VICTORIES

This encounter [the Battle of the Coral Sea] had an effect out of proportion to its tactical importance. Strategically, it was a welcome American victory, the first against Japan. Nothing like it had ever been seen before. It was the first battle at sea in which surface ships never exchanged a shot. . . .

THE SECOND WORLD WAR,

VOL. IV

AND

The annals of war at sea present no more intense, heart-shaking shock than these two battles [of the Coral Sea and Midway Island] in which the qualities of the U.S. Navy and Air Force and of the American race shone forth in splendour. The novel and hitherto utterly unmeasured conditions which air warfare had created made the speed of action and the twists of fortune more intense than ever has been witnessed before. But the bravery and self-devotion of the American airmen and sailors and the nerve and skill of their leaders was the foundation of all.

THE SECOND WORLD WAR,

VOL. IV

❊❊❊

President Roosevelt, who was eager to continue discussions at the White House on the draft declaration of the United Nations Pact sealing the first Washington (Arcadia) Conference, wheeled himself into W.S.C.'s room. There he found his guest, in the words of Harry Hopkins, "stark naked and gleaming pink from his bath," his valet waiting to wrap him in a towel. Faced with this vision President Roosevelt started to put his wheel chair in reverse.

PRIME MINISTER CHURCHILL (*to F.D.R.*): Pray enter—the Prime Minister has nothing to hide from the President of the United States.

ROOSEVELT AND HOPKINS, AN INTIMATE HISTORY

ALSO

PRIME MINISTER CHURCHILL: The President was wheeled in to me on the morning of January 1. I got out of my bath, and agreed to the draft [United Nations Pact].

IRREPRESSIBLE CHURCHILL

THE SECOND WORLD WAR,

VOL. III

✱✱✱

At the Teheran Conference in November–December 1943 Prime Minister Winston Churchill suggested that he and President Roosevelt have lunch together before the second plenary session. Roosevelt declined as he did not want the report spread that he and Mr. Churchill were matching their own schemes with Russia.

PRIME MINISTER CHURCHILL (*to Mr. Averell Harriman*): I shall insist on one thing: that I be host at dinner tomorrow evening. I think I have one or two claims to precedence. To begin with, I come first both in seniority and alphabetically. In the second place, I represent the longest established of the three governments. And, in the third place, tomorrow happens to be my birthday.

ROOSEVELT AND HOPKINS, AN INTIMATE HISTORY

✱✱✱

A MESSAGE TO THE UNITED STATES
CHAMBER OF COMMERCE
AT ITS ANNUAL DINNER IN NEW YORK
April 30, 1943

Please allow me to extend to American management and labour my warmest and deepest appreciation of what it has accomplished

since your last meeting in supplying the materials of war to the men
on the Allied fighting fronts.

We asked for the tools. You gave them to us. Without the constant flow from your factories to supplement our own output, the
Allied armies could not have gained the remarkable victories of the
last six months. Without the ships that you have built and are building on a prodigious scale, the life-lines of civilisation across the
oceans of the world would have worn thin, if indeed they had not
snapped. All our future efforts to accomplish the purposes of this
righteous war against aggression, and to bring it to a final decision
at the earliest moment, depend upon the faithful exertions of the
munition plants and kindred industries of every description. These
will assuredly be forthcoming in generous measure from all true
friends of freedom, and with them we may move forward together
in comradeship, and indeed in brotherhood, through the overthrow
of our embattled enemies in Europe and Asia, to that brighter age
which is our hearts' desire.

SPEECH—NEW YORK

✖✖✖

JOINT PRESS CONFERENCE WITH PRESIDENT ROOSEVELT
May 25, 1943

The Allies' future plans are to wage this war to the unconditional
surrender of all who have molested us—that applies to Asia as well
as to Europe.

The situation is very much more satisfactory than when I was
last here. It was in this house that I got the news of the fall of
Tobruk. I don't think any Englishman in the United States has
ever been so unhappy as I was that day; certainly no Englishman
since General Burgoyne surrendered at Saratoga.

Since the attack on Alamein and the descent on North Africa
we have had a great measure of success and a decisive victory.

A year ago Russia was subjected to such a heavy attack that it seemed she might lose the Caucasus; but she, too, recovered and gained another series of successes.

Hitler has been struck two tremendous, shattering blows—Stalingrad and Tunisia. In eleven months the Allies have given some examples of highly successful war-making, and have indisputably turned the balance.

I quote the words of your great general, Nathan Bedford Forrest, the eminently successful Confederate leader. Asked the secret of his victories, Forrest said, 'I git thar fustest with the mostest men.' The Allies can see a changed situation. Instead of, as hitherto, getting somewhere very late with very little, we are arriving first with most.

There is danger in wishful thinking that victory will come by internal collapse of the Axis. Victory depends on force of arms. I stand pat on a knock-out, but any windfalls in the way of internal collapses will be gratefully accepted.

❦❦❦

A TRIBUTE TO WEST POINT:
A LETTER TO MAJOR GENERAL F. B. WILBY,
SUPERINTENDENT OF THE UNITED STATES
MILITARY ACADEMY, WEST POINT,
FOR THE CORPS OF CADETS
May 29, 1944

I well remember in the winter of 1895, now quite a long time ago, being shown over the whole Academy at West Point by high authorities, and being enormously impressed with the efficiency of the teaching and the smartness of the cadets. As I had not long before come from Sandhurst, I considered myself an expert upon these points. I was particularly struck by the rule that all West Pointers must always show a crease down the hollow of their back. I do not know whether you have kept this up. Anyhow I am very glad it was not thought of by the British War Office during the time I was at Sandhurst. Certainly it seems to have had very fine results on your side of the Atlantic.

I send best wishes to you and to all at a moment when the grand feats and brotherhood in arms of our Armies are clearing so much evil and tyranny from the world.

THE DAWN OF LIBERATION

❈❈❈❈

FROM A REVIEW OF THE WAR
September 28, 1944

I must pay my tribute to the United States Army, not only in their valiant and ruthless battle-worthy qualities, but also in the skill of their commanders and the excellence of their supply arrangements. When one remembers that the United States four or five years ago was a peace-loving power, without any great body of troops, munitions, and with only a very small regular army to draw their commanders from, the American achievement is truly amazing. After the intense training they have received for nearly three years, or more than three years in some cases, their divisions are now composed of regular professional soldiers whose military quality is out of all comparison with hurriedly-raised wartime levies.

SPEECH—HOUSE OF COMMONS

❈❈❈❈

FORWARD TILL THE WHOLE TASK IS DONE
A WORLD BROADCAST
May 13, 1945

It may well be said that our strategy was conducted so that the best combinations, the closest concert, were imparted into the operations by the combined staffs of Britain and the United States, with whom, from Teheran onwards, the war leaders of Russia were joined. And it may also be said that never have the forces of two nations fought side by side and intermingled in the lines of battle with so much unity, comradeship and brotherhood as in the great

Anglo-American armies. Some people say: Well what would you expect, if both nations speak the same language, have the same laws, have a great part of their history in common, and have very much the same outlook upon life with all its hopes and glories? Isn't it just the sort of thing that would happen? And others may say: It would be an ill day for all the world and for the pair of them if they did not go on working together, and marching together and sailing together and flying together, whenever something has to be done for the sake of freedom and fair play all over the world. That is the great hope of the future.

BROADCAST

✼✼✼

A TRIBUTE TO EISENHOWER

A SPEECH AT THE MANSION HOUSE WHEN GENERAL EISENHOWER, SUPREME COMMANDER, RECEIVED THE FREEDOM OF THE CITY OF LONDON
June 12, 1945

I have been brought very closely in contact with General Eisenhower since the day early in 1942 when we first met at the White House after the attack on Pearl Harbour, and all the grave matters of the direction of the armies to the landings in French North Africa and all the great efforts which were called for a year ago had to be discussed and examined, and I had the opportunity of seeing at close quarters General 'Ike'—for that is what I call him—in action. I saw him at all sorts of times, because in war things do not always go as we wish. Another will breaks in, and there is a clash, and questions arise. Never have I seen a man so staunch in pursuing the purpose in hand, so ready to accept responsibility for misfortune, or so generous in victory.

There is one moment I would dwell on. It was just about a little more than a year ago that he had to decide whether to go across the Channel or put it off for, it might be, eleven days. It was a terrible decision. The Army had gathered. A million men in the front line had gathered, and thousands of craft and tens of thousands of aircraft, and the great ships were all arranged. You could not hold it. It was like trying to hold an avalanche in leash. Should it be launched or should it not be launched?

There were a great many people who had a chance of expressing their opinions. I was not one of them, because it was purely a technical matter. A great many generals and admirals were gathered in the High Command to express their opinions and views, but there was only one man on whom the awful brunt fell of saying 'Go' or 'Stay'. To say 'Stay' means keeping hundreds of thousands of men cooped up in wired enclosures so that the plans they had been told of might not leak out. It meant the problem of hundreds of thousands of men on board ship who had to be provided for and found accommodation. It might have meant that the air could not cover the landing or that the water was too rough for the many boats that were needed.

It was one of the most terrible decisions, and this decision was taken by this man—this very great man [prolonged applause].

It is one of many decision he has taken. Had he not said 'Go,' and eleven days had passed, the weather would have smiled, and all the groups of meteorologists would have been happy. The expedition would have started; and two days later the worst gale for forty years at that season of the year fell upon the beaches in Normandy. Not only did he take the risk and arrive at the fence, he cleared it in magnificent style.

There are many occasions when that kind of decision falls on the supreme commander. Many fearful tales come from the front line. A great deal of anxiety is felt by populations at home. Do we go forward? Do we fight in this area? Are we to push on? These decisions all resolved themselves into an 'Aye' or a 'No,' and all I can say about our guest is that in very many most important decisions, history will acclaim his decisions as right, and that the bias, the natural bias, that moved him in these matters was very much more in favour of 'Aye' than of 'No'.

I could go on for a very long time about your guest. There is no doubt whatever that we have among us today one of the greatest

Americans who have reached our shores and dwelt a considerable time among us. We honour him very much for his invariable consideration of the British point of view, for his impartial treatment of all the officers under his command. I know he will tell you when he rises that he never gave an order to a British officer which he could not immediately obey.

We also have made our contribution to the battles on the Continent, and I am quite sure that the influence he will wield in the world will be one always of bringing our countries together in the much more difficult task of peace in the same way as he brought them together in the grim and awful cataclysm of war. I have had personal acquaintance with him now for three years. It is not much, but three years of this sort may seem five-and-twenty. I feel we have here a great creative, constructive and combining genius, one from our sister nation across the ocean, one who will never speak evil but will always cherish his contact with the British people, and to whom I feel we should at this moment give the most cordial testimony in our power, of our admiration, of our affection, and of our heartfelt good wishes for everything that may happen to him in the future.

SPEECH—LONDON

❊❊❊

At the conclusion of the European war Prime Minister Churchill sent a number of messages about the great victory, including the following, to President Truman.

Your message is cherished by the British nation, and will be regarded as if it were a battle honour by all His Majesty's armed forces of all the races in all the lands. Particularly will this be true throughout the great armies which have fought together in France and Germany under General of the Army Eisenhower and in Italy under Field-Marshal Alexander.

In all theatres the men of our two countries were brothers-in-arms, and this was also true in the air, on the oceans, and in the narrow seas. In all our victorious armies in Europe we have fought as one. Looking at the staffs of General Eisenhower and Field-Marshal Alexander, anyone would suppose that they were the organization of one country, and certainly a band of men with one high purpose. Field-Marshal Montgomery's 21st Army Group, with its gallant Canadian Army, has played its part both in our glorious landing last June and in all the battles which it has fought, either as the hinge on which supreme operations turned or in guarding the northern flank, or advancing northward at the climax. All were together heart and soul.

You sent a few days ago your message to Field-Marshal Alexander, under whom, in command of the army front in Italy, is serving your doughty general, Mark Clark. Let me tell you what General Eisenhower has meant to us. In him we have had a man who set the unity of the Allied armies above all nationalistic thoughts. In his headquarters unity and strategy were the only reigning spirits. The unity reached such a point that British and American troops could be mixed in the line of battle, and that large masses could be transferred from one command to the other without the slightest difficulty. At no time has the principle of alliance between noble races been carried and maintained at so high a pitch. In the name of the British Empire and Commonwealth, I express to you our admiration of the firm, farsighted, and illuminating character and qualities of General of the Army Eisenhower.

I must also give expression to our British sentiments about all the valiant and magnanimous deeds of the United States of America, under the leadership of President Roosevelt, so steadfastly carried forward by you, Mr. President, since his death in action. They will for ever stir the hearts of Britons in all quarters of the world in which they dwell, and will, I am certain, lead to even closer affections and ties than those that have been created by the two world wars through which we have passed with harmony and elevation of mind.

VICTORY MESSAGE

✳✳✳

FROM MR. CHURCHILL'S FINAL REVIEW OF
THE WAR AND HIS FIRST MAJOR SPEECH
AS LEADER OF THE OPPOSITION IN THE
HOUSE OF COMMONS
August 16, 1945

On July 17 there came to us at Potsdam the eagerly-awaited news of the trial of the atomic bomb in the Mexican desert. Success beyond all dreams crowned this sombre, magnificent venture of our American Allies. The detailed reports of the Mexican desert experiment, which were brought to us a few days later by air, could leave no doubt in the minds of the very few who were informed, that we were in the presence of a new factor in human affairs, and possessed of powers which were irresistible. Great Britain had a right to be consulted in accordance with Anglo-American agreements. The decision to use the atomic bomb was taken by President Truman and myself at Potsdam, and we approved the military plans to unchain the dread, pent-up forces.

From that moment our outlook on the future was transformed. In preparation for the results of this experiment, the statements of the President and of Mr. Stimson and my own statement, which by the courtesy of the Prime Minister was subsequently read out on the broadcast, were framed in common agreement. Marshal Stalin was informed by President Truman that we contemplated using an explosive of incomparable power against Japan, and action proceeded in the way we all now know. It is to this atomic bomb more than to any other factor that we may ascribe the sudden and speedy ending of the war against Japan.

Before using it, it was necessary first of all to send a message in the form of an ultimatum to the Japanese which would apprise them of what unconditional surrender meant. This document was published on July 26—the same day that another event, differently viewed on each side of the House, occurred. [Note: The result of the General Election and the resignation of Mr. Churchill from the Premiership.] The assurances given to Japan about her future after her unconditional surrender had been made were generous in the extreme. When we remember the cruel and treacherous nature of the utterly unprovoked attack made by the Japanese warlords upon the United States and Great Britain, these assurances must be considered magnanimous in a high degree. In a nutshell, they implied 'Japan for the Japanese', and even access to raw materials, apart from their control, was not denied to their densely-populated homeland. We felt that in view of the new and fearful agencies of war-power about to be employed, every inducement to surrender, compatible with our declared policy, should be set before them. This we owed to our consciences before using this awful weapon.

Secondly, by repeated warnings, emphasized by heavy bombing attacks, an endeavor was made to procure the general exodus of the civil population from the threatened cities. Thus everything in human power, prior to using the atomic bomb, was done to spare the civil population of Japan. There are voices which assert that the bomb should never have been used at all. I cannot associate myself with such ideas. Six years of total war have convinced most people that had the Germans or Japanese discovered this new weapon, they would have used it upon us to our complete destruction with the utmost alacrity. I am surprised that very worthy people, but people who in most cases had no intention of proceeding to the Japanese front themselves, should adopt the position that rather than throw this bomb, we should have sacrificed a million American, and a quarter of a million British lives in the desperate battles and massacres of an invasion of Japan. Future generations will judge these dire decisions, and I believe that if they find themselves dwelling in a happier world from which war has been banished, and where freedom reigns, they will not condemn those who struggled for their benefit amid the horrors and miseries of this gruesome and ferocious epoch.

The bomb brought peace, but men alone can keep that peace, and henceforward they will keep it under penalties which threaten the survival, not only of civilization but of humanity itself. I may say that I am in entire agreement with the President that the secrets of the atomic bomb should so far as possible not be imparted at the present time to any other country in the world. This is in no design or wish for arbitrary power, but for the common safety of the world. Nothing can stop the progress of research and experiment in every country, but although research will no doubt proceed in many places, the construction of the immense plants necessary to transform theory into action cannot be improvised in any country.

For this and many other reasons the United States stand at this moment at the summit of the world. I rejoice that this should be so. Let them act up to the level of their power and their responsibility, not for themselves but for others, for all men in all lands, and then a brighter day may dawn upon human history. So far as we know, there are at least three and perhaps four years before the concrete progress made in the United States can be overtaken. In these three years we must remould the relationships of all men, wherever they dwell, in all the nations. We must remould them in such a way that these men do not wish or dare to fall upon each other for the sake of vulgar and out-dated ambitions or for passionate differences in ideology, and that international bodies of supreme authority may give peace on earth and decree justice among men. Our pilgrimage has brought us to a sublime moment in the history of the world. From the least to the greatest, all must strive to be worthy of these supreme opportunities. There is not an hour to be wasted; there is not a day to be lost. . . .

In those countries, torn and convulsed by war, there may be, for some months to come, the need of authoritarian government. The alternative would be anarchy. Therefore it would be unreasonable to ask or expect that liberal government—as spelt with a small 'l' —and British or United States democratic conditions, should be instituted immediately. They take their politics very seriously in those countries. A friend of mine, an officer, was in Zagreb when the results of the late General Election came in. An old lady said to him, 'Poor Mr. Churchill! I suppose now he will be shot.' My friend was able to reassure her. He said the sentence might be mitigated to one of the various forms of hard labour which are always open to His Majesty's subjects. Nevertheless we must know where we stand, and we must make clear where we stand, in these affairs of the Balkans and of Eastern Europe, and indeed of any country which comes into this field. Our ideal is government of the people by the people, for the people—the people being free without duress to express, by secret ballot without intimidation, their deep-seated wish as to the form and conditions of the Government under which they are to live . . .

Surely we can agree in this new Parliament, or the great majority of us, wherever we sit—there are naturally and rightly differences and cleavages of thought—but surely we can agree in this new Parliament, which will either fail the world or once again play a part in saving it, that it is the will of the people freely expressed by secret ballot, in universal suffrage elections, as to the form of their government and as to the laws which shall prevail, which is the first solution and safeguard. Let us then march steadily along that plain and simple line. I avow my faith in democracy, whatever course or view it may take with individuals and parties. They may make their mistakes, and they may profit from their mistakes. Democracy is now on trial as it never was before, and in these islands we must uphold it, as we upheld it in the dark days of 1940 and 1931, with all our hearts, with all our vigilance, and with all our enduring and inexhaustible strength. . . .

SPEECH—HOUSE OF COMMONS

❈❈❈

WRITING ON THE ATOMIC BOMB
August, 1945

The final decision now lay in the main with President Truman, who had the weapon; but I never doubted what it would be, nor have I ever doubted since that he was right. The historic fact remains, and must be judged in the after-time, that the decision whether or not to use the atomic bomb to compel the surrender of Japan was never even an issue. There was unanimous, automatic, unquestioned agreement around our table; nor did I ever hear the slightest suggestion that we should do otherwise.

THE SECOND WORLD WAR,

VOL. VI

✳✳✳

March 9, 1946

There have been many occasions when a powerful state has wished to raise great armies, and with money and time and discipline and loyalty that can be accomplished. Nevertheless the rate at which the small American Army of only a few hundred thousand men, not long before the war, created the mighty force of millions of soldiers, is a wonder in military history.

SPEECH—THE PENTAGON, WASHINGTON

✳✳✳

October 10, 1953

We are told the Locarno Treaty failed and did not prevent the war. There was a very good reason for that. The United States were not in it. Had the United States taken, before the First World War or between the wars, the same interest and made the same exertions to preserve peace and uphold freedom which I thank God she is doing now, there might never have been a first war and there would certainly never have been a second. With their mighty aid, I have a sure hope there will not be a third.

SPEECH—MARGATE

✳✳✳

ON THE AMERICAN AND
BRITISH CONSTITUTIONS

1932

Responding to question after a speech in New York City.

Q.:   Would you become an American citizen if we could make
you President of the United States? I know our Constitution
disqualifies you but we can amend that, as we did in the case
of Prohibition.

MR. CHURCHILL: There are various little difficulties in the way.
However, I have been treated so splendidly in the United
States that I should be disposed, if you can amend the Con-
stitution, seriously to consider the matter.

                    IRREPRESSIBLE CHURCHILL

                    ✳✳✳

WRITING ON YALTA
1945

This led the President [Roosevelt] to speak of the British Constitution. He said that I was always talking about what the
Constitution allowed and what it did not allow, but actually there
was no Constitution. However, an unwritten Constitution was better than a written one. It was like the Atlantic Charter; the document did not exist, yet all the world knew all about it. Among his
papers he had found one copy signed by himself and me, but

strange to say both signatures were in his own handwriting. I replied that the Atlantic Charter was not a law, but a star.

THE SECOND WORLD WAR,
VOL. VI

❇❇❇

November 11, 1947

The whole history of this country shows a British instinct—and, I think I may say, a genius—for the division of power. The American Constitution, with its checks and counter-checks, combined with its frequent appeals to the people, embodied much of the ancient wisdom of this Island. Of course, there must be proper executive power to any Government, but, our British, our English idea, in a special sense, has always been a system of balanced rights and divided authority, with many other persons and organized bodies having to be considered besides the Government of the day and the officials they employ. The essential British wisdom is expressed in many foreign Constitutions which followed our Parliamentary system, outside the totalitarian zone, but never was it so necessary as in a country which has no written Constitution. . . . Many forms of Government have been tried, and will be tried in this world of sin and woe. No one pretends that democracy is perfect or all-wise. Indeed, it has been said that democracy is the worst form of Government except all those other forms that have been tried from time to time; but there is the broad feeling in our country that the people should rule, continuously rule, and that public opinion, expressed by all constitutional means, should shape, guide and control the actions of Ministers who are their servants and their masters.

SPEECH—HOUSE OF COMMONS

❇❇❇

January 28, 1950

The British race have always abhorred arbitrary and absolute government in every form. The great men who founded the American Constitution expressed this same separation of authority in the strongest and most durable form. Not only did they divide executive, legislative and judicial functions, but also by instituting a federal system they preserved immense and sovereign rights to local communities and by all these means they have maintained—often at some inconvenience—a system of law and liberty under which they thrived and reached the physical and, at this moment, the moral leadership of the world.

SPEECH—WOODFORD

❄❄❄

AT THE CORONATION LUNCHEON, WESTMINSTER HALL
March 27, 1953

We must be very careful nowadays—I perhaps all the more because of my American forebears—in what we say about the American Constitution. I will, therefore, content myself with the observation that no Constitution was ever written in better English. The key thought alike of the British Constitutional Monarchy and the Republic of the United States of America is a hatred of dictatorship. Both here and across the ocean over the generations and the centuries, the idea of the division of power has lain deep at the root of our development. We do not want to live under a system dominated either by one man or one theme. Like nature, we follow in freedom the paths of variety and change.

SPEECH

❄❄❄

It must be remembered that Britain and the United States are united at this time upon the same ideologies, namely, freedom, and the principles set out in the American Constitution and humbly reproduced with modern variations in the Atlantic Charter. The Soviet Government have a different philosophy, namely, Communism, and use to the full the methods of police government, which they are applying in every State which has fallen a victim to their liberating arms. The Prime Minister cannot readily bring himself to accept the idea that the position of the United States is that Britain and Soviet Russia are just two foreign Powers, six of one and half a dozen of the other, with whom the troubles of the late war have to be adjusted. Except in so far as force is concerned, there is no equality between right and wrong. The great causes and principles for which Britain and the United States have suffered and triumphed are not mere matters of the balance of power. They in fact involve the salvation of the world.

THE SECOND WORLD WAR,

VOL. VI

LAST WORDS SPOKEN IN THE HOUSE OF COMMONS BY WINSTON CHURCHILL AS PRIME MINISTER

MARCH 31, 1955

[The debate in the House of Commons, on the North Atlantic Treaty Organization, turned on whether Prime Minister Churchill would consult with President Eisenhower and the governments of other countries on setting up some form of Assembly under NATO, similar to the Council of Europe. He resigned the Premiership six days later on April 6, 1955.]

MR. DE FREITAS: Whilst agreeing that it is undeniable that NATO should have this, may I ask the Prime Minister to consider consultations as to the evolution of the European Assembly so that Americans and Canadians could meet with European members and discuss common problems in debate?

PRIME MINISTER CHURCHILL: Certainly, I think the closer the contacts between the United States and Europe the better.

SPEECH—HOUSE OF COMMONS

SIGNIFICANT SPEECHES

BY

WINSTON CHURCHILL

IN

AMERICA

ON BRITISH-AMERICAN
ECONOMICS

WINSTON S. CHURCHILL LECTURED AT
PUBLIC MUSIC HALL, CLEVELAND, OHIO,

February 3, 1932

All that is necessary [to regain world prosperity] for the two or three principal governments of the world is to proclaim their desire to revalue commodities and services up to the level of 1927, then—call in their experts and order them to devise the methods and details.

[As to the theory that over-production is to blame for the Depression, Churchill commented sharply]: We are stripped bare by the curse of plenty.

[On tariff barriers—on the fact that large debts between nations are payable only in goods]: But when Germany attempted to pay back the war debts in reparations and goods, the other nations refused to take the goods, building tariff frontiers to protect their own industrial organizations.

And when Germany offered to pay France by sending workmen to help rebuild the devastated areas, France refused in horror at the threatened taking of jobs from her own workmen.

The problem was solved up until 1929 by the creditor nations lending back to Germany the money she paid. But when the 1929 crash came, the United States and others stopped lending back. The result was that Germany could pay only in gold.

. . . Unless Germany can pay her creditors in goods, or unless there is a great increase in prices, there is no hope of collecting the war's debts. . . .

The deflation now in progress is the greatest danger to capitalism, . . . deflation, if continued will isolate the nations completely, will bring repudiation of debts, will reduce the whole world to barbarism and barter of the Dark Ages.

Debts between nations can be paid only in goods but the victor nations did not want goods. Germany, for instance, offered to pay with workmen to rebuild the destroyed buildings but France indignantly cried, 'We saw enough of your men in the war.' Thus, there was only the process of paying in gold.

If the gold in France and the United States were put into circulation, instead of kept sterile in vaults, it would have driven prices up, . . . the high prices would make the tariff ineffective, and goods would pour in until the whole situation had resumed its economic balance.

The United States in 1928 was closer to bridging the gap between the consumer and the producer, which is what all economic systems have aimed at, and I propose that the two English-speaking nations of the world order their government experts to revalue commodities at the 1928 level and devise methods and details to keep the situation pliable.

It is the function of government to provide authority, it is for the government to declare what must be done, and the function of experts to provide the necessary steps. In this role it is not impossible that experts could devise the steps to revalue commodities and provide a stabilizer.

[On reparations]: Germany is not being bled white by the reparations demands . . . the United States did not bleed the world.

The United States immediately relent all she got as payment on war debts . . . Germany really has received a bonus. She has had an infusion of credits and commodities which she needed and desires and enjoys. She was in the position of the debtor who owes so much that he can see no other way but to go out and borrow more.

The system of war reparations was foolish, but I am not ready to believe yet that Germany cannot pay. Unquestionably she cannot pay now, but let us reserve judgment. Just now reparations are down to such a scale that they may not be beyond her power.

THE CLEVELAND PRESS

✻✻✻

RECOLLECTIONS OF WINSTON CHURCHILL'S 1932 CLEVELAND VISIT THIRTY-FOUR YEARS LATER IN 1966

by

EDITOR LOUIS B. SELTZER

It was a small gathering . . . thirty-four years ago, and most respectful in the presence of one of the world's truly great men.

So respectful, in fact, that, as we gathered around a table at the Mid-Day Club . . . guests of the late Sam Halle, the silence was rather painful.

"Now, come now," said Winston Churchill, blowing a cloud of cigar smoke straight ahead of him, "this isn't the American free speech I've heard so much about—or that my mother always boasted about."

That was all the gathering needed.

From that moment on, the immortal British visitor listened, asked questions, parried some, wittily taunted guests with some of America's international inconsistencies, and thoroughly enjoyed the whole afternoon's dialogue.

But, then, toward the conclusion, he suddenly became serious. His highly mobile face, which seemed to mirror his thoughts, had alternately been mischievous and light, somber and challenging; his lips pursing with his witticisms and his brow furrowing with his challenges.

"You know," he finally said, "that this is really an altogether new world in which we are all living—a world which when it moves into the 21st Century will look even more unlike the world which moved from the 19th into the 20th.

"All of this," he said, gesturing with his pudgy right hand, and directing our attention out of the window toward the Cleveland lakefront.

"All of this will be different. Who knows with what the skies may be filled—airplanes, yes—but tremendous airplanes; and helicopters, yes, and perhaps many thousands of them—and high buildings, yes, and hundreds more of them—and speed faster than sound, yes, and perhaps even faster than a flash of light."

The room was quiet. Here was a rare opportunity. Here was a great man moved to speak his thoughts. All listened intently.

Churchill, however, stopped. He felt that he had said enough on the subject. He tamped his cigar and reached for a match and lit it up again full blast, billowing the smoke, and watching the air currents carry it ceilingward.

"What about the world—what about war?" asked Sam Halle.

"I don't like it, Sam—I don't like it at all," Winston Churchill said, and his voice, conversational in tone up to this moment, carried increased emphasis.

"We are not through with wars. We will have another one. We cannot live in a fool's paradise. We must be realistic. Of course we should hope for and pray for and work for peace but we should not rule out the realism of men and nations and their ambitions and their obscure intentions.

"We must watch. We must prepare. We must not close our eyes to what is happening while our hopes are elevated with our objectives."

"At all times," Churchill said, after a pause, "we must separate the wish from the fact. We must wish—we must hope—we must move unceasingly forward toward the fulfillment of men's great dreams. We must not, however, as we do so, for so much as an instant take either our eye or our mind from the reality of the world in which we live—in a world of tumult, and change, and a world influenced, as always, by men's ambitions, and plans and conspiracies."

THE CLEVELAND PRESS

THE ATLANTIC CHARTER

A JOINT DECLARATION BY
MR. WINSTON CHURCHILL AND
AND PRESIDENT ROOSEVELT
AT THEIR MEETING IN THE ATLANTIC
August 14, 1941

The President of the United States and the Prime Minister, Mr. Churchill, representing His Majesty's Government in the United Kingdom, being met together, deem it right to make known certain common principles in the national policies of their respective countries on which they base their hopes for a better future for the world.

First, their countries seek no aggrandisement, territorial or other.

Second, they desire to see no territorial changes that do not accord with the freely expressed wishes of the peoples concerned.

Third, they respect the right of all peoples to choose the form of Government under which they will live; and they wish to see sovereign rights and self-government restored to those who have been forcibly deprived of them.

Fourth, they will endeavour, with due respect for their existing obligations, to further enjoyment by all States, great or small, victor or vanquished, of access, on equal terms, to the trade and to the raw materials of the world which are needed for their economic prosperity.

Fifth, they desire to bring about the fullest collaboration between all nations in the economic field, with the object of securing for all improved labour standards, economic advancement and social security.

Sixth, after the final destruction of Nazi tyranny, they hope to see established a peace which will afford to all nations the means of dwelling in safety within their own boundaries, and which will afford assurance that all the men in all the land may live out their lives in freedom from fear and want.

Seventh, such a peace should enable all men to traverse the high seas and oceans without hindrances.

Eighth, they believe all of the nations of the world, for realistic as well as spiritual reasons, must come to the abandonment of the use of force. Since no future peace can be maintained if land, sea, or air armaments continue to be employed by nations which threaten, or may threaten, aggression outside of their frontiers, they believe, pending the establishment of a wider and permanent system of general security, that the disarmament of such nations is essential. They will likewise aid and encourage all other practicable measures which will lighten for peace-loving peoples the crushing burden of armaments.

THE WHITE HOUSE CHRISTMAS TREE

Speech broadcast to the world from the White House, Washington, at the twentieth annual observance of the lighting of the community Christmas tree, December 24, 1941.

I spend this anniversary and festival far from my country, far from my family, yet I cannot truthfully say that I feel far from home. Whether it be the ties of blood on my mother's side, or the the friendships I have developed here over many years of active life, or the commanding sentiment of comradeship in the common cause of great peoples who speak the same language, who kneel at the same altars and, to a very large extent, pursue the same ideals, I cannot feel myself a stranger here in the centre and at the summit of the United States. I feel a sense of unity and fraternal association which, added to the kindliness of your welcome, convinces me that

I have a right to sit at your fireside and share your Christmas joys.

This is a strange Christmas Eve. Almost the whole world is locked in deadly struggle, and, with the most terrible weapons which science can devise, the nations advance upon each other. Ill would it be for us this Christmastide if we were not sure that no greed for the land or wealth of any other people, no vulgar ambition, no morbid lust for material gain at the expense of others, had led us to the field. Here, in the midst of war, raging and roaring over all the lands and seas, creeping nearer to our hearts and homes, here, amid all the tumult, we have tonight the peace of the spirit in each cottage home and in every generous heart. Therefore we may cast aside for this night at least the cares and dangers which beset us, and make for the children an evening of happiness in a world of storm. Here, then, for one night only, each home throughout the English-speaking world should be a brightly-lighted island of happiness and peace.

Let the children have their night of fun and laughter. Let the gifts of Father Christmas delight their play. Let us grown-ups share to the full in their unstinted pleasures before we turn again to the stern task and the formidable years that lie before us, resolved that, by our sacrifice and daring, these same children shall not be robbed of their inheritance or denied their right to live in a free and decent world.

And so, in God's mercy, a happy Christmas to you all.

ANGLO-AMERICAN UNITY

SPEECH ON RECEIVING AN HONORARY
DEGREE AT HARVARD UNIVERSITY
September 6, 1943

The last time I attended a ceremony of this character was in the spring of 1941, when, as Chancellor of Bristol University, I conferred a degree upon the United States Ambassador, Mr. Winant, and *in absentia* upon President Conant, our President, who is here today and presiding over this ceremony. The blitz was running hard at that time, and the night before, the raid on Bristol had been heavy. Several hundreds had been killed and wounded. Many houses were destroyed. Buildings next to the University were still burning and many of the University authorities who conducted the ceremony had pulled on their robes over uniforms begrimed and drenched; but all was presented with faultless ritual and appropriate decorum, and I sustained a very strong and invigorating impression of the superiority of man over the forces that can destroy him.

Here now, today, I am once again in academic groves—groves is, I believe, the right word—where knowledge is garnered, where learning is stimulated, where virtues are inculcated and thought encouraged. Here, in the broad United States, with a respectable ocean on either side of us, we can look upon the world in all its wonder and in all its woe. But what is this that I discern as I pass through your streets, as I look around this great company.

I see uniforms on every side. I understand that nearly the whole energies of the University have been drawn into the preparation of American youth for the battlefield. For this purpose all classes and courses have been transformed, and even the most sacred vacations have been swept away in a round-the-year and almost round-the-clock drive to make warriors and technicians for the fighting fronts.

Twice in my lifetime the long arm of destiny has searched across the oceans and involved the entire life and manhood of the United States in a deadly struggle. There was no use in saying 'We don't want it; we won't have it; our forebears left Europe to avoid these quarrels; we have founded a new world which has no contact with the old.' There was no use in that. The long arm reaches out remorselessly, and everyone's existence, environment, and outlook undergo a swift and irresistible change. What is the explanation, Mr. President, of these strange facts, and what are the deep laws to which they respond? I will offer you one explanation—there are others, but one will suffice. The price of greatness is responsibility. If the people of the United States had continued in a mediocre station, struggling with the wilderness, absorbed in their own affairs, and a factor of no consequence in the movement of the world, they might have remained forgotten and undisturbed beyond their protecting oceans: but one cannot rise to be in many ways the leading community in the civilized world without being involved in its problems, without being convulsed by its agonies and inspired by its causes.

If this has been proved in the past, as it has been, it will become indisputable in the future. The people of the United States cannot escape world responsibility. Although we live in a period so tumultuous that little can be predicted we may be quite sure that this process will be intensified with every forward step the United States make in wealth and in power. Not only are the responsibilities of this great republic growing, but the world over which they range is itself contracting in relation to our powers of locomotion at a positively alarming rate.

We have learned to fly. What prodigious changes are involved in that new accomplishment. Man has parted company with his trusty friend the horse and has sailed into the azure with the eagles, eagles being represented by the infernal (*loud laughter*)—I mean internal—combustion engine. Where, then, are those broad oceans, those vast staring deserts? They are shrinking beneath our very eyes. Even elderly Parliamentarians like myself are forced to acquire a high degree of mobility.

But to the youth of America, as to the youth of Britain, I say 'You cannot stop'. There is no halting-place at this point. We have now reached a stage in the journey where there can be no pause. We must go on. It must be world anarchy or world order. Throughout all this ordeal and struggle which is characteristic of our age, you will find in the British Commonwealth and Empire good comrades to whom you are united by other ties besides those of State policy and public need. To a large extent, they are the ties of blood and history. Naturally, I a child of both worlds, am conscious of these.

Law, language, literature—these are considerable factors. Common conceptions of what is right and decent, a marked regard for fair play, especially to the weak and poor, a stern sentiment of impartial justice, and above all the love of personal freedom, or as Kipling put it; 'Leave to live by no man's leave underneath the law' —these are common conceptions on both sides of the ocean among the English-speaking peoples. We hold to these conceptions as strongly as you do.

We do not war primarily with races as such. Tyranny is our foe, whatever trappings or disguise it wears, whatever language it speaks, be it external or internal, we must for ever be on our guard, ever mobilized, ever vigilant, always ready to spring at its throat. In all this, we march together. Not only do we march and strive shoulder to shoulder at this moment under the fire of the enemy on the fields of war or in the air, but also in those realms of thought which are consecrated to the rights and the dignity of man.

At the present time we have in continual vigorous action the British and United States Combined Chiefs of Staff Committee, which works immediately under the President and myself as representative of the British War Cabinet. This committee, with its elaborate organization of Staff officers of every grade, disposes of all our resources and, in practice, uses British and American troops, ships, aircraft, and munitions just as if they were the resources of a single State or nation.

I would not say there are never divergences of view among these high professional authorities. It would be unnatural if there were not. That is why it is necessary to have plenary meeting of principals every two or three months. All these men now know each other. They trust each other. They like each other, and most of them have been at work together for a long time. When they meet they thrash things out with great candour and plain, blunt speech, but after a few days the President and I find ourselves furnished with sincere and united advice.

This is a wonderful system. There was nothing like it in the last war. There never has been anything like it between two allies. It is reproduced in an even more tightly-knit form at General Eisenhower's headquarters in the Mediterranean, where everything is completely intermingled and soldiers are ordered into battle by the supreme commander or his deputy, General Alexander, without the slightest regard to whether they are British, American, or Canadian, but simply in accordance with the fighting need.

Now in my opinion it would be a most foolish and improvident act on the part of our two Governments, or either of them, to break up this smooth-running and immensely powerful machinery the moment the war is over. For our own safety, as well as for the security of the rest of the world, we are bound to keep it working and in running order after the war—probably for a good many years, not only until we have set up some world arrangement to keep the peace but until we know that it is an arrangement which will really give us that protection we must have from danger and aggression, a protection we have already had to seek across two vast world wars.

I am not qualified, of course, to judge whether or not this would become a party question in the United States, and I would not presume to discuss that point. I am sure, however, that it will not be a party question in Great Britain. We must not let go of the securities we have found necessary to preserve our lives and liberties until we are quite sure we have something else to put in their place which will give us an equally solid guarantee.

The great Bismarck—for there were once great men in Germany —is said to have observed towards the close of his life that the most potent factor in human society at the end of the nineteenth century was the fact that the British and American peoples spoke the same language. That was a pregnant saying. Certainly it has enabled us to wage war together with an intimacy and harmony never before achieved among allies.

The gift of a common tongue is a priceless inheritance and it may well some day become the foundation of a common citizenship. I like to think of British and Americans moving about freely over each other's wide estates with hardly a sense of being foreigners to one another. But I do not see why we should not try to spread our common language even more widely throughout the globe and, without seeking selfish advantage over any, possess ourselves of this invaluable amenity and birthright.

Some months ago I persuaded the British Cabinet to set up a

committee of Ministers to study and report upon Basic English. Here you have a plan. There are others, but here you have a very carefully wrought plan for an international language capable of a very wide transaction of practical business and interchange of ideas. The whole of it is comprised in about 650 nouns and 200 verbs or other parts of speech—no more indeed than can be written on one side of a single sheet of paper.

What was my delight when, the other evening, quite unexpectedly, I heard the President of the United States suddenly speak of the merits of Basic English, and is it not a coincidence that, with all this in mind, I should arrive at Harvard, in fulfillment of the long-dated invitations to receive this degree with which President Conant has honoured me? For Harvard has done more than any other American university to promote the extension of Basic English. The first work on Basic English was written by two Englishmen, Ivor Richards now of Harvard, and C. K. Ogden, of Cambridge University, England, working in association.

The Harvard Commission on English Language Studies is distinguished both for its research and its practical work, particularly in introducing the use of Basic English in Latin America; and this Commission, your Commission, is now, I am told, working with secondary schools in Boston on the use of Basic English in teaching the main language to American children and in teaching it to foreigners preparing for citizenship.

Gentlemen, I make you my compliments. I do not wish to exaggerate, but you are the head-stream of what might well be a mighty fertilizing and health-giving river. It would certainly be a grand convenience for us all to be able to move freely about the world—as we shall be able to do more freely than ever before as the science of the world develops—be able to move freely about the world, and be able to find everywhere a medium, albeit primitive, of intercourse and understanding. Might it not also be an advantage to many races, and an aid to the building-up of our new structure for preserving peace? All these are great possibilities, and I say: 'Let us go into this together. Let us have another Boston Tea Party about it.'

Let us go forward as with other matters and other measures

similar in aim and effect—let us go forward in malice to none and good will to all. Such plans offer far better prizes than taking away other people's provinces or lands or grinding them down in exploitation. The empires of the futures are the empires of the mind.

It would, of course, Mr. President, be lamentable if those who are charged with the duty of leading great nations forward in this grievous and obstinate war were to allow their minds and energies to be diverted from making the plans to achieve our righteous purposes without needless prolongation of slaughter and destruction.

Nevertheless, we are also bound, so far as life and strength allow, and without prejudice to our dominating military tasks, to look ahead to those days which will surely come when we shall have finally beaten down Satan under our feet and find ourselves with other great allies at once the masters and the servants of the future. Various schemes of achieving world security while yet preserving national rights, tradition and customs are being studied and probed.

We have all the fine work that was done a quarter of a century ago by those who devised and tried to make effective the League of Nations after the last war. It is said that the League of Nations failed. If so, that is largely because it was abandoned, and later on betrayed: because those who were its best friends were till a very late period infected with a futile pacifism: because the United States, the originating impulse, fell out of the line: because, while France had been bled white and England was supine and bewildered, a monstrous growth of aggression sprang up in Germany, in Italy and Japan.

We have learned from hard experiences that stronger, more efficient, more rigorous world institutions must be created to preserve peace and to forestall the causes of future wars. In this task the strongest victorious nations must be combined, and also those who have borne the burden and heat of the day and suffered under the flail of adversity; and, in this task, this creative task, there are some who say: 'Let us have a world council and under it regional or continental councils,' and there are others who prefer a somewhat different organization.

All these matters weigh with us now in spite of the war, which none can say has reached its climax, which is perhaps entering for us, British and Americans, upon its most severe and costly phase. But I am here to tell you that, whatever form your system of world security may take, however the nations are grouped and ranged, whatever derogations are made from national sovereignty for the sake of the large synthesis, nothing will work soundly or for long without the united effort of the British and American peoples.

If we are together nothing is impossible. If we are divided all will fail. I therefore preach continually the doctrine of the fraternal association of our two peoples, not for any purpose of gaining invidious material advantages for either of them, not for territorial aggrandisement or the vain pomp of earthly domination, but for the sake of service to mankind and for the honour that comes to those who faithfully serve great causes.

Here let me say how proud we ought to be, young and old alike, to live in this tremendous, thrilling, formative epoch in the human story, and how fortunate it was for the world that when these great trials came upon it there was a generation that terror could not conquer and brutal violence could not enslave. Let all who are here remember, as the words of the hymn we have just sung suggest, let all of us who are here remember that we are on the stage of history, and that whatever our station may be, and whatever part we have to play, great or small, our conduct is liable to be scrutinized not only by history but by our own descendants.

Let us rise to the full level of our duty and of our opportunity, and let us thank God for the spiritual rewards he has granted for all forms of valiant and faithful service.

SPEECH TO THE GENERAL ASSEMBLY OF VIRGINIA

March 8, 1946

Mr. Speaker, Members of the General Assembly of Virginia, Ladies and Gentlemen:

I was deeply moved by the glowing terms of the Joint Resolution of both branches of the Legislature inviting me here to address the General Assembly of Virginia. I take it as a high honour to be present here this morning ot discharge that task. I always value being asked to address a Parliament. I have already on two occasions in the war addressed the Congress of the United States. I have addressed the Canadian Parliament. I have addressed a Joint Session of the Belgian Legislature, more recently, and there is a place of which you may have heard across the ocean called the House of Commons, to which, invited or uninvited, I have, from time to time, had things to say. I have also had invitations, couched in terms for which I am most grateful, from the State Legislatures of South Carolina, Kentucky and Mississippi. It would have given me the greatest pleasure to accept and fulfil all these. But as I have not the life and strength to repay all the kindness which is offered me, I felt that these other States would be willing to accept the primacy of the Virginia Assembly, as the most ancient, law-making body on the mainland of the western hemisphere. And thus I find myself here before you this morning in Richmond, in the historic capitol of world-famous Virginia.

I am also about to visit Williamsburg. During the war, at one of our Conferences, General Marshall arranged to take the British Chiefs of Staff for a visit to Williamsburg and I had planned to go with them, but the work I had to do made it necessary for me to remain in Washington; and so, on this visit to the United States, I had promised myself the treat of seeing Williamsburg, and my friend, General Eisenhower, who is with us to-day, undertook to pilot me around. I have great satisfaction in meeting him over here. We had a lot of business to do together during what I believe has been called, in another connection, "the late unpleasantness" and I have formed impressions that will last me all my days of his single-hearted purpose, wide and profound views on military science and his great power of making the soldiers and officers of our two countries work together under all the shocks and strains of war as if they were the soldiers of one single nation.

I hope I shall acquit myself to your satisfaction but the respon-

sibility for what may happen is yours. Do you not think you are
running some risk in inviting me to give you my faithful counsel
on this occasion? You have not asked to see beforehand what I am
going to say. I might easily, for instance, blurt out a lot of things,
which people know in their hearts are true, but are a bit shy of
saying in public, and this might cause a regular commotion and get
you all into trouble. However, the people of Virginia and, above
all, the people of Richmond have proved in the past that they have
strong nerves and that they can face not only facts but fate with
fortitude and pride. Of course my mind goes back into the past so
much of which we have in common. The light of the Elizabethan
age, which Shakespeare, Raleigh and Grenville adorned, casts its
unfading lustre upon our scene here and in Williamsburg nearby.
This was a cradle of the Great Republic in which more than 150
years afterwards the strong champions of freedom and independence were found to have been nursed. With what care did these
early Fathers of our modern inspiration preserve the title deeds of
freedom in Parliamentary privilege, in trial by jury, in the Habeas
Corpus, in Magna Carta, and in the English Common Law! With
what vigilance did Thomas Jefferson, Patrick Henry and Robert
Henry Lee, and even George Washington, the Father of his country, defend these title deeds in later, unhappy but pregnant times!
The theme of individual liberty and of the rights of citizens so
painfully evolved across the centuries in England was upheld
through every stress and confusion by Virginia and that theme
lights the English-speaking world to-day. It lights our world and it
is also a beacon shining through the mists and storms to many
lands, where the rights of man—his honour, his happiness, his
freedom—are yearned for or are so far enjoyed only precariously.
I salute you here in this General Assembly as the guardians of the
sacred flame.

Another century passes across our minds and we see Virginia
and Richmond the centre of a tragedy which, however agonising
at the time, is now for ever illuminated by drama and romance.
I have visited most of your battlefields on the peninsula, on the
Rappahannock in the Wilderness, and I was guided there some years

ago by your distinguished historian Mr. Freeman,* who is, I believe, here to-day, and whose works are a solid contribution, not only to the fame of the south but to the whole strength of the indissoluble Union. Yet it is in the words of an English General Officer that I shall express myself to you this morning. General Henderson, the author of *The Life of Stonewall Jackson* and of *The Campaign of Fredericksburg,* was a man I knew nearly 40 years ago, and this is what he wrote:—

> Far and Wide, between the mountains and the sea stretches the fair Virginia for which Lee and Jackson and their soldiers,
> 'One equal temper of heroic hearts',
> fought so well and unavailingly; . . . . yet her brows are bound with glory, the legacy of her lost children; and her spotless name, uplifted by their victories and manhood, is high among the nations. Surely she may rest content, knowing that so long as men turn to the records of history will their deeds live, giving to all time one of the noblest examples of unyielding courage and devotion the world has known.

My grandfather** was a Northerner in the state of New York, and you would not expect me to belie the cause for which he strove. We have moved on into a broader age and larger combinations. Old battles are remembered not as sources of bitterness but to celebrate the martial virtues and civic fidelity of both sides in that immortal struggle. Out of this story have also come examples of high character in which Americans have shown themselves in no wise wanting in the new trials and tribulations through which we have just passed.

To-day the American Union is the most powerful champion of national and individual freedom and it carries with it a large portion of the hopes of men. There was about General Robert E. Lee a quality of selflessness which raises him to the very highest rank of men, whether soldiers or statesmen, who have been concerned with the fortunes of nations. And in General Marshall and in General

* Mr. Douglas Southall Freeman, Editor-Author.
** Mr. Leonard Jerome.

Eisenhower, and others of the Army and Navy of the United States whom I could mention, that character, that quality of self-lessness has been a bond uniting all Allied Armies and the key to the victory which we have gained together.

It has been said that the dominant lesson of history is that mankind is unteachable. You will remember how my dear friend, the late President Roosevelt, had to argue only a few years ago, that Americans were not what is called "soft" and how he asserted that this was "The land of unending challenge"; and I myself have read in secret documents German reports which spoke before they met them of "these ridiculous American troops". Surely these European countries should not have forgotten or ignored so soon the example of tenacity, willpower and self-devotion which shines through all the records of the great war between the American States. We, too, in our British islands and in our great self-governing Empire spread about the world, have proved that our race when stirred to its depth has qualities deserving of respect.

In fact, in proportion to our numbers, our efforts, our sacrifices and our losses have not been surpassed. Moreover, it fell to us to have the honour of standing alone for a whole year against the main strength of the mighty Axis and the time for preparation which was thus gained was, as I am sure General Eisenhower will agree, a vital service to the United States and to the common cause.

But it is upon the future rather than upon the past that I wish to rest this morning. In these last years of my life there is a message of which I conceive myself to be a bearer. It is a very simple message which can be well understood by the people of both our countries. It is that we should stand together. We should stand together in malice to none, in greed for nothing but in defence of those causes which we hold dear not only for our own benefit, but because we believe they mean the honour and the happiness of long generations of men. We ought, as I said to the Congress of the United States in a dark hour in 1941, to walk together in majesty and peace. That I am sure is the wish of the overwhelming majority of the 200 million Britons and Americans who are spread about the globe. That this is our destiny, or, as most of us would put it, the Will of God, seems sure and certain. How is it to be expressed, in what way and in what hour it is to be achieved I cannot tell.

I read the other day that an English nobleman, whose name is new to me, has stated that England would have to become the 49th state of the American Union. I read yesterday that an able American editor had written that the United States ought not to be asked to re-enter the British Empire. It seems to me and I dare say it seems to you, that the path of wisdom lies somewhere between these scarecrow extremes. We must find the means and the method of working together not only in times of war and mortal anguish but in times of peace with all its bewilderments and clamour and clatter of tongues. It is in the years of peace that wars are prevented and that those foundations are laid upon which the noble structures of the future can be built. But peace will not be preserved without the virtues that make victory possible in war. Peace will not be preserved by pious sentiments expressed in terms of platitudes or by official grimaces and diplomatic correctitude, however desirable this may be from time to time. It will not be preserved by casting aside in dangerous years the panoply of warlike strength. There must be earnest thought. There must also be faithful perseverance and forsight. Greatheart must have his sword and armour to guard the pilgrims on their way. Above all, among the English-speaking peoples, there must be the union of hearts based upon conviction and common ideals. That is what I offer. That is what I seek.

ADDRESS TO AMERICAN AND BRITISH SERVICE MEMBERS

THE PENTAGON, WASHINGTON, D.C.

March 9, 1946

General of the Army Eisenhower, Fleet Admiral Leahy, Fleet Admiral Nimitz, and General of the Air Spaatz. It is indeed a very great pleasure and honour to me that the Secretary of War and General Eisenhower should have asked me here to-day and have given me an opportunity, before going home, to meet the high officers of the United States services and to express to them on behalf of my country and of the British services our admiration and gratitude for all they have done in this great common struggle carried to absolute victory in arms. The prevailing feature of our work together was the intimacy of association. Language is a great bridge. There are many, many ideas we have in common and also practice: but there was a spirit of loyalty, of good will, of comradeship which never has been seen in all the history of war between Allied Armies, Navies, Air Forces fighting together side by side. On General Eisenhower's staff, which I saw often and closely in Africa, in France and in Germany, it was carried to extreme perfection. And, as you know, the best people were picked for the various posts, and they gave orders and took orders without regard to which country their next neighbour or opposite number belonged to. I used the word "opposite number" by mistake, because there were no "opposite numbers"—there was absolute intermingling of staff work, and the same was true in the commands in the field. Many British and American troops served with perfect confidence under the commanders of the other country. And speaking for our own people, we always had more than fair treatment and felt absolute confidence in those to whom we confided the lives of our soldiers.

I am certain that our effective unity saved scores of thousands of lives, perhaps far more, and abridged the course of the struggle, as nothing else could have done. That must be regarded as a precious possession which we have in common and which whenever circumstances may require it—I cannot think they will do so in our lifetime—will be available to strengthen any joint efforts our Governments may order in some future period. No one was more the champion and embodiment of this unity than General Eisenhower. I never had a chance to visit the Pacific but I am told the same conditions prevailed there as were established by him at SHAEF Headquarters and in the field. Of course, when people are on different ships they don't come so closely together as they do in the camps and billets. But it was one great force that overthrew the mighty powers with which we were confronted and which were dashed to ruin and helplessness by our exertions.

I have been thinking a great deal about the work of the United States services. I will speak a little more of the Army than of the others because I saw more of it. I greatly admired the manner in which the American Army was formed. I think it was a prodigy of organisation, of improvisation. There have been many occasions when a powerful state has wished to raise great armies, and with money and time and discipline and loyalty that can be accomplished. Nevertheless the rate at which the small American Army of only a few hundred thousand men, not long before the war, created the mighty force of millions of soldiers, is a wonder in military history.

I was here two or three years ago and visited with General Marshall, from whom I received a most delightful telegram just now, an Army Corps being trained in South Carolina, and we saw there the spectacle of what you may call the mass production of divisions. In great and rapid rotation they were formed, and moved on to further stages of their perfection. I saw the creation of this mighty force—this mighty Army, victorious in every theatre against the enemy in so short a time and from such a very small parent stock. This is an achievement which the soldiers of every other country will always study with admiration and with envy.

But that is not the whole story, nor even the greatest part of the story. To create great Armies is one thing; to lead them and to handle them is another. It remains to me a mystery as yet unexplained how the very small staffs which the United States kept during the years of peace were able not only to build up the Armies and Air Force units, but also to find the leaders and vast staffs capable of handling enormous masses and of moving them faster and farther than masses have ever been moved in war before.

The United States owes a debt to its officer corps. In time of peace in this country, as in my own, the military profession is very often required to pass a considerable number of years in the cool shade. One of Marlborough's veterans wrote the lines, now nearly 250 years ago,

God and the soldier we adore
In time of danger, not before;
The danger passed and all things righted,
God is forgotten and the soldier slighted.

Undoubtedly the military profession in the great Western democracies, which wholeheartedly desire peace, is one which has required great sacrifices from those who devote themselves to it. All around them goes the busy exciting world of business and politics with all its varieties, but the officers frugally, modestly, industriously, faithfully pursue their professional studies and duties, very often for long periods at a time, without the public notice. That you should have been able to preserve the art not only of creating mighty armies almost at the stroke of a wand—but of leading and guiding those armies upon a scale incomparably greater than anything that was prepared for or even dreamed of, constitutes a gift made by the Officer Corps of the United States to their nation in time of trouble, which I earnestly hope will never be forgotten here, and it certainly never will be forgotten in the island from which I come. You will, I am sure, permit me to associate with this amazing feat, the name of General Marshall, the creator of this Instrument of Victory.

I offer you gentlemen my most earnest congratulations on the manner in which, when the danger came, you were not found wanting. We talk a great deal about the future of armies and we are studying this matter across the ocean ourselves, and the relation between the officers and the other ranks. I speak not entirely as an amateur. I went through five years of professional training at the beginning of my life, in those impressionable years, and I have had the good fortune to be in all the wars that Great Britain has been engaged in in one capacity or another during my lifetime. We now have to choose very carefully the line of division between the officers and other ranks upon which authority should stand. There is only one line in my view, and that is professional attainment. The men have a right to feel that their officers know far better than they do how to bring them safely and victoriously through the terribly difficult decisions which arise in war. And for my part as far as

Great Britain is concerned, I shall always urge that the tendency in the future should be to prolong the courses of instruction at the colleges rather than to abridge them and to equip our young officers with that special technical professional knowledge which soldiers have a right to expect from those who can give them orders, if necessary, to go to their deaths. It is quite clear that class or wealth or favour will not be allowed in the modern world to afford dividing lines. Professional attainment, based upon prolonged study, and collective study at colleges, rank by rank, and age by age—those are the title deeds of the commanders of the future armies, and the secret of future victories.

I venture to use these few words to you this afternoon because I have had a very varied experience in peace and war, and have met so many men who have played great parts, and I felt it a high honour to be invited to meet you again this afternoon, and to revive old acquaintances and shake hands with new ones. I thought these few observations I ventured to make might not be thought unfitting or unacceptable.

꙰꙰꙰

SPEECH AT A DINNER GIVEN BY MR. HENRY R. LUCE AT THE RITZ-CARLTON HOTEL IN NEW YORK CITY

March 25, 1949

I am extremely complimented to be invited here tonight and to find myself your guest amidst a gathering of Americans among whom I can discern many doughty comrades in our common struggle and who, taken together, represent a powerful living element in the future and in the power of the United States. I thank you very much for all the kind things that you have said.

You yourself have rendered great services. The wonderful publications which spread so widely through the land and put quality and art and point and pith and so forth in their vanguard, these are in themselves great contributions to the life and strength not only of the United States but of the English-speaking world. This great company, these old friends and comrades, gives me confidence and I am glad to come here and express my profound thanks on behalf of Britain and on behalf of Western Europe, of free Europe, as I have some credentials to do—for all you have done and are doing.

Gentlemen—many nations have arrived at the summit of the world but none, before the United States, on this occasion, has chosen that moment of triumph, not for aggrandizement, but for further self-sacrifice—sacrifice for the causes by which the life and strength of mankind is refreshed. The United States has shown itself more worthy of trust and honour than any government of men or associations of nations, that has ever reached pre-eminence by their action on the morrow of the common victory won by all. I wish to express the thanks of my own dear island and of its Empire, Commonwealth and also of the many countries in Western Europe who are drawing together on the broad ideals of Anglo-Saxon, British-American, call it what you will, unity, which alone gives an opportunity for the further advance of the human race.

Gentlemen, some time ago, you may possibly remember, I made a speech in Missouri at Fulton—I got into great trouble for that. But now not so much. Now it is thought better of. And I was very glad to see that General Marshall, that great statesman and soldier —I do not know whether you put soldier or statesman first in regard to so eminent a man—General Marshall has created this policy of the Marshall Aid, which shall ever bear his name—not because of what happens in the three or four years of the Aid but because of its effect as a turning point in the history of the world. General Marshall played his part, and then, we have now come to the Atlantic Pact, which when Mr. Attlee kindly showed it to me before it became public—but after it was settled—I thought it was one of the most important documents ever signed by large communities of human beings and certainly indicates a very considerable advance in opinion as far as the United States of America are concerned. Well, there you are—you're in it now, because there's no way out, but still if we pool our luck and share our fortunes I think you will have no reason to regret it.

But what has brought this great change from the time when I was so scolded three years ago for what I said at Fulton? And I do remember Governor Dewey coming down here to back me up at that rather bleak and raw moment when I spoke here in New York. The Governor knows how to take a bump and I've had some of that, too. My father—I remember some words that my father spake when I was an urchin—I remember that he said a man who can't take a knockdown blow isn't worth a damn. Well, I've always tried to live up to that and on the whole it's quite a healthy process. How has this great change from the atmosphere three years ago, when I spoke at Fulton, and now address you here—this distinguished gathering here—how has that great change been accomplished? No one could possibly have done it but Mr. Stalin. He is the one. No enemy of Russia, no—and I was never an enemy of Russia—no anti-Communist or no Conservative Republican gathering, missionaries, agitators, propaganda—none of them—if they worked night and day could ever have achieved the extraordinary change of opinion, change of conviction, change of mood, change of attitude and policy which has taken place in the last two years except the Soviet Government.

And that brings me to a question which we must ask ourselves. What is the explanation of the Soviet policy? Why have they deliberately united the free world against them? I will hazard the answer. These men in the Kremlin are very capable men; they do not act on the spur of the moment; profound deliberations take place in conclaves long welded together and any mistake made by any member of the company may be seriously viewed and punished. Yes—they do not let themselves go like some of us politicians do in the democratic countries. Well, how is it then—that they have deliberately united the free world against them? It is, I am sure, because they feared the friendship of the West more than they do its hostility. They can't afford to allow free and friendly intercourse between their country and those they control, and the rest of the world. They daren't see it develop—the coming and going and all the easements and tolerances which come from the agreeable contacts of nations and of individuals. They can't afford it. The Russians must not see what goes on outside and the world must not see what goes on inside the Soviet domain. That is, in my opinion, the explanation. After all if you were one of the fourteen men in the Kremlin—holding down hundreds of millions of people, aiming at the rule of the world—you might well feel that your prime interest was, at all costs, to keep up the barriers. I believe that their motive is self-preservation—not for Russia—but for themselves. Of course going out of office in Russia isn't quite as easy a business as it may be here or over the other side of the ocean. You lose the election, you may lose your life. It's very high stakes they play for—these fourteen men—and I'm sure that self-preservation for themselves lies at the root of this strange, extraordinary, unreasonable policy which has caused them deliberately to alienate all the generous sympathy there was for the brave Russian armies who fought so nobly in the war.

And thus we have come to what is called the cold war, a form of relationship between nations unprecedented in history, unparalleled in history. Never have there been such things that are happening now published all over the world. The insults, the taunts, the affronts, the ultimatums, the holdings up and so forth, and American bombers based in British airports and Soviet plans being pushed in every country to undermine or overthrow the existing state of civilization. All this—never in peace has been possible, but it is going on now and it called the cold war.

You would like me to examine some of these question with you tonight because I don't want to trespass upon so important an audience except to put to them points of real vital consequence. And I put this question. Are we winning the cold war?

It's a very important one for all of us, and for our families and our children. We wonder what world they will inherit and come into. Are we winning the cold war? Well this can't be decided, I think, by looking at Europe alone. We must first look to the East. The worst event, I'm sure Mr. Luce will agree with me in this—I'm sure the worst event since the fighting stopped has been the subjugation of a large part of China by Communism. There's your most formidable event. Now mind you, I think you have done quite right not to be diverted to make great undue efforts there at this moment, but the American interest in China is enormous. I was very much astonished when I came over here after Pearl Harbour to find the estimate of values which seemed to prevail in high American quarters, even in the highest, about China. Some of them thought that China would make as great a contribution to victory in the war as the whole British Empire together. Well, that astonishmed me very much. Nothing that I picked up afterwards led me to think that my astonishment was ill-founded. And it was said to me—well, China is an immense factor in the world, an immense population of intelligent, gifted, cultivated people, charming people with so many virtues, and so on. Well, I was thinking what part they would be able to play in our victory. I think on the whole you will not find a large profit item entered on that side of the ledger, but that doesn't alter our regard for the Chinese people. But what has happened now? It's very important, and while I think the decision of the United States is quite right, I am astonished they are not more concerned about it than they appear to be. Here I would like to congratulate you upon, and pay a tribute to, the work of General MacArthur in Japan. He has seemed to show a genius in peace equal to the high renown he gained in war.

In my view you don't want to knock a man down except to pick him up in a better frame of mind. That is my view about all these things that happen in the world—and you may pick him up in a better frame of mind. And that is a thing to think about. I say that the Atlantic Pact, in my view, would naturally be followed at no lengthy interval by a Pacific Pact which would deal with that immense portion of the globe.

Well, so much for the East. But a great advance has been made in the West in this cold war. Take the success of the Berlin Airlift, which arose largely from American conviction that it could be done. I will say, quite frankly, without any special knowledge, I wondered really whether it could be done and on the face of it, it seemed rather odd—I mean, carrying coal by air, and so on. But still it has been a great success. Time has been gained for peace. The efficiency of the American and British air forces has been greatly sustained by the enormous practice in almost active service conditions which they have had and are having over all these long months, not without their sacrifices in life. And lastly, and this I care about very much, the airlift into Berlin has won the heart of Germany—gathered the heart of Germany over to us—as nothing else could have done and shown them that their choice should be with the Western Nations and with progress and with freedom and that they should not be drawn into the hideous, Communist entanglement which many of them might in their despair otherwise have succumbed to. I think it is a wonderful thing, although when we look at the record of crimes that have been brought out, it seems hard to forget at all the past. I assure you you must forget the past. You must obliterate all parts of the past which are not useful to the future. You must regard the re-entry of Germany into the family of European nations as an event which the Western World must desire and must, if possible, achieve.

Gentlemen—three weeks ago I was in Brussels. I was addressing a meeting of 30,000 people—very friendly, even enthusiastic; 250 Communists were removed or thought it better to be silent—but there were these 30,000 people in this great square at Brussels, and I could feel their anxiety. I could feel, as I spoke, their anxiety —their fear. After all, they haven't got the Atlantic Ocean between them and danger. They haven't even got the Channel and the Channel is pretty good, as we showed you in the last war—and showed others. In ten days—in ten days perhaps the Soviet armour might be in Brussels. Here were these 30,000 people—good, faithful, decent people—naturally they know about it all. The Soviets have a new technique developing for what they do to countries they overrun, and what they will do to the countries they expect to overrun. It is a very elaborate technique—a Swedish professor came and explained it to me at length—he's writing a book about it—it is to liquidate all outstanding personalities in every class and walk of life. To liquidate them so as to have nothing below but a mass of ordinary people whom they can rule like the Communist Party in Russia rules the enormous mass of unfortunate Russian serfs. That is their technique, and they have got lists all made out of the different countries outside the Iron Curtain and of the people and so on. I don't suppose they've troubled to make a list here but they might find quite a lot in this room. But it's a grim thing to have that peril so little away. And while I was talking to these people— in the beautiful surroundings there—I could feel their fear and anxiety, but when I spoke of the United States being with us in this matter of European freedom, I felt a wave of hope in this great concourse and I know you will not let them down in regard to any matter in which you have pledged the word of the great Republic.

Well, gentlemen, it isn't only in Belgium. You look at Europe. The hideous process of the subjugation of Czechoslovakia should be studied in the utmost detail. It's a work of art—the methods and so on. Well, the Czechs live on and no nation in bondage should despair, but I was glad to see the American veterans to-night displaying a placard on which is written 'Uncle Joe, what happened to Masaryk?'—a friend of ours and fighter in the war, a struggler for freedom. There is terrible danger and peril and if you have not got these great barriers of salt water or short effective barriers, fear must come into their hearts, but that fear is removed because they are relying upon the valour, virtue and the giant strength of the United States.

And France—they have a situation with Thorez, this deserter, saying that this third of the population who vote Communist will fight against their country if the Russians have to invade it or have a chance of invading it. Italy—shattered and ruined in many ways but making a great recovery. In all these countries under direst peril they do look to you to give them the strength, not only to protect them, but to give them the strength to stand up for their own liberties. I don't want to have the whole of the world, of Britain and all that hanging on to the United States to be kept going by them, but you must do enough to animate them—that is what you are doing and that is what the Marshall Aid and the Atlantic Pact have done—is to animate these countries and enable them to come forward more and more in their own strength.

If it was not for the aid of the United States, and, I will say, of Great Britain (which counts), they would all go down like ninepins before the Communist menace. I tell you—it's no use arguing with a Communist. It's no good trying to convert a Communist, or persuade him. You can only deal with them on the following basis. I have had some experience in direct contact with the highest authorities, under the most favourable conditions, and I can tell you that you can only do it by having superior force on your side on the matter in question—and they must also be convinced that you will use—you will not hesitate to use—these forces, if necessary, in the most ruthless manner. You have not only to convince the Soviet Government that you have superior force—that they are confronted by superior force—but that you are not restrained by any moral consideration if the case arose from using that force with complete material ruthlessness. And that is the greatest chance of peace, the surest road to peace. Then the Communists will make a bargain—I have made bargains with them and they will keep the bargains so long as it suits them—and a good bargain—I mean good in the best sense of the word—may well last for quite a long time—may well suit both parties for quite a long time. I cannot tell how it will go but this I am sure, that if you wish for peace, it is absolutely necessary that you should be the stronger—I say you —we, all of us, we're in it—we should be the stronger and that they should know that we stop at nothing that honour allows. But you will ask—I will press this a little more if you will permit me, and my argument is a whole, is integral—you will ask: Is time on our side and the question whether more decided action should be taken?—Now I have reached a conclusion for the moment upon that. And I do not think any violent or precipitate action should be taken now. I do not regard war as inevitable. I do not think so. I think we still have control to preserve our cause without the world being plunged in another frightful struggle.

Well, now, do not let us however delude ourselves with the idea that we can make armies strong enough in the next year or two which could hold the front of civilization in Europe. I do not think we can. But they're all getting welded together under this pressure. Unities are being formed which would never otherwise have been formed. Give them a little time to knit and set. Let us have it. Our forces are getting stronger, actually and relatively, than they were a year ago. We have probably a year or two before other people are able to make the atomic bomb. And once they are able to make it, then they have to make it, which is another phase, measured by considerable time periods. Well, I heard a lot about that. But— gentlemen, it is sad after all our victory and triumph and all that we hoped for and so on, to find not peace and ease and hope and comfort, but only the summons to further endeavour. But that is life; After our great victory we did hope that the struggle for freedom would be decided in our time, but however long the struggle lasts, British and American people will not weary of it, or if weary of it, they will not desist from it, because victory or defeat are things which happen, but duty is a thing which is compulsory and has to go on irrespective, and carries with it its own rewards whatever the upshot of the struggle may be.

We are now confronted with something which is quite as wicked but much more formidable than Hitler, because Hitler had only the Herrenvolk stuff and anti-Semitism. Well, somebody said about that —a good starter, but a bad stayer. That's all he had. He had no theme. But these fourteen men in the Kremlin have their hierarchy and a church of Communist adepts whose missionaries are in every country as a fifth column, and not only a fifth column, in your country, ours, everywhere, and so on, with a feeling that they may be running a risk, but if their gamble comes off they will be the masters of the whole land in which they are a minority at the present time. They will be the Quislings with power to rule and dominate all the rest of their fellow countrymen. Therefore they have a good prospective advantage. It is certain in my opinion that Europe would have been communized and London would have been under bombardment some time ago, but for the deterrent of the atomic bomb in the hands of the United States. That is my firm belief and that governs the situation today. Sometimes one looks at the terrible alternative. Fancy if they had got it first. Well, I feel that sense that we all should have in our troubled journey—pilgrimage—that Divine protection has shielded those who faithfully sustained the causes of freedom and of justice.

One comfort I've got today is that the democratic nations are not fooled so easily by Stalin as they were by Hitler. You must have noticed that. Whenever Hitler said 'this is the last territorial claim I shall make, I need no more Czechs' and so on—they all used to turn around upon me in those days and say, there are you, now you see how wrong you were! Now you see it's all settled, it's all happy! Look, this is a peace move, it's all friendly, and so on. Well, once bit, twice shy—and I notice now that a very different and far more critical mood about manoeuvring offers by dictators prevails in the most enlightened circles on this side of the Atlantic.

I will say just a word about my own country before I sit down—a word or two about the British scene. Now I'm opposed to the—you might have heard perhaps—I'm opposed to the present Government. But that's our own affair. Like you, we settle our own affairs in our own way by our own political system. We don't want foreigners interfering any more than you would like any of us to interfere with you. That's all right. And I'm grateful for all the aid you have given to my country, but I say—do not underrate the strength of Britain. And do not ever lose sight of the fact that Britain is an absolutely vital necessity to the strength and future of the United States.

You may be larger and we may be the older. You may be the stronger, sometimes we may be the wiser. But let us talk it out like friends and brothers, as we shall, as we can, because we can understand each other with greater perfection than any two great groupings of the human race have ever been able to before. I said at this speech I made at Fulton, which I got scolded for, I said—don't suppose that half a century from now you will not see 70,000,000 or 80,000,000 of Britons spread about the world and united in defence of our traditions, our way of life and the world causes which you and we espouse. Well, added to all that, you have the power in this world, that fraternal association of the English-speaking world which I plead, far greater than alliances and not so formal, that fraternal association will give the freedom and security that is needed, that we demand for ourselves, and that we together, perhaps alone, can bestow on other mortals.

Forward then! Forward, let us go forward, without fear into the future and let us dread naught when duty calls!

꘎꘎꘎꘎

THE TWENTIETH CENTURY— ITS PROMISE AND ITS REALIZATION

SPEECH AT THE MASSACHUSETTS INSTITUTE OF TECHNOLOGY, BOSTON
March 31, 1949

I am honoured by your wish that I should take part in the discussions of the Massachusetts Institute of Technology. We have suffered in Great Britain by the lack of colleges of university rank in which engineering and the allied subjects are taught. Industrial production depends on technology and it is because the Americans, like the pre-war Germans, have realized this and created institutions for the advanced training of large numbers of high-grade engineers to translate the advances of pure science into industrial technique, it is for that reason that their output per head and consequent standard of life are so high. It is surprising that England, which was the first country to be industrialized, has nothing of comparable stature. If tonight I strike other notes than those of material progress, it implies no want of admiration for all the work you have done and are doing. My aim, like yours, is to be guided by balance and proportion.

The outstanding feature of the twentieth century has been the

enormous expansion in the numbers who are given the opportunity
to share in the larger and more varied life which in previous periods
was reserved for the few and for the very few. This process must
continue at an increasing rate. If we are to bring the broad masses
of the people in every land to the table of abundance, it can only
be by the tireless improvement of all our means of technical production, and by the diffusion in every form of education of an improved quality to scores of millions of men and women. Yea, even
in this darkling hour I have faith that this process will go on. I rejoice in Tennyson's celebrated lines:

> Men, my brothers, men, the workers,
>   ever reaping something new;
> That which they have done but earnest of the
>   things that they shall do.

I was, however, a little disquieted, I must admit, that you find it
necessary to debate the question, to quote Dean Burchard's opening
address, 'whether the problem of world production yielding at least
a minimum living to the whole population can be solved, and
whether man has so destroyed the resources of his world that he
may be doomed to die of starvation'. If, with all the resources of
modern science, we find ourselves unable to avert world famine,
we shall all be to blame, but a peculiar responsibility would rest
upon the scientists. I do not believe they will fail, but if they do,
or perhaps were not allowed to succeed, the consequences would
be very unpleasant because it is quite certain that mankind would
not agree to starve equally, and there might be some very sharp
disagreements about how the last crust was to be shared. This
would simplify our problem, as our greatest intellectual authorities
here will readily admit, in an unduly primordial manner.

I frankly confess that I feel somewhat overawed in addressing
this vast scientific and learned audience on the subject which your
panels are discussing. I have no technical and no university education, and have just had to pick up a few things as I went along.
Therefore I speak with a diffidence, which I hope to overcome as
I proceed, on these profound scientific, social and philosophic

issues, each of which claims a lifelong study for itself, and are now to be examined, as schoolmen would say, not only in their integrity but in their relationship, meaning thereby not only one by one but all together.

I was so glad that in the first instance you asked me to talk about the past rather than to peer into the future, because I know more about the past than I do about the future, and I was well content that the President of the United States [Harry Truman], whose gift of prophecy was so remarkably vindicated by recent electoral results, should have accepted that task. We all regret that his heavy State duties prevent him from being here tonight. I shall therefore have to try to do a little of the peering myself.

For us in Britain, the nineteenth century ended amid the glories of the Victorian era, and we entered upon the dawn of the twentieth in high hope for our country, our Empire and the world. The latter and larger part of the nineteenth century had been the period of liberal advance (liberal with a small 'l'). In 1900 a sense of moving hopefully forward to brighter, broader, easier days predominated. Little did we guess that what has been called the Century of the Common Man would witness as its outstanding feature more common men killing each other with greater facilities than any other five centuries put together in the history of the world. But we entered this terrible twentieth century with confidence. We thought that with improving transportation nations would get to know each other better. We believed that as they got to know each other better they would like each other more, and that national rivalries would fade in a growing international consciousness. We took it almost for granted that science would confer continual boons and blessings upon us, would give us better meals, better garments and better dwellings for less trouble, and thus steadily shorten the hours of labour and leave more time for play and cultures. In the name of ordered but unceasing progress, we saluted the age of democracy expressing itself ever more widely through parliaments freely and fairly elected on a broad or universal franchise. We saw no reason then why men and women should not shape their own home life and careers without being cramped by the growing complexity of the State, which was to be their servant and the protector of their rights. You had the famous American maxim 'Governments derive their just powers from the consent of the governed', and we both noticed that the world was divided into peoples that owned the governments and governments that owned the peoples. At least I heard all this around that time and liked some of it very much.

I was a Minister in the British Liberal Government (with a large 'L' please this time), returned with a great majority in 1906. That new Liberal Government arrived in power with much of its message already delivered and most of its aims already achieved. The days of hereditary aristocratic privilege were ended or numbered. The path was opened for talent in every field of endeavour. Primary education was compulsory, universal and free, or was about to become so. New problems arising, as problems do from former successes, awaited the new adminstration. The independence of the proletariat from thraldom involved at least a minimum standard of life and labour, and security for old age, sickness and the death of the family breadwinner. It was to these tasks of social reform and insurance that we addressed ourselves. The name of Lloyd George will ever be associated in Great Britain with this new departure, and I am proud to have been his lieutenant in this work and also, later, as a Conservative Chancellor of the Exchequer and later, still, as head of the wartime National Coalition to have carried these same themes forward on a magnified scale.

That is how we began the century. Science presently placed novel and dangerous facilities in the hands of the most powerful countries. Humanity was informed that it could make machines that would fly through the air and vessels which could swim beneath the surface of the seas. The conquest of the air and the perfection of the art of flying fulfilled the dream which for thousands of years had glittered in human imagination. Certainly it was a marvellous and romantic event. Whether the bestowal of this gift upon an immature civilization composed of competing nations whose nationalization grew with every advance of democracy and who were as yet devoid of international organization, whether this gift was a blessing or a curse has yet to be proved. On the whole I remain an optimist. For good, or for ill, air mastery is today the supreme expression of military power, and fleets and armies, however vital and important, must accept a subordinate rank. This is a memorable milestone in the march of man.

The submarine, to do it justice, has never made any claim to be a blessing or even a convenience. I well remember when it became an accomplished fact of peculiar military significance to the British Isles and to the British Navy, there was a general belief even in the Admiralty where I presided, that no nation would ever be so wicked as to use these underwater vessels to sink merchantmen at sea. How could a submarine, it was asked, provide for the safety of the crews of the merchant ships it sank, and public opinion was shocked when old Admiral Fisher bluntly declared that this would be no bar to the submarine being used by the new and growing German Navy in the most ruthless manner. His prediction was certainly not stultified by what was soon to happen.

Here then we have these two novel and potent weapons placed in the hands of highly nationalized sovereign States in the early part of the twentieth century, and both of them dwell with us today for our future edification. A third unmeasured sphere opened to us as the years passed, which, for the sake of comprehensive brevity, I will describe as radar. This radar, with its innumerable variants and possibilities, has so far been the handmaiden of the air, but it has also been the enemy of the submarine, and in alliance with the air may well prove its exterminator. Thus we see the changes which were wrought upon our society.

In the first half of the twentieth century, fanned by the crimson wings of war, the conquest of the air affected profoundly human affairs. It made the globe seem much bigger to the mind and much smaller to the body. The human biped was able to travel about far more quickly. This greatly reduced the size of his estate, while at the same time creating an even keener sense of its exploitable value. In the nineteenth century Jules Verne wrote *Round the World in Eighty Days*. It seemed a prodigy. Now you can get around it in four; but you do not see much of it on the way. The whole prospect and outlook of mankind grew immeasurably larger, and the multiplication of ideas also proceeded at an incredible rate. This vast expansion was unhappily not accompanied by any noticeable advance in the stature of man, either in his mental faculties, or his moral character. His brain got no better, but it buzzed the more. The scale of events around him assumed gigantic proportions while he remained about the same size. By comparison therefore he actually became much smaller. We no longer had great men directing manageable affairs. Our need was to discipline an array of gigantic and turbulent facts. To this task we have certainly so far proved unequal. Science bestowed immense new powers on man, and, at the same time, created conditions which were largely beyond his comprehension and still more beyond his control. While he nursed the illusion of growing mastery and exulted in his new trappings, he became the sport and presently the victim of tides, and currents, of whirlpools and tornadoes amid which he was far more helpless than he had been for a long time.

Hopeful developments in many directions were proceeding in 1914 on both sides of the Atlantic and they seemed to point to an age of peace and plenty when suddenly violent events broke in upon them. A spirit of adventure stirred the minds of men and was by no means allayed by the general advance of prosperity and science. On the contrary prosperity meant power, and science offered weapons. We read in the Bible, and I hope you still read the Bible, 'Jeshurun waxed fat and kicked'.

For several generations Britannia had ruled the waves—for long periods at less cost annually than that of a single modern battleship. History, I think, will say that this great trust was not abused. American testimony about the early period of the Monroe Doctrine is upon record. There was the suppression of the slave trade. During our prolonged naval supremacy undeterred by the rise of foreign tariffs, we kept our ports freely open to the commerce of the world. Our Colonial and Oriental Empire, even our coastal trade, was free to the shipping of all the nations on equal terms. We in no way sought to obstruct the rise of other States or navies. For nearly the whole of the nineteenth century the monopoly of sea power in British hands was a trust discharged faithfully in the general interest. But in the first decade of the twentieth century with new patterns of warships, naval rivalries became acute and fierce. Civilized governments began to think in dreadnoughts. It was in such a setting very difficult to prevent the First World War, far more difficult than it would have been to prevent the second.

There was of course one way to prevent it—one way then as now —the creation of an international instrument strong enough to adjust the disputes of nations and enforce its decisions against an aggressor. Much wisdom, eloquence and earnest effort was devoted to this theme in which the United States took the lead, but they only got as far as the World Court at The Hague and improvements in the Geneva Convention. The impulses toward a trial of strength in Europe were far stronger at this time. Germany, demanding her 'place in the sun', was faced by a resolute France with her military honour to regain. England, in accordance with her foreign policy of 300 years, sustained the weaker side. France found an ally in the Russia of the Czars and Germany in the crumbling Empire of the Hapsburgs. The United States, for reasons which were natural and traditional, but no longer so valid as in the past, stood aloof and expected to be able to watch as a spectator, the thrilling, fearful drama unfold from across what was then called 'the broad Atlantic.' These expectations, as you perhaps may remember, were not borne out by what happened.

After four and a half years of hideous mechanical slaughter, illuminated by infinite sacrifice, but not remarkably relieved by strategy or generalship, high hopes and spacious opportunities awaited the victorious Allies when they assembled at Versailles. War, stripped of every pretension of glamour or romance had been brought home to the masses of the peoples and brought home in forms never before experienced except by the defeated. To stop another war was the supreme object and duty of the statesmen who met as friends and allies around the Peace Table. They made great errors. The doctrine of self-determination was not the remedy for Europe, which needed then, above all things, unity and larger groupings. The idea that the vanquished could pay the expenses of the victors was a destructive and crazy delusion. The failure to strangle Bolshevism at its birth and to bring Russia, then prostrate, by one means or another, into the general democratic system lies heavy upon us today. Nevertheless, the statesmen of Versailles, largely at the inspiration of President Wilson, an inspiration implemented effectively by British thought, created the League of Nations. This is their defence before history, and had the League been resolutely sustained and used, it would have saved us all.

This was not to be. Another ordeal even more appalling than the first lay before us. Even when so much else had failed we could have obtained a prolonged peace, lasting all our lives at least, simply by keeping Germany disarmed in accordance with the Treaty, and by treating her with justice and magnanimity. This latter condition was very nearly achieved at Locarno in 1925, but the failure to enforce the disarmament clauses and above all to sustain the League of Nations, both of which purposes could easily have been accomplished, brought upon us the Second World War. Once again the English-speaking world gloriously but narrowly emerged, bleeding and breathless, but united as we never were before. This unity is our present salvation, because after all our victories, we are now faced by perils, both grave and near, and by problems more dire than have ever confronted Christian civilization, even in this twentieth century of storm and change.

There remains however a key of deliverance. It is the same key which was searched for by those who laboured to set up the World Court at The Hague in the early years of the century. It is the same conception which animated President Wilson and his colleagues at Versailles, namely the creation of a world instrument capable at least of giving to all its members security against aggression. The United Nations Organization which has been erected under the inspiring leadership of my great wartime friend, President Roosevelt, which took the place of the former League, has so far been rent and distracted by the antagonism of Soviet Russia and by the fundamental schism which has opened between Communism and the rest of mankind. But we must not despair. We must persevere, and if the gulf continues to widen, we must make sure that the cause of freedom is defended by all the resources of combined forethought and superior science. Here lies the best hope of averting a third world struggle.

One of the questions which you are debating here is defined as 'the failure of social and political institutions to keep pace with material and technical change.' Scientists should never underrate the deep-seated qualities of human nature and how, repressed in one direction, they will certainly break out in another. The *genus homo*—if I may display my Latin—is a tough creature who has travelled here by a very long road. His nature has been shaped and his virtues ingrained by many millions of years of struggle, fear and pain, and his spirit has, from the earliest dawn of history, shown itself upon occasion capable of mounting to the sublime, far above material conditions or mortal terrors. He still remains man—still remains as Pope described him 200 years ago.

> Placed on this Isthmus of a middle State,
> A being darkly wise and rudely great, . . .
> Created half to rise and half to fall;
> Great Lord of all things, yet a prey to all;
> Sole judge of truth, in endless error hurled;
> The glory, jest and riddle of the world.

In his introductory address, Mr. Burchard, the Dean of Humanities, spoke with awe of 'an approaching scientific ability to control men's thoughts with precision.' I shall be very content personally if my task in this world is done before that happens. Laws just or unjust may govern men's actions. Tyrannies may restrain or regulate their words. The machinery of propaganda may pack their minds with falsehood and deny them truth for many generations of time. But the soul of man thus held in trance or frozen in a long night can be awakened by a spark coming from God knows where and in a moment the whole structure of lies and oppression is on trial for its life. Peoples in bondage need never despair. Let them hope and trust in the genius of mankind. Science no doubt could if sufficiently perverted exterminate us all, but it is not in the power of material forces in any period which the youngest here tonight need take into practical account, to alter the main elements in human nature or restrict the infinite variety of forms in which the soul and genius of the human race can and will express itself.

How right you are, Dr. Compton, in this great institution of technical study and achievement, to keep a dean of humanities in the gaining of which philosophy and history walk hand in hand. Our inheritance of well-founded, slowly conceived codes of honour, morals and manners, the passionate convictions which so many hundreds of millions share together of the principles of freedom and justice, are far more precious to us than anything which scientific discoveries could bestow. Those whose minds are attracted or compelled to rigid and symmetrical systems of government should remember that logic, like science, must be the servant and not the master of man. Human beings and human societies are not structures that are built or machines that are forged. They are plants that grow and must be tended as such. Life is a test and this world a place of trial. Always the problems, or it may be the same problem, will be presented to every generation in different forms. The problems of victory may be even more baffling than those of defeat. However much the conditions change, the supreme question is how we live and grow and bloom and die, and how far each human life conforms to standards which are not wholly related to space or time.

And here I speak not only to those who enjoy the blessings and consolation of revealed religion but also to those who face the mysteries of human destiny alone. The flame of Christian ethics is still our highest guide. To guard and cherish it is our first interest, both spiritually and materially. The fulfilment of spiritual duty in our daily life is vital to our survival. Only by bringing it into perfect application can we hope to solve for ourselves the problems of this world and not of this world alone.

I cannot speak to you here tonight without expressing to the United States—as I have perhaps some right to do—the thanks of Britain and of Europe for the splendid part America is playing in the world. Many nations have risen to the summit of human affairs, but here is a great example where new-won supremacy has not been used for self-aggrandizement but only for further sacrifice.

Three years ago I made a speech at Fulton under the auspices of President Truman. Many people here and in my own country were startled and even shocked by what I said. But events have vindicated and fulfilled in much detail the warnings which I deemed it my duty to give at that time. Today there is a very different climate of opinion. I am in cordial accord with much that is being done. We have, as dominating facts, the famous Marshall Aid, the new unity in Western Europe and now the Atlantic Pact. Let us inquire into that. The responsible ministers in all the countries concerned deserve high credit. There is credit enough for all. In my own country the Foreign Secretary, Mr. Bevin, who has come here to sign the Atlantic Pact, has shown himself indifferent to mere party popularity in dealing with these great national issues. He has shown himself, like many American public men, above mere partisan interest in dealing with these national and world issues. No one could, however, have brought about these immense changes in the feeling of the United States, Great Britain and Europe but for the astounding policy of the Russian Soviet Government. We may well ask: 'Why have they deliberately acted so as to unite the free world against them?' It is certainly not because there are not very able men among them. Why have they done it? It is because they fear the friendship of the West more than its hostility. They cannot afford to allow free and friendly intercourse to grow up between the vast areas they control and the civilized nations of the West. The Russian people must not see what is going on outside, and the world must not see what goes on inside the Soviet domain. Thirteen or fourteen men in the Kremlin, holding down hundreds of millions of people and aiming at the rule of the world, feel that at all costs they must keep up the barriers. Self-preservation, not for Russia but for themselves, lies at the root and is the explanation of their sinister and malignant policy.

In consequence of the Soviet conduct the relations of Communist Russia with the other great powers of the world are without precedent in history. Measures and countermeasures have been taken on many occasions which in any previous period could only have meant or accompanied armed conflict. The situation has been well described by distinguished Americans as the 'cold war'. And the question is asked: 'Are we winning the cold war?' Well, this cannot be decided by looking at Europe alone. We must also look at Asia. The worst disaster since our victory has been the collapse of China under Communist attack and intrigue. China, in which the United States has always taken a high interest, comprises an immense part of the population of the world. The absorption of China and of India into the Kremlin-controlled Communist Empire, would certainly bring measureless bloodshed and misery to 800,000,000 or 900,000,000 people.

On the other hand the position in Europe has so far been successfully maintained. The prodigious effort of the Berlin Airlift has carried us through the winter. Time, though dearly bought, has been gained for peace. The efficiency of the American and British Air Forces has been proved and improved. Most of all, the spectacle of the British and Americans trying to feed the 2,000,000 Germans in Berlin, in their zone in Berlin, while the Soviet Government was trying to starve them out, has been an object lesson to the German people far beyond anything that words could convey. I trust that small and needless provocations of German sentiment may be avoided by the Western Powers. The revival and union of Europe cannot be achieved without the earnest and freely given aid of the German people.

This has certainly been demonstrated by the Berlin Airlift, which has fully justified itself. Nevertheless, fear and its shadows brood over Western Europe today. A month ago in Brussels I spoke to a meeting of 30,000 Belgians. I could feel at once their friendship and anxiety. They have no Atlantic Ocean, no English Channel, between them and the Russian Communist armoured divisions. Yet they bravely and ardently support the cause of United Europe. I was also conscious of the hope and faith which they, like the Greek people, place in the United States. I can see the movement of this vast crowd when I spoke of the hands—strong hands—stretched out across the ocean. You have great responsibilities there for much faith is placed upon you.

We are now confronted with something quite as wicked but in

some ways more formidable than Hitler, because Hitler had only the Herrenvolk pride and anti-Semitic hatred to exploit. He had no fundamental theme. But these thirteen men in the Kremlin have their hierarchy and a church of Communist adepts, whose missionaries are in every country as a fifth column, obscure people, but awaiting the day when they hope to be the absolute masters of their fellow countrymen and pay off old scores. They have their anti-God religion and their Communist doctrine of the entire subjugation of the individual to the State and behind this stands the largest army in the world, in the hands of a Government pursuing imperialist expansion, as no Czar or Kaiser has ever done. I must not conceal from you tonight the truth as I see it. It is certain that Europe would have been Communized, like Czechoslovakia, and London under bombardment some time ago but for the deterrent of the atomic bomb in the hands of the United States.

Another question is also asked. Is time on our side? This is not a question that can be answered except within strict limits. We have certainly not an unlimited period of time before a settlement should be achieved. The utmost vigilance should be practised but I do not think myself that violent or precipitate action should be taken now. War is not inevitable. The Germans have a wise saying, 'The trees do not grow up to the sky.'

Often something happens to turn or mitigate the course of events. Four or five hundred years ago Europe seemed about to be conquered by the Mongols. Two great battles were fought almost on the same day near Vienna and in Poland. In both of these the chivalry and armed power of Europe were completely shattered by the Asiatic hordes and mounted archers. It seemed that nothing could avert the doom of the famous continent from which modern civilization and culture had spread throughout the world. But at the critical moment the Great Khan died. The succession was vacant and the Mongol armies and their leaders trooped back on their ponies across the 7,000 miles which separated them from their capital in order to choose a successor. They never returned till now.

We need not abandon hope or patience. Many favourable processes are on foot. Under the impact of Communism all the free nations are being welded together as they never have been before and never could be, but for the harsh external pressure to which they are being subjected. We have no hostility to the Russian people and no desire to deny them their legitimate rights and security. I hoped that Russia, after the war, would have access, through un-frozen waters, into every ocean, guaranteed by the world organiza-tion of which she would be a leading member; I hoped that she should have the freest access, which indeed she has at the present time, to raw materials of every kind; and that the Russians every-where would be received as brothers in the human family. That still remains our aim and ideal. We seek nothing from Russia but goodwill and fair play. If, however, there is to be a war of nerves let us make sure our nerves are strong and are fortified by the deep-est convictions of our hearts. If we persevere steadfastly together, and allow no appeasement of tyranny and wrongdoing in any form; it may not be our nerve or the structure of our civilization which will break, and peace may yet be preserved.

This is a hard experience in the life of the world. After our great victory, which we believed would decide the struggle for freedom for our time at least, we thought we had deserved better of fortune. But unities and associations are being established by many nations throughout the free world with a speed and reality which would not have been achieved perhaps for generations. Of all these unities the one most precious to me is, to use an expression I used first at Har-vard six years ago, and one most precious to me, the fraternal association between the British Commonwealth of Nations and the United States. Do not, my friends, I beg of you, underrate the strength of Britain. As I said at Fulton, 'Do not suppose that half a century from now you will not see 70,000,000 or 80,000,000 of Britons spread about the world and united in defence of our tradi-tions, our way of life, and the world causes which you and we espouse.' United we stand secure. Let us then move forward to-gether in discharge of our mission and our duty, fearing God and nothing else.

SPEECHES
TO AND ABOUT
AMERICA
BY
WINSTON
CHURCHILL
FROM
LONDON

THE BIRTH THROES
OF A SUBLIME RESOLVE

A RADIO SPEECH TO AMERICA ON
RECEIVING THE HONORARY DEGREE OF
DOCTOR OF LAWS OF THE UNIVERSITY
OF ROCHESTER, NEW YORK

June 16, 1941

I am grateful, President Valentine, for the honour which you have conferred upon me in making me a Doctor of Laws of Rochester University in the State of New York. I am extremely complimented by the expressions of praise and commendation in which you have addressed me, not because I am or ever can be worthy of them, but because they are an expression of American confidence and affection which I shall ever strive to deserve.

But what touches me most in this ceremony is that sense of kinship and of unity which I feel exists between us this afternoon. As I speak from Downing Street to Rochester University and through you to the people of the United States, I almost feel I have the right to do so, because my mother, as you have stated, was born in your city, and here my grandfather, Leonard Jerome, lived for so many years, conducting as a prominent and rising citizen a newspaper with the excellent eighteenth-century title of the *Plain Dealer*.

The great Burke has truly said, 'People will not look forward to posterity who never look backward to their ancestors', and I feel it most agreeable to recall to you that the Jeromes were rooted for many generations in American soil, and fought in Washington's armies for the independence of the American Colonies and the foundation of the United States. I expect I was on both sides then. And I must say I feel on both sides of the Atlantic Ocean now.

At intervals during the last forty years I have addressed scores of great American audiences in almost every part of the Union. I have learnt to admire the courtesy of these audiences; their sense of fair play; their sovereign sense of humour, never minding the joke that is turned against themselves; their earnest, voracious desire to come to the root of the matter and to be well and truly informed on Old World affairs.

And now, in this time of world storm, when I have been called upon by King and Parliament and with the support of all parties in the State to bear the chief responsibility in Great Britain, and when I have had the supreme honour of speaking for the British nation in its most deadly danger and in its finest hour, it has given me comfort and inspiration to feel that I think as you do, that our hands are joined across the oceans, and that our pulses throb and beat as one. Indeed I will make so bold as to say that here at least, in my mother's birth city of Rochester, I hold a latchkey to American hearts.

Strong tides of emotion, fierce surges of passion, sweep the broad expanses of the Union in this year of fate. In that prodigious travail there are many elemental forces, there is much heart-searching and self-questioning; some pangs, some sorrow, some conflict of voices, but no fear. The world is witnessing the birth throes of a sublime resolve. I shall presume to confess to you that I have no doubts what that resolve will be.

The destiny of mankind is not decided by material computation. When great causes are on the move in the world, stirring all men's souls, drawing them from their firesides, casting aside comfort, wealth and the pursuit of happiness in response to impulses at once awe-striking and irresistible, we learn that we are spirits, not animals, and that something is going on in space and time, and beyond space and time, which, whether we like it or not, spells duty.

A wonderful story is unfolding before our eyes. How it will end we are not allowed to know. But on both sides of the Atlantic we all feel, I repeat, all, that we are a part of it, that our future and that of many generations is at stake. We are sure that the character of human society will be shaped by the resolves we take and the deeds we do. We need not bewail the fact that we have been called upon to face such solemn responsibilities. We may be proud, and even rejoice amid our tribulations, that we have been born at this cardinal time for so great an age and so splendid an opportunity of service here below.

Wickedness, enormous, panoplied, embattled, seemingly triumphant, casts its shadow over Europe and Asia. Laws, customs and traditions are broken up. Justice is cast from her seat. The rights of the weak are trampled down. The grand freedoms of which the President of the United States has spoken so movingly are spurned and chained. The whole stature of man, his genius, his initiative and his nobility, is ground down under systems of mechanical barbarism and of organized and scheduled terror.

For more than a year we British have stood alone, uplifted by your sympathy and respect and sustained by our own unconquerable will-power and by the increasing growth and hopes of your massive aid. In these British Islands that look so small upon the map we stand, the faithful guardians of the rights and dearest hopes of a dozen States and nations now gripped and tormented in a base and cruel servitude. Whatever happens we shall endure to the end.

But what is the explanation of the enslavement of Europe by the German Nazi regime? How did they do it? It is but a few years ago since one united gesture by the peoples, great and small, who are now broken in the dust, would have warded off from mankind the fearful ordeal it has had to undergo. But there was no unity. There was no vision. The nations were pulled down one by one while the others gaped and chattered. One by one, each in his turn, they let themselves be caught. One after another they were felled by brutal violence or poisoned from within by subtle intrigue.

And now the old lion with her lion cubs at her side stands alone against hunters who are armed with deadly weapons and impelled by desperate and destructive rage. Is the tragedy to repeat itself once more? Ah no! This is not the end of the tale. The stars in their courses proclaim the deliverance of mankind. Not so easily shall the onward progress of the peoples be barred. Not so easily shall the lights of freedom die.

But time is short. Every month that passes adds to the length and to the perils of the journey that will have to be made. United we stand. Divided we fall. Divided, the dark age returns. United, we can save and guide the world.

❊❊❊

THE MEETING WITH
PRESIDENT ROOSEVELT

A BROADCAST ADDRESS
August 24, 1941

I thought you would like me to tell you something about the voyage which I made across the ocean to meet our great friend, the

President of the United States. Exactly where we met is a secret, but I don't think I shall be indiscreet if I go so far as to say that it was 'somewhere in the Atlantic.'

In a spacious, landlocked bay which reminded me of the West Coast of Scotland, powerful American warships protected by strong flotillas and far-ranging aircraft awaited our arrival, and, as it were, stretched out a hand to help us in. Our party arrived in the newest, or almost the newest, British battleship, the *Prince of Wales,* with a modern escort of British and Canadian destroyers, and there for three days I spent my time in company, and I think I may say in comradeship, with Mr. Roosevelt; while all the time the chiefs of the staff and the naval and military commanders both of the British Empire and of the United States sat together in continual council.

President Roosevelt is the thrice-chosen head of the most powerful state and community in the world. I am the servant of King and Parliament at present charged with the principal direction of our affairs in these fateful times, and it is my duty also to make sure, as I have made sure, that anything I say or do in the exercise of my office is approved and sustained by the whole British Commonwealth of Nations. Therefore this meeting was bound to be important, because of the enormous forces at present only partially mobilized but steadily mobilizing which are at the disposal of these two major groupings of the human family: the British Empire and the United States, who, fortunately for the progress of mankind, happen to speak the same language, and very largely think the same thoughts, or anyhow think a lot of the same thoughts.

The meeting was therefore symbolic. That is its prime importance. It symbolizes, in a form and manner which everyone can understand in every land and in every clime, the deep underlying unities which stir and at decisive moments rule the English-speaking peoples throughout the world. Would it be presumptuous for me to say that it symbolizes something even more majestic—namely; the marshalling of the good forces of the world against the evil forces which are now so formidable and triumphant and which have cast their cruel spell over the whole of Europe and a large part of Asia?

This was a meeting which marks for ever in the pages of history the taking-up by the English-speaking nations, amid all this peril, tumult and confusion, of the guidance of the fortunes of the broad toiling masses in all the continents; and our loyal effort without any clog of selfish interest to lead them forward out of the miseries into which they have been plunged back to the broad highroad of freedom and justice. This is the highest honour and the most glorious opportunity which could ever have come to any branch of the human race.

When one beholds how many currents of extraordinary and terrible events have flowed together to make this harmony, even the most sceptical person must have the feeling that we all have the chance to play our part and do our duty in some great design, the end of which no mortal can foresee. Awful and horrible things are happening in these days. The whole of Europe has been wrecked and trampled down by the mechanical weapons and barbaric fury of the Nazis; the most deadly instruments of war-science have been joined to the extreme refinements of treachery and the most brutal exhibitions of ruthlessness, and thus have formed a combine of aggression the like of which has never been known, before which the rights, the traditions, the characteristics and the structure of many ancient honoured states and peoples have been laid prostrate and are now ground down under the heel and terror of a monster. The Austrians, the Czechs, the Poles, the Norwegians, the Danes, the Belgians, the Dutch, the Greeks, the Croats and the Serbs, above all the great French nation, have been stunned and pinioned. Italy, Hungary, Rumania, Bulgaria have bought a shameful respite by becoming the jackals of the tiger, but their situation is very little different and will presently be indistinguishable from that of his victims. Sweden, Spain and Turkey stand appalled, wondering which will be struck down next.

Here, then, is the vast pit into which all the most famous states and races of Europe have been flung and from which unaided they can never climb. But all this did not satiate Adolf Hitler; he made a treaty of non-aggression with Soviet Russia, just as he made one with Turkey, in order to keep them quiet till he was ready to attack them, and then, nine weeks ago today, without a vestige of provocation, he hurled millions of soldiers, with all their apparatus, upon the neighbour he had called his friend, with the avowed object of destroying Russia and tearing her in pieces. This frightful business is now unfolding day by day before our eyes. Here is a devil who, in a mere spasm of his pride and lust for domination, can condemn two or three millions, perhaps it may be many more, of human beings, to speedy and violent death. 'Let Russia be blotted out— Let Russia be destroyed. Order the armies to advance.' Such were his decrees. Accordingly from the Arctic Ocean to the Black Sea, six or seven millions of soldiers are locked in mortal struggle. Ah, but this time it was not so easy.

This time it was not all one way. The Russian armies and all the peoples of the Russian Republic have rallied to the defence of their hearths and homes. For the first time Nazi blood has flowed in a fearful torrent. Certainly 1,500,000, perhaps 2,000,000 of Nazi cannon-fodder have bit the dust of the endless plains of Russia. The tremendous battle rages along nearly 2,000 miles of front. The Russians fight with magnificent devotion; not only that, our generals who have visited the Russian front line report with admiration the efficiency of their military organization and the excellence of their equipment. The aggressor is surprised, startled, staggered. For the first time in his experience mass murder has become unprofitable. He retaliates by the most frightful cruelties. As his armies advance, whole districts are being exterminated. Scores of thousands—literally scores of thousands—of executions in cold blood are being perpetrated by the German police-troops upon the Russian patriots who defend their native soil. Since the Mongol invasions of Europe in the sixteenth century, there has never been methodical, merciless butchery on such a scale, or approaching such a scale. And this is but the beginning. Famine and pestilence have yet to follow in the bloody ruts of Hitler's tanks. We are in the presence of a crime without a name.

But Europe is not the only continent to be tormented and devastated by aggressions. For five long years the Japanese military factions, seeking to emulate the style of Hitler and Mussolini, taking all their posturing as if it were a new European revelation, have been invading and harrying the 500,000,000 inhabitants of China.

Japanese armies have been wandering about that vast land in futile excursions, carrying with them carnage, ruin and corruption and calling it the 'Chinese Incident.' Now they stretch a grasping hand into the southern seas of China; they snatch Indo-China from the wretched Vichy French; they menace by their movements Siam; menace Singapore, the British link with Australia; and menace the Philippine Islands under the protection of the United States. It is certain that this has got to stop. Every effort will be made to secure a peaceful settlement. The United States are labouring with infinite patience to arrive at a fair and amicable settlement which will give Japan the utmost reassurance for her legitimate interests. We earnestly hope these negotiations will succeed. But this I must say: that if these hopes should fail we shall of course range ourselves unhesitatingly at the side of the United States.

And thus we come back to the quiet bay somewhere in the Atlantic where misty sunshine plays on great ships which carry the White Ensign, or the Stars and Stripes. We had the idea, when we met there—the President and I—that without attempting to draw up final and formal peace aims, or war aims, it was necessary to give all peoples, especially the oppressed and conquered peoples, a simple, rough-and-ready wartime statement of the goal towards which the British Commonwealth and the United States mean to make their way, and thus make a way for others to march with them upon a road which will certainly be painful, and may be long!

There are, however, two distinct and marked differences in this joint declaration from the attitude adopted by the Allies during the latter part of the last war; and no one should overlook them. The United States and Great Britain do not now assume that there will never be any more war again. On the contrary, we intend to take ample precautions to prevent its renewal in any period we can foresee by effectively disarming the guilty nations while remaining suitably protected ourselves.

The second difference is this: that instead of trying to ruin German trade by all kinds of additional trade barriers and hindrances as was the mood of 1917, we have definitely adopted the view that it is not in the interests of the world and of our two countries that any large nation should be unprosperous or shut out from the means of making a decent living for itself and its people by its industry and enterprise. These are far-reaching changes of principle upon which all countries should ponder. Above all, it was necessary to give hope and the assurance of final victory to those many scores of millions of men and women who are battling for life and freedom, or who are already bent down under the Nazi yoke. Hitler and his confederates have for some time past been adjuring, bullying and beseeching the populations whom they have wronged and injured, to bow to their fate, to resign themselves to their servitude, and for the sake of some mitigations and indulgences, to 'collaborate'—that is the word—in what is called the New Order in Europe.

What is this New Order which they seek to fasten first upon Europe and if possible—for their ambitions are boundless—upon all the continents of the globe? It is the rule of the *Herrenvolk*—the master-race—who are to put an end to democracy, to parliaments, to the fundamental freedoms and decencies of ordinary men and women, to the historic rights of nations; and give them in exchange the iron rule of Prussia, the universal goose-step, and a strict, efficient discipline enforced upon the working-class by the political police, with the German concentration camps and firing parties, now so busy in a dozen lands, always handy in the background. There is the New Order.

Napoleon in his glory and his genius spread his Empire far and wide. There was a time when only the snows of Russia and the white cliffs of Dover with their guardian fleets stood between him and the dominion of the world. Napoleon's armies had a theme: they carried with them the surges of the French Revolution. Liberty, Equality and Fraternity—that was the cry. There was a sweeping away of outworn medieval systems and aristocratic privilege. There was the land for the people, a new code of law. Nevertheless, Napoleon's Empire vanished like a dream. But Hitler, Hitler has no theme, naught but mania, appetite and exploitation. He has, however, weapons and machinery for grinding down and for holding down conquered countries which are the product, the sadly perverted product, of modern science.

The ordeals, therefore, of the conquered peoples will be hard. We must give them hope; we must give them the conviction that their sufferings and their resistances will not be in vain. The tunnel may be dark and long, but at the end there is light. That is the symbolism and that is the message of the Atlantic meeting. Do not despair, brave Norwegians: your land shall be cleansed not only from the invader but from the filthy quislings who are his tools. Be sure of yourselves, Czechs: your independence shall be restored. Poles, the heroism of your people standing up to cruel oppressors, the courage of your soldiers, sailors and airmen, shall not be forgotten: your country shall live again and resume its rightful part in the new organization of Europe. Lift up your heads, gallant Frenchmen: not all the infamies of Darlan and of Laval shall stand between you and the restoration of your birthright. Tough, stouthearted Dutch, Belgians, Luxembergers, tormented, mishandled, shamefully castaway peoples of Yugoslavia, glorious Greece, now subjected to the crowning insult of the rule of the Italian jackanapes; yield not an inch! Keep your souls clean from all contact with the Nazis; make them feel even in their fleeting hour of brutish triumph that they are the moral outcasts of mankind. Help is coming; mighty forces are arming in your behalf. Have faith. Have hope. Deliverance is sure.

There is the signal which we have flashed across the water; and if it reaches the hearts of those to whom it is sent, they will endure with fortitude and tenacity their present misfortunes in the sure faith that they, too, are still serving the common cause, and that their efforts will not be in vain.

You will perhaps have noticed that the President of the United States and the British representative, in what is aptly called the 'Atlantic Charter,' have jointly pledged their countries to the final destruction of the Nazi tyranny. That is a solemn and grave undertaking. It must be made good; it will be made good. And, of course, many practical arrangements to fulfil that purpose have been and are being organized and set in motion.

The question has been asked: how near is the United States to war? There is certainly one man who knows the answer to that question. If Hitler has not yet declared war upon the United States, it is surely not out of his love for American institutions; it is certainly not because he could not find a pretext. He has murdered half a dozen countries for far less. Fear of immediately redoubling the tremendous energies now being employed against him is no doubt a restraining influence. But the real reason is, I am sure, to be found in the method to which he has so faithfully adhered and by which he has gained so much.

What is that method? It is a very simple method. One by one: that is his plan; that is his guiding rule; that is the trick by which he has enslaved so large a portion of the world. Three and a half years ago I appealed to my fellow countrymen to take the lead in weaving together a strong defensive union within the principles of the League of Nations, a union of all the countries who felt themselves in ever-growing danger. But none would listen; all stood idle while Germany rearmed. Czechoslovakia was subjugated; a French Government deserted their faithful ally and broke a plighted word in that ally's hour of need. Russia was cajoled and deceived into a kind of neutrality or partnership, while the French Army was being annihilated. The Low Countries and the Scandinavian countries, acting with France and Great Britain in good time, even after the war had begun, might have altered its course, and would have had, at any rate, a fighting chance. The Balkan States had only to stand together to save themselves from the ruin by which they are now engulfed. But one by one they were undermined and overwhelmed. Never was the career of crime made more smooth.

Now Hitler is striking at Russia with all his might, well knowing the difficulties of geography which stand between Russia and the aid which the Western Democracies are trying to bring. We shall strive our utmost to overcome all obstacles and to bring this aid. We have arranged for a conference in Moscow between the United States, British and Russian authorities to settle the whole plan. No barrier must stand in the way. But why is Hitler striking at Russia, and inflicting and suffering himself or, rather, making his soldiers suffer, this frightful slaughter? It is with the declared object of turning his whole force upon the British Islands, and if he could succeed in beating the life and the strength out of us, which is not so easy, then is the moment when he will settle his account, and it is already a long one, with the people of the United States and generally with the Western Hemisphere. One by one, there is the process; there is the simple, dismal plan which has served Hitler so well. It needs but one final successful application to make him the master of the world. I am devoutly thankful that some eyes at least are fully opened to it while time remains. I rejoiced to find that the President saw in their true light and proportion the extreme dangers by which the American people as well as the British people are now beset. It was indeed by the mercy of God that he began eight years ago that revival of the strength of the American Navy without which the New World today would have to take its orders from the European dictators, but with which the United States still retains the power to marshal her gigantic strength, and in saving herself to render an incomparable service to mankind.

We had a church parade on the Sunday in our Atlantic bay. The President came on to the quarter-deck of the *Prince of Wales,* where there were mingled together many hundreds of American and British sailors and marines. The sun shone bright and warm while we all sang the old hymns which are our common inheritance and which we learned as children in our homes. We sang the hymn founded on the psalm which John Hampden's soldiers sang when they bore his body to the grave, and in which the brief, precarious span of human life is contrasted with the immutability of Him to Whom a thousand ages are but as yesterday, and as a watch in the night. We sang the sailors' hymn 'For those in peril'—and there are very many—'on the sea.' We sang 'Onward Christian Soldiers.' And indeed I felt that this was no vain presumption, but that we had the right to feel that we were serving a cause for the sake of which a trumpet has sounded from on high.

When I looked upon that densely-packed congregation of fighting men of the same language, of the same faith, of the same fundamental laws and the same ideals, and now to a large extent of the same interests, and certainly in different degrees facing the same dangers, it swept across me that here was the only hope, but also the sure hope, of saving the world from measureless degradation.

And so we came back across the ocean waves, uplifted in spirit, fortified in resolve. Some American destroyers which were carrying mails to the United States marines in Iceland happened to be going the same way, too, so we made a goodly company at sea together.

And when we were right out in mid-passage one afternoon a noble sight broke on the view. We overtook one of the convoys which carry the munitions and supplies of the New World to sustain the champions of freedom in the Old. The whole broad horizon seemed filled with ships; seventy or eighty ships of all kinds and sizes, arrayed in fourteen lines, each of which could have been drawn with a ruler, hardly a wisp of smoke, not a straggler, but all bristling with cannons and other precautions on which I will not dwell, and all surrounded by their British escorting vessels, while overhead the far-ranging Catalina air-boats soared—vigilant, protecting eagles in the sky. Then I felt that—hard and terrible and long drawn-out as this struggle may be—we shall not be denied the strength to do our duty to the end.

✻✻✻

OUR GREAT
AMERICAN ALLY

SPEECH DELIVERED AT AN INSPECTION
OF AN AMERICAN FORCE IN BRITAIN
March 23, 1944

It is with feelings of emotion and of profound encouragement that I have the honour to review you here today. In these weeks that are passing so swiftly I see gathered here on English soil these soldiers of our great American ally preparing themselves to strike a blow for a cause which is a greater cause than either of our two countries has ever fought for in bygone days.

It is a world cause because though no one can tell how the future of the world will shape itself, we are determined that the dark tyrannies which have overclouded our lives and drawn our people from their homes shall be broken and battered down, and that an example shall be made of the guilty which will prevent such tyrannies being inflicted again upon the masses of the people.

You have a great part to play. You are specially trained. You are the most modern expression of war. Soon you will have the opportunity of testifying your faith in all those inspiring phrases of the American Constitution, and of striking a blow which, however it may leave the world, will, as we are determined, make it a better and a broader world for all.

You have come across the ocean. Here you are on this little island wrapped in northern mist. I cannot give you any guarantee about the weather, but I can assure you that you are greeted with warm hearts on every side.

Our troops, British and American, are at this moment shedding their blood side by side in Italy, at Cassino, or in the Anzio bridgehead, fighting hard and losing heavily in the struggle. And now here this comradeship in arms is repeated, and I am confident that not only will the enemy feel the shock of our joint exertions, but that there will be left behind a core of good feeling and mutual understanding and a unity which will in itself be of priceless advantage to the good will which has united us now for so many years.

I thank God you are here, and from the bottom of my heart I wish you all good fortune and success.

TRIBUTE TO
PRESIDENT ROOSEVELT

SPEECH TO THE HOUSE OF COMMONS
April 17, 1945

I beg to move:

'That an humble Address be presented to His Majesty to convey to His Majesty the deep sorrow with which this House has learned of the death of the President of the United States of America, and to pray His Majesty that in communicating his own sentiments of grief to the United States Government, he will also be generously pleased to express on the part of this House their sense of the loss which the British Commonwealth and Empire and the cause of the Allied nations have sustained, and their profound sympathy with Mrs. Roosevelt and the late President's family, and with the Government and people of the United States of America.'

My friendship with the great man to whose work and fame we pay our tribute today began and ripened during this war. I had met him, but only for a few minutes, after the close of the last war, and as soon as I went to the Admiralty in September 1939, he telegraphed inviting me to correspond with him direct on naval or other matters if at any time I felt inclined. Having obtained the permission of the Prime Minister, I did so. Knowing President Roosevelt's keen interest in sea warfare, I furnished him with a stream of information about our naval affairs, and about the various actions, including especially the action of the Plate River, which lighted the first gloomy winter of the war.

When I became Prime Minister, and the war broke out in all its hideous fury, when our own life and survival hung in the balance, I was already in a position to telegraph to the President on terms of an association which had become most intimate and, to me, most agreeable. This continued through all the ups and downs of the world struggle until Thursday last, when I received my last messages from him. These messages showed no falling off in his accustomed clear vision and vigour upon perplexing and complicated matters. I may mention that this correspondence which, of course, was greatly increased after the United States entry into the war, comprises to and fro between us, over 1,700 messages. Many of these were lengthy messages, and the majority dealt with those more difficult points which come to be discussed upon the level of heads of Governments only after official solutions have not been reached at other stages. To this correspondence there must be added our nine meetings—at Argentia, three in Washington, at Casablanca, at Teheran, two at Quebec and, last of all, at Yalta, comprising in all about 120 days of close personal contact, during a great part of which I stayed with him at the White House or at his home at Hyde Park or in his retreat in the Blue Mountains, which he called Shangri-la.

I conceived an admiration for him as a statesman, a man of affairs, and a war leader. I felt the utmost confidence in his upright, inspiring character and outlook, and a personal regard—affection I must say—for him beyond my power to express today. His love of his own country, his respect for its constitution, his power of gauging the tides and currents of its mobile public opinion, were always evident, but added to these were the beatings of that generous heart which was always stirred to anger and to action by spectacles of aggression and oppression by the strong against the weak. It is, indeed, a loss, a bitter loss to humanity that those heart-beats are stilled for ever.

President Roosevelt's physical affliction lay heavily upon him. It was a marvel that he bore up against it through all the many years of tumult and storm. Not one man in ten millions, stricken and crippled as he was, would have attempted to plunge into a life of physical and mental exertion and of hard, ceaseless political controversy. Not one in ten millions would have tried, not one in a generation would have succeeded, not only in entering this sphere, not only in acting vehemently in it, but in becoming indisputable master of the scene. In this extraordinary effort of the spirit over the flesh, of will-power over physical infirmity, he was inspired and sustained by that noble woman his devoted wife, whose high ideals marched with his own, and to whom the deep and respectful sympathy of the House of Commons flows out today in all fullness.

There is no doubt that the President foresaw the great dangers closing in upon the pre-war world with far more prescience than most well-informed people on either side of the Atlantic, and that he urged forward with all his power such precautionary military preparations as peacetime opinion in the United States could be brought to accept. There never was a moment's doubt, as the quarrel opened, upon which side his sympathies lay. The fall of France, and what seemed to most people outside this island, the impending destruction of Great Britain, were to him an agony, although he never lost faith in us. They were an agony to him not only on account of Europe, but because of the serious perils to which the United States herself would have been exposed had we been overwhelmed or the survivors cast down under the German yoke. The bearing of the British nation at that time of stress, when we were all alone, filled him and vast numbers of his countrymen with the warmest sentiments towards our people. He and they felt the blitz of the stern winter of 1940–41, when Hitler set himself to rub out the cities of our country, as much as any of us did, and perhaps more indeed, for imagination is often more torturing than reality. There is no doubt that the bearing of the British and, above all, of the Londoners, kindled fires in American bosoms far harder to quench than the conflagrations from which we were suffering. There was also at that time, in spite of General Wavell's victories—all the more, indeed, because of the reinforcements which were sent from this country to him—the apprehension widespread in the United States that we should be invaded by Germany after the fullest preparation in the spring of 1941. It was in February that the President sent to England the late Mr. Wendell Willkie, who, although a political rival and an opposing candidate, felt as he did on many important points. Mr. Willkie brought a letter from Mr. Roosevelt, which the President had written in his own hand, and this letter contained the famous lines of Longfellow:

'. . . Sail on, O ship of State!
Sail on, O Union, strong and great!
Humanity with all its fears,
With all the hopes of future years,
Is hanging breathless on thy fate!'

At about that same time he devised the extraordinary measure of assistance called Lend-Lease, which will stand forth as the most unselfish and unsordid financial act of any country in all history. The effect of this was greatly to increase British fighting power, and for all the purpose of the war effort to make us, as it were, a much more numerous community. In that autumn I met the President for the first time during the war at Argentia in Newfoundland, and together we drew up the declaration which has since been called the Atlantic Charter, and which will, I trust, long remain a guide for both our peoples and for other people of the world.

All this time in deep and dark and deadly secrecy, the Japanese were preparing their act of treachery and greed. When next we met in Washington, Japan, Germany and Italy had declared war upon the United States, and both our countries were in arms, shoulder to shoulder. Since then we have advanced over the land and over the sea through many difficulties and disappointments, but always with a broadening measure of success. I need not dwell upon the series of great operations which have taken place in the Western Hemisphere, to say nothing of that other immense war proceeding on the other side of the world. Nor need I speak of the plans which we made with our great ally, Russia, at Teheran, for these have now been carried out for all the world to see.

But at Yalta I noticed that the President was ailing. His captivating smile, his gay and charming manner, had not deserted him, but his face had a transparency, an air of purification, and often there was a faraway look in his eyes. When I took my leave of him in Alexandria harbour I must confess that I had an indefinable sense of fear that his health and his strength were on the ebb. But nothing altered his inflexible sense of duty. To the end he faced his innumerable tasks unflinching. One of the tasks of the President is to sign maybe a hundred or two State papers with his own hand every day, commissions and so forth. All this he continued to carry out with the utmost strictness. When death came suddenly upon him 'he had finished his mail.' That portion of his day's work was done. As the saying goes, he died in harness, and we may well say in battle harness, like his soldiers, sailors, and airmen, who side by side with ours are carrying on their task to the end all over the world. What an enviable death was his! He had brought his country through the worst of its perils and the heaviest of its toils. Victory had cast its sure and steady beam upon him.

In the days of peace he had broadened and stabilized the foundations of American life and union. In war he had raised the strength, might and glory of the great Republic to a height never attained by any nation in history. With her left hand she was leading the advance of the conquering Allied armies into the heart of Germany, and with her right, on the other side of the globe, she was irresistibly and swiftly breaking up the power of Japan. And all the time ships, munitions, supplies, and food of every kind were aiding on a gigantic scale her allies, great and small, in the course of the long struggle.

But all this was no more than worldly power and grandeur, had it not been that the causes of human freedom and of social justice, to which so much of his life had been given, added a lustre to this power and pomp and warlike might, a lustre which will long be discernible among men. He has left behind him a band of resolute and able men handling the numerous interrelated parts of the vast American war machine. He has left a successor who comes forward with firm step and sure conviction to carry on the task to its appointed end. For us, it remains only to say that in Franklin Roosevelt there died the greatest American friend we have ever known, and the greatest champion of freedom who has ever brought help and comfort from the new world to the old.

❉❉❉

STATEMENT ON THE ATOMIC BOMB

August 6, 1945

On August 6, 1945, President Truman announced that British and American scientists had produced the atomic bomb and that the first had been dropped that day on Japan. Mr. Attlee then issued from No. 10 Downing Street, the following statement, written by Mr. Churchill before the change of government.

By the year 1939 it had become widely recognized among scientists of many nations that the release of energy by atomic fission was a possibility. The problems which remained to be solved before this possibility could be turned into practical achievement were, however, manifold and immense; and few scientists would at that time have ventured to predict that an atomic bomb could be ready for use by 1945. Nevertheless, the potentialities of the project were so great that His Majesty's Government thought it right that research should be carried on in spite of the many competing claims on our scientific man-power. At this stage the research was carried out mainly in our Universities, principally Oxford, Cambridge, London (Imperial College), Liverpool, and Birmingham. At the time of the formation of the Coalition Government, responsibility for co-ordinating the work and pressing it forward lay with the Ministry of Aircraft Production, advised by a committee of leading scientists presided over by Sir George Thomson.

At the same time, under the general arrangements then in force for the pooling of scientific information, there was a full interchange of ideas between the scientists carrying out this work in the United Kingdom and those in the United States.

Such progress was made that by the summer of 1941 Sir George Thomson's committee was able to report that, in their view, there was a reasonable chance that an atomic bomb could be produced before the end of the war. At the end of August, 1941, Lord Cherwell, whose duty it was to keep me informed on all these and other technical developments, reported the substantial progress which was being made. The general responsibility for the scientific research carried on under the various technical committees lay with the then Lord President of the Council, Sir John Anderson. In these circumstances (having in mind also the effect of ordinary high explosive, which we had recently experienced), I referred the matter on August 30, 1941, to the Chiefs of Staff Committee in the following minute:

'General Ismay, for Chiefs of Staff Committee: Although personally I am quite content with the existing explosives, I feel we must not stand in the path of improvement, and I therefore think that action should be taken in the sense proposed by Lord Cherwell, and that the Cabinet Minister responsible should be Sir John Anderson.

I shall be glad to know what the Chiefs of Staff Committee think.'

The Chiefs of the Staff recommended immediate action with the maximum priority.

It was then decided to set up within the Department of Scientific and Industrial Research a special division to direct the work, and Imperial Chemical Industries Limited agreed to release Mr. W. A. Akers to take charge of this directorate, which we called, for purposes of secrecy, the Directorate of 'Tube Alloys'. After Sir John Anderson had ceased to be Lord President and became Chancellor of the Exchequer I asked him to continue to supervise this work, for which he has special qualifications. To advise him, there was set up under his chairmanship a consultative council composed of the President of the Royal Society, the Chairman of the Scientific Advisory Committee of the Cabinet, the Secretary of the Department of Scientific and Industrial Research, and Lord Cherwell. The Minister of Aircraft Production, at that time Lord Brabazon, also served on this committee.

Under the chairmanship of Mr. Akers there was also a technical committee, on which sat the scientists who were directing the different sections of the work and some others. This committee was originally composed of Sir James Chadwick, Professor Peierls, and Drs. Halban, Simon and Slade. Later it was joined by Sir Charles Darwin and Professors Cockcroft, Oliphant and Feather. Full use was also made of university and industrial laboratories.

On October 11, 1941, President Roosevelt sent me a letter suggesting that any extended efforts on this important matter might usefully be co-ordinated, or even jointly conducted. Accordingly, all British and American efforts were joined, and a number of British scientists concerned proceeded to the United States. Apart from these contacts, complete secrecy guarded all these activities, and no single person was informed whose work was not indispensable to progress.

By the summer of 1942 this expanded programme of research had confirmed with surer and broader foundations the promising forecasts which had been made a year earlier, and the time had come when a decision must be made whether or not to proceed with the construction of large-scale production plants. Meanwhile it had become apparent from the preliminary experiments that these plants would have to be on something like the vast scale described in the American statements which have been published today.

Great Britain at this period was fully extended in war production, and we could not afford such grave interference with the current munitions programmes on which our warlike operations depended. Moreover, Great Britain was within easy range of German bombers, and the risk of raiders from the sea or air could not be ignored. The United States, however, where parallel or similar progress had been made, was free from these dangers. The decision was therefore taken to build the full-scale production plants in America.

In the United States the erection of the immense plants was placed under the responsibility of Mr. Stimson, United States Secretary of War, and the American Army Administration, whose wonderful work and marvellous secrecy cannot be sufficiently admired. The main practical effort and virtually the whole of its prodigious cost now fell upon the United States authorities, who were assisted by a number of British scientists. The relationship of the British and American contributions was regulated by discussion between the late President Roosevelt and myself, and a combined policy committee was set up.

The Canadian Government, whose contribution was most valuable, provided both indispensable raw material for the project as a whole and also necessary facilities for the work on one section of the project, which has been carried out in Canada by the three Governments in partnership.

The smoothness with which the arrangements for co-operation which were made in 1943 have been carried into effect is a happy augury for our future relations, and reflects great credit on all concerned—on the members of the combined policy committee which we set up; on the enthusiasm with which our scientists and technicians gave of their best—particularly Sir James Chadwick, who gave up his work at Liverpool to serve as technical adviser to the United Kingdom members of the policy committee and spared no effort; and, not least, on the generous spirit with which the whole United States organization welcomed our men and made it possible for them to make their contribution.

By God's mercy British and American science outpaced all German efforts. These were on a considerable scale, but far behind. The possession of these powers by the Germans at any time might have altered the result of the war, and profound anxiety was felt by those who were informed. Every effort was made by our Intelligence Service and by the Air Force to locate in Germany anything resembling the plants which were being created in the United States. In the winter of 1942-43 most gallant attacks were made in Norway on two occasions by small parties of volunteers from the British Commandos and Norwegian forces, at very heavy loss of life, upon stores of what is called 'heavy water', an element in one of the possible processes. The second of these two attacks was completely successful.

The whole burden of execution, including the setting-up of the plants and many technical processes connected therewith in the practical sphere, constitutes one of the greatest triumphs of American—or indeed human—genius of which there is record. Moreover, the decision to make these enormous expenditures upon a project which, however hopefully established by American and British research, remained nevertheless a heart-shaking risk, stands to the everlasting honour of President Roosevelt and his advisers.

It is now for Japan to realize, in the glare of the first atomic bomb which has smitten her, what the consequences will be of an indefinite continuance of this terrible means of maintaining a rule of law in the world.

This revelation of the secrets of nature, long mercifully withheld from man, should arouse the most solemn reflections in the mind and conscience of every human being capable of comprehension. We must indeed pray that these awful agencies will be made to conduce to peace among the nations, and that instead of wreaking measureless havoc upon the entire globe they may become a perennial fountain of world prosperity. . . .

⌘⌘⌘

U.S. AND BRITAIN'S SPECIAL RELATIONSHIP

FROM A SPEECH TO THE HOUSE OF COMMONS
November 7, 1945

I think the speech of the President of the United States on October 27th is the dominant factor in the present world situation. This was the speech of the head of a State and nation, which has proved its ability to maintain armies of millions, in constant victorious battle in both hemispheres at the same time. If I read him and understand him correctly, President Truman said, in effect, that the United States would maintain its vast military power and potentialities, and would join with any like-minded nations, not only to resist but to prevent aggression no matter from what quarter it came, or in what form it presented itself. Further, he made it plain that in regions which have come under the control of the Allies, unfair tyrannical Governments not in accordance with the broad principles of democracy as we understand them, would not receive recognition from the Government of the United States. Finally, he made it clear that the United States must prepare to abandon oldfashioned isolation and accept the duty of joining with other friendly, and well-disposed nations, to prevent, and to carry out those high purposes, if necessary, by the use of force carried to its extreme limits.

It is, of course, true that all these propositions and purposes have been set forth in the Declaration of the United Nations at San Francisco in May. None the less, this reaffirmation by the President of the United States on October 27th is of transcendant importance. If such a statement had been made in the Summer of 1914, the Kaiser would never have launched an aggressive war over a Balkan incident. All would have come to a great parley, between the most powerful Governments of those days. In the face of such a declaration, the world war of 1914 would not have occurred. Such a declaration in 1919, would have led to a real Treaty of Peace and a real armed League of Nations. Such a declaration at any time between the two wars, would have prevented the second. It would have made the League of Nations, or a world League strong enough to prevent this re-arming of Germany which has led all of us through so much tribulation and danger, and Germany herself to punishment and ruin which may well shock the soul of man. Therefore, I feel it is our duty to-day in the most definite manner, to welcome and salute the noble declaration made by the President of the United States and to make it plain that upon the principles set forth in the 12 Articles, which follow so closely upon those of the Atlantic Charter, we stand by the United States with a conviction which overrides all other considerations. I cannot bring myself to visualise, in its frightful character, another world war, but none of us knows what would happen if such a thing occurred. It is a sombre thought that, so long as the new world organisation is so loosely formed, such possibilities and their consequences are practically beyond human control.

There is a general opinion which I have noticed, that it would be a serious disaster if the particular minor planet which we inhabit blew itself to pieces, or if all human life were extinguished upon its surface, apart that is to say, from fierce beings, armed with obsolescent firearms, dwelling in the caverns of the Stone Age. There is a general feeling that that would be a regrettable event. Perhaps, however, we flatter ourselves. Perhaps we are biased: but everyone realises how far scientific knowledge has outstripped human virtue. We all hope that men are better, wiser, more merciful than they were 10,000 years ago. There is certainly a great atmosphere of comprehension. There is a growing factor which one may call world public opinion, most powerful, most persuasive, most valuable. We understand our unhappy lot, even if we have no power to control it.

Those same deep, uncontrollable anxieties which some of us felt in the years before the war recur, but we have also a hope that we had not got then. That hope is the strength and resolve of the

United States to play a leading part in world affairs. There is this mighty State and nation, which offers power and sacrifice in order to bring mankind out of the dark valley through which we have been travelling. The valley is indeed dark, and the dangers most menacing, but we know that not so far away are the broad uplands of assured peace. Can we reach them? We must reach them. This is our sole duty.

I am sure we should now make it clear to the United States that we will march at their side in the cause that President Truman has devised, that we add our strength to their strength, and that their stern sober effort shall be matched by our own. After all, if everything else fails—which we must not assume—here is the best chance of survival. Personally, I feel that it is more than survival. It may even be safety, and, with safety, a vast expansion of prosperity. Having regard to all these facts of which many of us here are aware at the present time, we may confidently believe that with the British Empire and Commonwealth standing at the side of the United States, we shall together be strong enough to prevent another world catastrophe. As long as our peoples act in absolute faith and honour to each other, and to all other nations, they need fear none and they need fear nothing. The British and American peoples come together naturally, and without the need of policy or design. That is because they speak the same language, were brought up on the same common law, and have similar institutions and an equal love of individual liberty. There is often no need for policy or statecraft to make British and Americans agree together at an international council table. They can hardly help agreeing on three out of four things. They look at things in the same way. No policies, no pacts, no secret understandings are needed between them. On many of the main issues affecting our conduct and our existence, the English-speaking peoples of the world are in general agreement.

It would be a mistake to suppose that increasingly close and friendly relations between Great Britain and the United States imply an adverse outlook towards any other Power. Our friendship may be special, but it is not exclusive. On the contrary, every problem dealing with other Powers is simplified by Anglo-American agreement and harmony. That is a fact which I do not think the Foreign Secretary, or any one who took part in the recent Conference, would doubt. It is not as if it were necessary to work out some arrangement between British and Americans at a conference. In nearly every case where there is not some special difficulty between them, they take the same view of the same set of circumstances, and the fact that it is so, makes it all the more hopeful that other Powers gathered at the Conference will be drawn into the circle of agreement which must precede action.

It is on this basis I come to the atomic bomb. According to our present understanding with the United States, neither country is entitled to disclose its secrets to a third country without the approval of the other. A great deal has already been disclosed by the United States in agreement with us. An elaborate document giving an immense amount of information on the scientific and theoretical aspects was published by the Americans several weeks ago. A great deal of information is also common property all over the world. We are told by those who advocate immediate public disclosure, that the Soviet Government are already possessed of the scientific knowledge, and that they will be able to make atomic bombs in a very short time. This, I may point out, is somewhat inconsistent with the argument that they have a grievance, and also with the argument, for what it is worth, that we and the United States have at this moment, any great gift to bestow, such as would induce a complete melting of hearts and create some entirely new relationship.

What the United States do not wish to disclose is the practical production method which they have developed, at enormous expense and on a gigantic scale. This would not be an affair of scientists or diplomatists handing over envelopes containing formulæ. If effective, any such disclosure would have to take the form of a considerable number of Soviet specialists, engineers and scientists visiting the United States arsenals, for that is what the manufacturing centres of the atomic bomb really are. They would have to visit them, and they would have to dwell there amid the plant, so that it could all be explained to them at length and at leisure. These specialists would then return to their own country, carrying with them the blue-prints and all the information which they had obtained together, no doubt, with any further improvements which might have occurred to them. I trust that we are not going to put pressure on the United States to adopt such a course. I am sure that if the circumstances were reversed, and we or the Americans asked for similar access to the Russian arsenals, it would not be granted. During the war we imparted many secrets to the Russians especially in connection with Radar, but we were not conscious of any adequate reciprocity. Even in the heat of the war both countries acted under considerable reserve.

Therefore, I hope that Great Britain, Canada and the United States will adhere to the policy proclaimed by President Truman, and will treat their knowledge and processes as a sacred trust to be guarded for the benefit of all nations and as a deterrent against aggressive war. I myself, as a British subject, cannot feel the slightest anxiety that these great powers should at the present moment be in the hands of the United States. I am sure they will not use them in any aggressive sense, or in the indulgence of territorial or commercial appetites. They, like Great Britain, have no need or desire for territorial gains. Personally, I feel it must be in most men's minds to-day that it is a matter for rejoicing that these powers of manufacture are in such good hands. The possession of these powers will help the United States and our Allies to build up the structure of world security. It may be the necessary lever which is required to build up that great structure of world security.

How long, we may ask, is it likely that this advantage will rest with the United States? In the Debate on the Address I hazarded the estimate that it would be three or four years. According to the best information I have been able to obtain, I see no reason to alter that estimate, and certainly none to diminish it. But even when that period is over, whatever it may prove to be, the progress made by the United States' scientists and, I trust, by our own, both in experiment and manufacture, may well leave us and them with the prime power and responsibility for the use of these dire superhuman weapons. I also agree with President Truman when he says that those who argue that, because of the atomic bomb, there is no need for armies, navies and air forces, are at present 100 per cent wrong. I should be glad to hear, in whatever terms His Majesty's Ministers care to express themselves, that this is also the view of His Majesty's Government.

I cannot leave this subject without referring to another aspect which is forced upon me by speeches made in a recent Debate on the Adjournment. It was said that unless all knowledge of atomic energy, whether of theory or production, were shared among all the nations of the world, some of the British and American scientists would act independently, by which, I suppose, is meant that they would betray to foreign countries whatever secrets remained. In that case, I hope the law would be used against those men with the utmost rigour. Whatever may be decided on these matters should surely be decided by Parliaments and responsible governments, and not by scientists, however eminent and however ardent they may be. Mr. Gladstone said that expert knowledge is limited knowledge. On many occasions in the past we have seen attempts to rule the world by experts of one kind and another. There have been theocratic governments, military governments and aristocratic governments. It is now suggested that we should have scientistic —not scientific—governments. It is the duty of scientists, like all other people, to serve the State and not to rule it because they are scientists. If they want to rule the State and must get elected to Parliament or win distinction in the Upper House and so gain access to some of the various administrations which are formed from time to time. Most people in the English-speaking world will, I believe, think it much better that great decisions should rest with governments lawfully elected on democratic lines. I associate myself with the majority in that opinion.

May I in conclusion submit to the House a few simple points which, it seems to me, should gain its approval? First, we should fortify in every way our special and friendly connections with the United States, aiming always at a fraternal association for the purpose of common protection and world peace. Secondly, this association should in no way have a point against any other country, great or small, in the world, but should, on the contrary, be used to draw the leading victorious Powers ever more closely together on equal terms and in all good faith and good will. Thirdly, we should not abandon our special relationship with the United States and Canada about the atomic bomb, and we should aid the United States to guard this weapon as a sacred trust for the maintenance of peace. Fourthly, we should seek constantly to promote and strengthen the world organisation of the United Nations, so that, in due course, it may eventually be fitted to become the safe and trusted repository of these great agents. Fifthly, and this, I take it, is already agreed, we should make atomic bombs, and have them here, even if manufactured elsewhere, in suitable safe storage with the least possible delay. Finally, let me say on behalf of the whole House that we wish the Prime Minister the utmost success in his forthcoming highly important visit to Washington.

※※※

THE AL SMITH MEMORIAL

A SPEECH RECORDED IN LONDON AND
BROADCAST AT A PUBLIC DINNER IN
NEW YORK
October 14, 1947

Mr. Chairman, Your Eminence Cardinal Spellman, Ambassador Austin, Secretary Forrestal, Governor Dewey, Mayor O'Dwyer, and friends of Governor Smith:—

This gathering has for its purpose a salutation to the memory of Al Smith by those who knew him or who have carefully studied his character and life's work. I had the pleasure to meet him several times and enjoyed long talks with him on men and things. In those days he had been four times Governor of the State of

New York and had been defeated as candidate for the Presidency. He spoke to me, not without feeling, of the lack of continuity in American public life for party leaders. The unsuccessful candidate for the Presidency, although he commands the hopes and esteem of nearly half the nation, often has no public sphere in which he can carry forward all the prestige and allegiances he has gathered in a nationwide campaign. With us, over here, it is different, and in many cases a Prime Minister falls from power only to walk four or five yards across the floor of the House of Commons and carry forward his work as Leader of the Opposition. I have a great respect for the American Constitution, but in this instance, I must confess that I definitely prefer the British system, or perhaps I should say custom, for we have no system.

I had followed Al Smith's contest for the Presidency with keen interest and sympathy. I was in the fullest agreement with his attitude on Prohibition. I even suggested to him a slogan—"All for Al and Al for All". He certainly was a man of the highest quality of brain and heart, who rose under the free institutions of America, as anyone has a right to do, from humble beginnings to high, long, and successful executive office. To be chosen four times Governor remains a record for the Empire State. His devotion to the religion he had learned as a child was perhaps a hindrance to him in a political appeal to the vast and varied American democracy, but it was the comfort and inspiration of his life, and his many private virtues and gaiety of nature and personal charm hung on this golden thread. He loved his fellow men and was capable of giving them the noblest forms of service and sacrifice. Long may his memory be cherished in the mighty city of which he was a shining and faithful son.

Let me turn from this great American to the Causes which I am sure, were he with us now, he would have made his own. We have travelled a long way in opinion since I spoke at Fulton under the auspices of the President eighteen months ago, and many things which were startling or disputable then have now become the foundation of dominant Anglo-American thought. During all this time the Soviet Government have poured out, through their radio

in twenty-six languages, and in all the speeches made on their behalf, an unceasing stream of abuse upon the Western World, and
they have accompanied this virulent propaganda by every action
which could prevent the world settling down into a durable peace
or the United Nations Organisation plying its part as a great world
instrument to prevent war. Indeed the Conferences at Lake Success
—perhaps prematurely named—have become a forum in which
reproaches and insults are hurled at each other by the greatest
States, hurled at each other for all mankind to hear if they care to
listen. But some of them are getting tired.

I have been much puzzled to know why it is that the Soviet
Government have taken this violently aggressive line. From an external point of view it seems so foolish that we wonder what is the
real motive behind it. I cannot believe that it is the prelude to war.
These fourteen men in the Kremlin, who rule with despotic power
the vast populations and territories of which they are the masters,
are very capable and well-informed. If their minds were set on war,
I cannot believe that they would not lull the easy-going democracies
into a false sense of security. Hitler was a master of this and always,
before or during some act of aggression, he uttered soothing words
or made non-aggression pacts. Therefore, while I cannot exclude
the danger of war, I do not think the violent abuse which the Soviet
Government and their Communist adherents all over the world
lavish on all existing forms of civilization, is necessarily a sign of
danger. It is more likely, in my opinion, being used for internal
purposes. If there are only fourteen men, all eyeing one another
and deeply conscious of the enormous populations they hold in
chains of mind and spirit enforced by terror, it may well be that
they think it pays them and helps them to perpetrate their rule by
representing to the otherwise blind-folded masses of the brave and
good-hearted Russian people, that the Soviet Government stands
between them and a repetition of the horror of invasion which they
withstood when it came, so manfully. I devoutly hope that this view
of mine may prove to be correct.

But the United States and the western democracies of Europe
would fail to profit by the hard experiences they have undergone

if they did not take every measure of prudent, defensive preparation which is open to them. While taking all necessary steps and above all, maintaining a solid front, we should not however be hasty in abandoning our hope in the United Nations Organisation. It may be that the Soviet Government and their Communist Fifth Columns in so many countries will, at some moment or other, quit the United Nations Organisation. Then there would be what is called "Two Worlds". We should all be sorry to see that, but if one of these worlds is far more powerful than the other, and is equally vigilant and is also sincerely desirous of maintaining peace, there is no reason why a two-world system should lead to war. Great wars come when both sides believe they are more or less equal, when each thinks it has a good chance of victory. No such conditions of equality would be established if the Soviet Government and their Communist devotees were to make a separate organization of their own. Indeed the two great systems might even begin to be polite to one another and speak again the measured language of diplomacy. Therefore it seems to me we should not be unduly depressed if the Soviet-Communist forces should decide to part company with the World Organization. Certainly we ought not to give away anything which is essential to our security in order to persuade them to linger with us for the purpose of paralyzing the joint harmonious action of three-quarters of mankind.

I must now say a word about my own country and yours. First of all I ask you to pay no attention to the many insulting things which are said about the United States by the Communists and crypto-Communists and fellow-travellers in our Island. Their interest and their instructions naturally lead them to say everything in their power to make division between us. You should completely ignore their taunts and jeers. For instance, I noticed in the newspapers bitter words from a Mr. Priestley,* who gained some acceptance in the war from the fact that we used him for broadcasting

* Mr. J. B. Priestley, the author and dramatist, had written in an American magazine: "The most powerful Government on earth seems to have no continuing policy, no tradition to guide it, and is clearly swayed by what is largely an irresponsible sensation-loving Press and an electorate that can be stampeded like cattle. Imagine our feelings. It is like being locked in a house with a whimsical drunken giant."

purposes. He has no influence. No American should allow himself to be irritated or offended by such diatribes. They do not represent in the slightest degree the feeling of the British nation or, I may say, of His Majesty's Government. We have a Socialist Government —you may have heard of that—and I am the Leader of the Conservative Party in opposition to it—perhaps you have heard of that, too. But I can tell you that there is no country in Europe which makes a firmer or more solid front against Soviet and Communist encroachments than Great Britain. There is no doubt whatever that the Government and the overwhelming mass of the British people, at home and throughout our Commonwealth, if any great issue should arise affecting human freedom, would act with the United States in the same solidarity and fraternal intimacy which has, so lately, given us victory against the combined dictatorships of Germany, Italy and Japan.

I believe that Britain will rise again with even higher influence in the world than she now exercises. I work for the revival of a United Europe. I am sure that the English-speaking world can weather all the storms that blow, and that above all these a world instrument, in Al Smith's words "to weld the democracies together", can be erected, which will be all powerful, so long as it is founded on freedom, justice and mercy—and is well armed.

✷✷✷

AMERICAN SOCIETY IN LONDON

A SPEECH AT THE INDEPENDENCE DAY DINNER
HELD AT THE DORCHESTER HOTEL
July 4, 1950

Your Excellencies, My Lords, Ladies and Gentlemen:
I was glad when you asked me to join you tonight in celebrating

Independence Day. Among Englishmen I have a special qualification for such an occasion, I am directly descended through my mother from an officer who served in Washington's Army. And as such I have been made a member of your strictly selected Society of the Cincinnati. I have my pedigree supported by affidavits at every stage if it is challenged. So what? Well, Ladies and Gentlemen, it is a long time since the War of Independence and quite a lot of things have happened, and keep on happening. There is no doubt that I was on both sides then and it gives me a comfortable feeling of simplification as the years have passed to feel that we're all on the same side now. The drawing together in fraternal association of the British and American peoples, and of all the peoples of the English-speaking world may well be regarded as the best of the few good things that have happened to us and to the world in this century of tragedy and storm.

It was Bismarck who said in the closing years of his life that the most potent factor in human society at the end of the nineteenth century was the fact that the British and American peoples spoke the same language. He might well have added, what was already then apparent, that we had in common a very wide measure of purpose and ideals arising from our institutions, our literature and our common law. Since then, on the anvil of war, we have become so welded together that what might have remained for generations an interesting historical coincidence has become the living and vital force which preserves Christian civilization and the rights and freedom of mankind. Nearly two months have passed since the Ambassador talked over with me the invitation with which you have honoured me. Mr. Lew Douglas is an intimate war comrade of mine, and one of the best friends from across the Atlantic which our country had in the struggle; and that is saying a lot. He is esteemed throughout this island and we all have felt the utmost sympathy for him in his accident, and admiration for the courage with which he has surmounted so much physical pain. No one I am sure can do more to prevent misunderstandings—diplomatic or otherwise—between our two countries than His Excellency the American Ambassador.

When I accepted your invitation I could not foresee that when the date arrived we should once again be brothers in arms, engaged in fighting for exactly the same cause that we thought we had carried to victory five years ago. The British and Americans do not war with races or governments as such. Tyranny, external or internal, is our foe whatever trappings or disguises it wears, whatever language it speaks, or perverts. We must forever be on our guard, and always vigilant against it—in all this we march together. Not only, if need be, under the fire of the enemy but also in those realms of thought which are consecrated to the rights and the dignity of man, and which are so amazingly laid down in the Declaration of Independence, which has become a common creed on both sides of the Atlantic Ocean.

The inheritance of the English-speaking world, vast and majestic though it is in territory and resources, derives its glory as a moral unity from thought and vision widely spread in the minds of our people and cherished by all of those who understand our destiny. As you may have heard (I don't want to give away any secrets) we had a General Election here a few months ago by which a Parliament was returned very evenly balanced but still more sharply divided; but divided not by small matters but by issues which cut deep into our national life. We have not developed to any extent over here the bipartisan conduct of external policy by both great parties like that which has in these later years so greatly helped the United States. Nevertheless, once the deep gong of comradeship between kindred nations strikes, resounds and reverberates, and when our obligations of the United Nations are staring us in the face, we shall allow no domestic party quarrels—grievous though they may be—to mar the unity of our national or international action. You can count on Britain, and not only Britain. Four years ago, when President Truman, whom we salute tonight, took me to Westminster College at Fulton in Missouri I ventured to offer the American people my counsel, and I said, 'Let no man underrate the abiding power of the British Empire and Commonwealth. Do not suppose that we shall not come through these dark years of privation as we came through the glorious years of agony, or that half a century from now will not see 70,000,000 or 80,000,000 Britons spread throughout the world and united in defence of our traditions, our way of life, and the world causes which you and we espouse.' In the increasing unity of the Anglo-American thought and action resides the main foundation of the freedom and progress of all men in all the lands. Let us not weary, let us not lose confidence in our mission, let us not fail in our duty in times of stress, let us not flinch if danger comes.

We must ask ourselves whether danger—I mean the danger of a third world war, has come nearer because of what has happened in the last week and is happening now. I do not think, myself, that the danger has grown greater. But then, I thought it very serious before. It all depends where you start thinking in these matters. I must say that we—Britons and Americans—and the many States and nations associated with us have had hard luck. The Russian Communists have built up an empire far beyond the dreams of the Tsars out of a war in which they might have been conquered or driven beyond the Ural mountains in spite of the bravery with which the Russian Army fought for its native soil. They would have been conquered or driven out but for the immense diversionary aid of Britain and the United States on land and sea and, above all, in the air. And also the vital supplies which had cost so much self-denial, and peril—and the Ambassador knows a lot about all that because the shipping on which everything depended was throughout influenced in the most effective manner by his personal care and courage. Not only do the Soviets hold at the present time all the famous capitals of Europe east of the line—which I call 'the Iron Curtain' drawn from Stettin to Trieste, not only are they endeavouring with great cruelties to compel these many States and countries to adopt the Communist system and become incorporated in the Soviet mass, but they have gained also vast populations in Asia, including practically the whole of China. And they are pressing forward in insatiable, imperialist ambition wherever any weakness on the part of the free world gives them an opportunity.

Thus, I say we have had hard luck, just when we thought we had finished with Hitler and Mussolini, with Nazism and Fascism, we have Stalin and Communism lumping up against us representing the former Hitler tyranny in barbaric form and Asiatic guise. We had hoped that the task of this hard-pressed generation was done. Your poet Walt Whitman said: 'Now understand me well it is provided in the essence of things that from any fruition of success, no matter what, shall come forth something to make a greater struggle necessary.' We pray this may not be so. These hard decrees may be the lot of the human race in its unending struggle for existence, but the question which we have to consider tonight, and in regard to which the Ambassador laid before you in a cogently related argument many essential facts, is whether our dangers have been increased by the Communist act of aggression in Korea. I agree with the British Government speakers that they have not been increased. How does this new menace differ in principle from the Berlin blockade, two years ago, which together we faced with composure and overcame by the Allied airlift, mainly carried by American planes but in which we bore an important share? It differs in one major fact. We are told that the Kremlin oligarchy now know how to make the atomic bomb. That is the one new fact. To that extent there is a change to our disadvantage. It certainly seems to me that there is a better hope of a general settlement with Soviet Russia following on the defeat of aggression in Korea on a localized scale, than that we should drift on while large quantities of these devastating weapons are accumulated. Indeed I feel that there is nothing more likely to bring on a third world war than drift.

It is always difficult for free democracies, governed in the main by public opinion from day to day, to cope with the designs of dictator States and totalitarian systems. But hitherto we have held our own, or we should not be here tonight. We have only to be morally united and fearless, to give mankind the best hope of avoiding another supreme catastrophe. But I must say one thing before I sit down. It is of vital consequence to these hopes of world peace that what the Communists have begun in Korea should not end in their triumph. If that were to happen a third world war, under conditions even more deadly than now exist, would certainly be forced upon us, or hurled upon us before long. It is fortunate that the path of duty, and of safety, is so plainly marked out before our eyes, and so widely recognized by both our nations and governments, and by the large majority, the overwhelming majority of the member States comprised in the United Nations Organization.

We owe it not only to ourselves, but to our faith in an institution, if not a world government at least a world protection from aggressive war, not to fail in our duty now. Thus we shall find the best hopes of peace and surest proof of honour. The League of Nations failed not because of its noble conceptions, but because these were abandoned by its members. We must not ask to be taught this hard lesson twice. Looking around this obscure, tumultuous scene, with all its uncertainties as it presents itself to us tonight, I am sure we shall not be guilty of such incurable folly; we shall go forward; we shall do our duty; we shall save the world from a third world war. And should it come in spite of all our efforts, we shall not be trampled down into serfdom and ruin.

⌘⌘⌘

PILGRIMS' DINNER
IN HONOR OF
GENERAL RIDGWAY

A SPEECH AT THE SAVOY HOTEL
October 14, 1952

We all regret the absence from our dinner this evening of Lord Halifax, whose career as British Ambassador to the United States added lustre to his long record of eminent service. Tonight we have a distinguished gathering at the Pilgrims' Dinner. You will note, by the way, that in this well-known and long-known island we have succeeded for nearly a thousand years in preventing any invaders from coming in. But you should also note—as pilgrims—that we have never prevented any from going out—not even in the *Mayflower*—and speaking as a Briton I must admit that some quite good ones have gone out. But now larger syntheses (if I may use the kind of learned jargon which is fashionable) are bringing together by forces, which are primarily moral and intellectual, all the individuals and all the nations who would die rather than submit to Communist rule. But there is no reason why the free world should die. On the contrary, it has only to remain united and progressive not only to survive, but to preserve its right to live in its own way without the need of another hideous catastrophe.

Here tonight we have two of our famous British Commanders, Alex and Monty. I am sure that in their separate spheres they are going to do all in their power to help our guest of the evening, General Ridgway, to carry out the enormous task which he has undertaken. General Ridgway had a predecessor. I am afraid that I might get into trouble if I told you his name. All I will say is that those who understand the work he did in Europe will ever remember it with thankfulness. We are fortunate indeed that General Ridgeway has come to our aid in this critical period with his record in the war and in Korea as soldier and statesman.

We have also been forced to spare from the Cabinet Lord Ismay (his international status prevents my using his pet name) who is doing the same sort of thing for NATO as he did for me in the war —to make all things go as well as possible between the military and the politicians and to weave together many diverse elements into the harmonious structure of a machine capable of giving decisions for millions of men.

All down the ages many and varied, but not always wholly successful, have been the expedients which have tried to bring the nations together in peace or war. It may be that NATO, our shield against war, can also unite us for peace. There are hopeful stirrings in Europe today, most of which find their inspiration directly or indirectly in the leadership which NATO has given. From small beginnings who can tell what blessings they may bring us? Come what will, at the present time it is in NATO that wise men in

Europe and America will do well to place their trust as a benevolent combination of the free peoples for their defence against mortal danger.

Our policy, the policy of the English-speaking world, the policy of NATO, and of all who prefer Parliamentary democracy with its many defects—never concealed—to totalitarian rule wherever it comes from, our policy is by hard sacrifice and constant toil to increase the deterrents against an aggressor. I can assure you tonight that we shall do our utmost, short of going bankrupt, to increase these deterrents and also to convince the other side that we are planning no assault on them.

We all hate and fear war. Let me tell you why in my opinion, and it is only an opinion, not a prophecy, a third World War is unlikely to happen. It is because, among other reasons, it would be entirely different in certain vital aspects from any other war that has ever taken place. Both sides know that it would begin with horrors of a kind and on a scale never dreamed of before by human beings. It would begin by both sides in Europe suffering in this first stage exactly what they dread the most. It would also be different because the main decisions would probably come in the first month or even in the first week. The quarrel might continue for an indefinite period, but after the first month it would be a broken-backed war in which no great armies could be moved over long distances. The torments would fall in increasing measure upon the whole civilian population of the globe, and Governments dependent upon long distance communications by land would find they had lost their power to dominate events.

These are only a few of the grave facts which rule our destinies; but we can be sure that this proved and experienced General of the United States Army, whom we welcome here tonight as our guest of honour, will do his utmost for our common cause, and it is with sincere feelings of hope that I support our President in asking you to drink the health of our distinguished guests at these tables tonight, and first and foremost of General Ridgeway.

※※※

DOCTORATE OF NEW YORK UNIVERSITY

A SPEECH AT No. 10 DOWNING STREET ON
ACCEPTING, *IN ABSENTIA*, A DOCTORATE
OF LAW FROM THE UNIVERSITY OF
THE STATE OF NEW YORK
April 7, 1954

Rochester was the home of my grandparents, and my mother was born in Brooklyn, so it is with both pride and emotion that I accept the degree of Doctor of Laws from the Board of Regents of the University of the State of New York. I take it as a remarkable honour that now, for the first time in one hundred and seventy years, you confer a degree *in absentia*. I am only sorry for the *absentia*. Three thousand miles of sea keep us apart, but science, in one of its more beneficial manifestations, is able to record my thanks to you in person, and certainly no ocean divides me or indeed my countrymen, from you in thought and spirit to-night.

I am not a lawyer, but I have obeyed a lot of laws, and helped to make a few. Law, language, and literature unite the English-speaking world, and all sorts of other things are happening which fortify these mighty traditions with ever-growing practical considerations of safety and survival. The rule of law, calm, without prejudice, swayed neither to the right nor to the left however political tides or party currents may flow, is the foundation of freedom. The independence of the judiciary from the executive is the prime defence against the tyranny and retrogression of totalitarian government. Trial by jury, the right of every man to be judged by his equals, is among the most precious gifts that England has bequeathed to America.

Great have been our divergencies since 1776. But in respect of the law and the maintenance of the English common law, Great Britain and the United States have marched together. Indeed it is a fact that American law is more wedded to the older versions of English law than is the case in Britain, where in the first half of the nineteenth century a great deal of technical modernization was effected. Although I like old things better than new, I believe our revised version has many conveniences in procedure. Going back to 1776, you may have heard that as a lineal descendant on my mother's side from a Captain in Washington's armies, I am a member of the Cincinnati. As I told them when admitted to the Society I must have been on both sides then. Certainly in judging that historic quarrel I am on both sides now. Sex was not born till protoplasm—or protozoa if you prefer—divided itself. But for this split the sexes would not have had all the fun of coming together again.

Naturally we have our differences. They are differences of method rather than of purpose. I am a great believer in democracy and free speech. Naturally when immense masses of people speak the same language and enjoy the fullest rights of free speech they often say some things that all the others do not agree to. If speech were always to be wise it could never be free, and even where it is most strictly regulated it is not always wise. But where British and American relations are concerned I remain an incurable optimist.

I remember when I first came over here in 1895 I was a guest of your great lawyer and orator, Mr. Bourke Cockran. I was only a young Cavalry subaltern but he poured out all his wealth of mind and eloquence to me. Some of his sentences are deeply rooted in my mind. 'The earth,' he said, 'is a generous mother. She will produce in plentiful abundance food for all her children if they will but cultivate her soil in justice and in peace.' I used to repeat it so frequently on British platforms that I had to give it a holiday. But now to-day it seems to come back with new pregnancy and force, for never was the choice between blessing and cursing more vehemently presented to the human race. There was another thing Bourke Cockran used to say to me. I cannot remember his actual words but they amounted to this: 'In a society where there is democratic tolerance and freedom under the law, many kinds of evils will crop up, but give them a little time and they usually breed their own cure.' I do not see any reason to doubt the truth of that.

There is no country in the world where the process of self-criticism and self-correction is more active than in the United States. You must not think I am talking politics. I make it a rule never to meddle in the internal or party politics of any friendly country. It is hard enough to understand the party politics of your own. I end where I began in my thanks to you for the compliment you pay me to-night. Your country and your population are far bigger than ours even when our sister Commonwealths are added, but whenever we are working together we seem to be more than twice as strong. It is my faith that if we work together there are no problems that we cannot solve, no dangers which we cannot ward off from ourselves, and no tangles through which we cannot guide the freedom-loving peoples of the world.

❊❊❊

ANGLO-AMERICAN FRIENDSHIP

A SPEECH AT A DINNER OF THE ENGLISH-SPEAKING UNION IN HONOR OF GENERAL GRUENTHER
June 8, 1954

We are deeply indebted to the Duke of Edinburgh* for presiding at this gathering of the English-Speaking Union and for expressing our welcome to General Gruenther in such just and powerful terms. This is a memorable and well-chosen occasion. Ten years ago last Sunday, the greatest expeditionary force that has ever sailed from any shores set out from our South Coast, for the Normandy beaches. A million men owing allegiance to the King were concentrated in a few weeks into the British bridgehead. They were matched by a million American citizens who had crossed the Atlantic like their fathers twenty-seven years before. They had come

* Prince Philip, consort of Queen Elizabeth II. [K.H.]

to help us liberate Europe, and as we hoped *all* Europe, from the grip of Hitler's tyranny and save the ancient civilization from which they themselves had sprung.

To-day General Gruenther, standing where Eisenhower stood, commands forces not of two nations only but of fourteen. He also commands the respect and confidence of us all. He is a wise and skilful leader of a widespread military coalition which has been built up for the defence of law and freedom. We all earnestly pray that he will never be called upon to lead his armies into battle. It is the strength of the organized free world, personified at this great gathering by General Gruenther, with its measureless reserves and resources as yet unmobilized, which give us the right to hope that none will dare assail us.

The English-Speaking Union plays an active and vital part in the whole vast process of bringing the English-speaking nations of the world into unity and keeping them in effective harmony. We are entitled to-night to fix our thoughts on the might, and I think I may say majesty, of the unwritten alliance which binds the British Commonwealth and Empire to the great republic of the United States. It is an alliance far closer in fact than many which exist in writing. It is a treaty with more enduring elements than clauses and protocols. We have history, law, philosophy, and literature; we have sentiment and common interest; we have a language which even the Scottish Nationalists will not mind me referring to as English. We are often in agreement on current events and we stand on the same foundation of the supreme realities of the modern world.

When great and buoyant communities enjoy free speech in the same language, it is not surprising that they often say different things about the confused and tangled age in which we dwell. But nothing must divide us as we march together along the path of destiny. If the world is to be split in twain we know which side we are on and we believe that our unbreakable unity is the core to the safety and survival and to the freedom and peaceful progress of mankind. As I have several times said, our policy is 'Peace through Strength'. There is nothing contradictory in that. In fact I believe the two are inseparable.

When I spoke in the House of Commons on 11 May of last year,

Stalin had just died and new minds controlled the fortunes of
Russia. I hoped that we should see from them a more realistic and
less pedantic approach to world problems. But I added:

> This would be the most fatal moment for the free nations to relax
> their comradeship and preparedness. To fail to maintain our de-
> fence effort up to the limit of our strength would be to paralyse
> every beneficial tendency towards peace both in Europe and in
> Asia. For us to become divided among ourselves because of di-
> vergencies of opinion or local interests, or to slacken our com-
> bined efforts would be to end for ever such new hope as may
> have broken upon mankind and lead instead to their general ruin
> and enslavement. Unity, vigilance, and fidelity are the only founda-
> tions upon which hope can live.

Nothing that has happened in the past twelve months has made me
alter my view that peace through strength must be our guiding star.
It is the duty and also the interest of the Communist and free
worlds that they should live in peace together and strive untiringly
to remove or outlive their differences. Humanity stands to-day at
its most fateful milestone. On the one hand science opens a chasm
of self-destruction beyond limit. On the other hand she displays
a vision of plenty and comfort of which the masses of no race have
ever known or even dreamed. We in the West know which we would
choose, but also that we can only reach it at the price of eternal
vigilance. While persevering at great sacrifice and cost in building
our military strength, we must never lose sight of the importance
of a peaceful and friendly settlement of our differences with Russia.

What a vista would be open to all if the treasure and toil consumed on weapons of destruction could be devoted to simple and
peaceful ends. It is not only the West who would benefit from it.
The people of Russia have had to live a hard and tragic life and
the twentieth century has been full of agony for them. They would
dearly love the easement and the leisure, the comfort and the diver-
sions, which could be theirs should those who rule them so decide.
The English-speaking world, united in itself, and supported by its
allies, is an unconquerable force. It asks nothing more than that it

should be allowed in safety and freedom to use its wealth, its genius, and its power for the furtherance of peace, progress for all.

⌘⌘⌘

THE WILLIAMSBURG
AWARD–A SPEECH
IN DRAPER'S HALL

A SPEECH IN DRAPER'S HALL, LONDON
December 7, 1955

I am honoured by the Award which the Williamsburg Trustees have made to me, and I am glad indeed to be the first to receive it. I saw myself nine years ago the wonderful memorial which Mr. Rockefeller's father has raised to the history of the United States, and the link which he has provided with the past. No more fascinating gleam exists of a vanished world, embodying as it does the grace, the ease, and the charm of bygone colonial days.

I am also profoundly touched by the personal kindness which has led so many Americans, when I was unable to go to them, to come over here and give this truly remarkable dinner in the Drapers' Hall in London. This memorable event is a proof—if proof were needed—of the unity of thought and sentiment which has come into being between us during this tragic century, and which, I venture to say, is the most important thing in the world. The horizons of life are dark and confused, but I think that most of us here have the sort of feeling that we shall not go far wrong if we keep together. I am very glad to learn that Sir Anthony Eden and the Foreign Secretary, Mr. Harold Macmillan, whom we are all so glad to see here to-night, are going over in the New Year for another talk about all those tiresome and difficult matters in which our common interests are involved. They will talk about them on foundations strong, and ever growing stronger, and which will never be broken by force or the threat of force.

Colonial Williamsburg has added a new element to our strength and unity. The Award, and the conception which Mr. Rockefeller's father embraced, transcends the bounds of race, creed, and geography, and brings the whole free world within its sphere. The choice is world wide. This, in my view, constitutes the strength of its appeal, and the fact that you should give your first Award to one who is a British subject establishes an even higher and wider level than those bounded by nationality.

I am, however, by blood half American and on my mother's side I have the right to enjoy the early memories of Colonial Williamsburg as much as anyone here. I delight in my American ancestry which gave me in five generation a claim to membership of several celebrated historical institutions across the Atlantic. Jerome Park in New York shows that my grandfather took an interest in horse-racing.

It gave me extreme pleasure to hear you read the message which President Eisenhower has sent on this occasion. He is a great friend of mine. For the last fourteen years we have worked together, and it is but a week ago that I had the honour to receive from him the Medallion which bore the imprint of a picture painted with his own hands. His message to-night comes from Gettysburg, and there we have one of those famous names which teach us to forget and forgive as well as to remember.

The Trustees of Colonial Williamsburg have come in a body and have brought with them distinguished guests. Mr. Baruch, Mr. Harriman, General Bedell Smith were prevented at the last moment from joining our company to-night. I am very glad, however, that we have Admiral 'Betty' Stark and Lew Douglas, who works so tirelessly for Anglo-American unity, and General Gruenther, the N.A.T.O. Supreme Allied Commander in Europe. My own British friends, comrades, and colleagues are too numerous for me to attempt to mention, and I can only express my gratitude that they should be here to-night. It has been to me an occasion I shall never forget.

Mr. Winthrop Rockefeller, you have presented to me a Town Crier's Bell as it was made at Colonial Williamsburg in the days of our forefathers. The words you have inscribed on it are inspiring. Its silver tone is gentle. I shall ring it whenever I feel there is duty to be done.

THE UNWRITTEN ALLIANCE

✖✖✖

AMERICAN HISTORY RETOLD

BY

WINSTON CHURCHILL

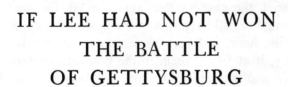

IF LEE HAD NOT WON
THE BATTLE
OF GETTYSBURG

On July 1, 1863, General Lee's invasion of the North had brought
several components of his army into the vicinity of Gettysburg,
in southern Pennsylvania, where he determined to concentrate
them. The Union Commander, Meade, held the town with only
a small force, as a screen to a manœuvre elsewhere. Advance
guard actions precipitated a general engagement, which endured
furiously for three days. On the third, Lee, after suffering several

repulses, decided to attempt the envelopment of the Union right, while his fresh reserves under General Pickett were to attempt a direct break through the Union centre at Cemetery Hill. The former operation broke down, but the latter, in one of the fiercest actions in military history, all but succeeded—the Northern line was actually penetrated and only a lack of further reserves prevented Lee from following up Pickett's charge with the rout of the Union army. Lee was compelled to fall back into Virginia, and no further general invasion of the North was ever attempted. The Battle of Gettysburg, together with Grant's capture of Vicksburg, which occurred next day, is considered the turning-point of the war. From then on final victory for the Union became inevitable. Had Lee won, there is little doubt that in a few days he would have held Washington and a large portion of Northern territory.

The quaint conceit of imagining what would have happened if some important or unimportant event had settled itself differently has become so fashionable that I am encouraged to enter upon an absurd speculation. What would have happened if Lee had not won the Battle of Gettysburg? Once a great victory is won it dominates not only the future but the past. All the chains of consequence clink out as if they never could stop. The hopes that were shattered, the passions that were quelled, the sacrifices that were ineffectual are all swept out of the land of reality. Still it may amuse an idle hour, and perhaps serve as a corrective to undue complacency, if at this moment in the twentieth century—so rich in assurance and prosperity, so calm and buoyant—we meditate for a spell upon the debt we owe to those Confederate soldiers who by a deathless feat of arms broke the Union front at Gettysburg and laid open a fair future to the world.

It always amuses historians and philosophers to pick out the tiny things, the sharp agate points, on which the ponderous balance of destiny turns; and certainly the details of the famous Confederate victory of Gettysburg furnish a fertile theme. There can be at this date no conceivable doubt that Pickett's charge would have been defeated, if Stuart with his encircling cavalry had not arrived in the rear of the Union position at the supreme moment. Stuart might have been arrested in his decisive swoop if any one of twenty commonplace incidents had occurred. If, for instance, General Meade had organized his lines of communication with posts for defence against raids, or if he had used his cavalry to scout upon his flanks, he would have received a timely warning. If General Warren had only thought of sending a battalion to hold Little Round Top, the rapid advance of the masses of Confederate cavalry must have been detected. If only President Davis's letter to General Lee, captured by Captain Dahlgren, revealing the Confederacy's plans, had reached Meade a few hours earlier, he might have escaped Lee's clutches.

Anything, we repeat, might have prevented Lee's magnificent combinations from synchronizing, and if so Pickett's repulse was sure. Gettysburg would have been a great Northern victory. It might have well been a final victory. Lee might, indeed, have made a successful retreat from the field. The Confederacy with its skilful generals and fierce armies might have survived for another year, or even two, but, once defeated decisively at Gettysburg, its doom was inevitable. The fall of Vicksburg, which happened only two days after Lee's immortal triumph, would in itself, by opening the Mississippi to the river fleets of the Union, have cut the Secessionist States almost in half. Without wishing to dogmatize, we feel we are on solid ground in saying that the Southern States could not have survived the loss of a great battle in Pennsylvania, and the almost simultaneous bursting open of the Mississippi.

However, all went well. Once again by the narrowest of margins the compulsive pinch of military genius and soldiery valour produced a perfect result. The panic which engulfed the whole left of Meade's massive army has never been made a reproach against the Yankee troops. Everyone knows they were stout fellows. But defeat is defeat, and rout is ruin. Three days only were required after the cannon at Gettysburg had ceased to thunder before General Lee fixed his headquarters in Washington. We need not here dwell upon the ludicrous features of the hurried flight to New York of all the politicians, place hunters, contractors, sentimentalists, and their retinues, which was so successfully accomplished. It is more agreeable to remember how Lincoln, "greatly falling with a falling State," preserved the poise and dignity of a nation. Never did his rugged yet sublime common sense render a finer service to his countrymen. He was never greater than in the hour of fatal defeat.

But, of course, there is no doubt whatever that the mere military victory which Lee gained at Gettysburg would not by itself have altered the history of the world. The loss of Washington would not have affected the immense numerical preponderance of the Union States. The advanced situation of their capital and its fall would have exposed them to a grave injury, would no doubt have considerably prolonged the war; but standing by itself this military episode, dazzling though it may be, could not have prevented the ultimate victory of the North. It is in the political sphere that we have to look to find the explanation of the triumphs begun upon the battlefield.

Curiously enough, Lee furnishes an almost unique example of a regular and professional soldier who achieved the highest excellence both as a general and as a statesman. His ascendancy throughout the Confederate States on the morrow of his Gettysburg victory threw Jefferson Davis and his civil government irresistibly, indeed almost unconsciously, into the shade. The beloved and victorious commander, arriving in the capital of his mighty antagonists, found there the title deeds which enabled him to pronounce the grand decrees of peace. Thus it happened that the guns of Gettysburg fired virtually the last shots in the American Civil War.

The movement of events then shifted to the other side of the Atlantic Ocean, England—the name by which the British Empire was then commonly described—had been riven morally in twain by the drama of the American struggle. We have always admired the steadfastness with which the Lancashire cotton operatives, though starved of cotton by the Northern blockade—our most prosperous county reduced to penury, almost become dependent upon the charity of the rest of England—nevertheless adhered to the Northern cause. The British working classes on the whole judged the quarrel through the eyes of Disraeli and rested solidly upon the side of the abolition of slavery. Indeed, all Mr. Gladstone's democratic flair and noble eloquence would have failed, even upon the then restricted franchise, to carry England into the Confederate camp as a measure of policy. If Lee after his triumphal entry into Washington had merely been the soldier, his achievements would have ended on the battlefield. It was his august declaration that the victorious Confederacy would pursue no policy towards the African negroes which was not in harmony with the moral conceptions of western Europe, that opened the high roads along which we are now marching so prosperously.

But even this famous gesture might have failed if it had not been caught up and implemented by the practical genius and trained Parliamentary aptitudes of Gladstone. There is practically no doubt at this stage that the basic principle upon which the colour question in the Southern States of America has been so happily settled owed its origin mainly to Gladstonian ingenuity, and to the long statecraft of Britain in dealing with alien and more primitive populations. There was not only the need to declare the new fundamental relationship between master and servant, but the creation for the liberated slaves of institutions suited to their own cultural development and capable of affording them a different, yet honourable, status in a commonwealth destined eventually to become almost world-wide.

Let us only think what would have happened supposing the liberation of the slaves had been followed by some idiotic assertion of racial equality, and even by attempts to graft white democratic institutions upon the simple, docile, gifted African race belonging to a much earlier chapter in human history. We might have seen the whole of the Southern States invaded by gangs of carpetbagging politicians exploiting the ignorant and untutored coloured vote against the white inhabitants and bringing the time-honoured forms of Parliamentary government into unmerited disrepute. We might have seen the sorry farce of black legislatures attempting to govern their former masters. Upon the rebound from this there must inevitably have been a strong reassertion of local white supremacy. By one device or another the franchises accorded to the negroes would have been taken from them. The constitutional principles of the

Republic would have been proclaimed, only to be evaded or subverted; and many a warm-hearted philanthropist would have found his sojourn in the South no better than "A Fool's Errand."

But we must return to our main theme and to the procession of tremendous events which followed the Northern defeat at Gettysburg and the surrender of Washington. Lee's declaration abolishing slavery, coupled as it was with the inflexible resolve to secede from the American Union, opened the way for British intervention.

Within a month the formal treaty of alliance between the British Empire and the Confederacy had been signed. The terms of this alliance being both offensive and defensive, revolutionized the military and naval situation. The Northern blockade could not be maintained even for a day in the face of the immense naval power of Britain. The opening of the Southern ports released the pent-up cotton, restored the finances and replenished the arsenals of the Confederacy. The Northern forces at New Orleans were themselves immediately cut off and forced to capitulate. There could be no doubt of the power of the new allies to clear the Mississippi of Northern vessels throughout the whole of its course through the Confederate States. The prospect of a considerable British army embarking for Canada threatened the Union with a new military front.

But none of these formidable events in the sphere of arms and material force would have daunted the resolution of President Lincoln, or weakened the fidelity of the Northern States and armies. It was Lee's declaration abolishing slavery which by a single masterstroke gained the Confederacy an all-powerful ally, and spread a moral paralysis far and wide through the ranks of their enemies. The North was waging war against Secession, but as the struggle had proceeded, the moral issue of slavery had first sustained and then dominated the political quarrel. Now that the moral issue was withdrawn, now that the noble cause which inspired the Union armies and the Governments behind them was gained, there was nothing left but a war of reconquest to be waged under circumstances infinitely more difficult and anxious than those which had already led to so much disappointment and defeat. Here was the South victorious, reinvigorated, reinforced, offering of her own free will to make a more complete abolition of the servile status on the American continent than even Lincoln had himself seen fit to demand. Was the war to continue against what soon must be heavy odds merely to assert the domination of one set of English-speaking people over another; was blood to flow indefinitely in an ever-broadening stream to gratify national pride or martial revenge?

It was this deprivation of the moral issue which undermined the obduracy of the Northern States. Lincoln no longer rejected the Southern appeal for independence. "If," he declared in his famous speech in Madison Square Garden in New York, "our brothers in the South are willing faithfully to cleanse this continent of negro slavery, and if they will dwell beside us in neighbourly goodwill as an independent but friendly nation, it would not be right to prolong the slaughter on the question of sovereignty alone."

Thus peace came more swiftly than war had come. The Treaty of Harper's Ferry which was signed between the Union and Confederate States on September 6, 1863 embodied the two fundamental propositions: that the South was independent, and the slaves were free. If the spirit of old John Brown had revisited the battle-scarred township which had been the scene of his life and death, it would have seen his cause victorious; but at a cost to the United States terrible indeed. Apart from the loss of blood and treasure, the American Union was riven in twain. Henceforth there would be two Americas in the same northern continent. One of them would have renewed in a modern and embattled form its old ties of kinship and affiliation with the Mother Country across the ocean. It was evident, though peace might be signed and soldiers furl their flags, that profound antagonisms, social, economic, and military, underlay the life of the English-speaking world. Still, slavery was abolished. As John Bright said, "At last after the smoke of the battlefield has cleared away, the horrid shape which had cast its shadow over the whole continent, has vanished and is gone for ever."

At this date, when all seems so simple and clear, one has hardly the patience to chronicle the bitter and lamentable developments which occupied the two succeeding generations.

But we may turn aside in our speculation to note how strangely the careers of Mr. Gladstone and Mr. Disraeli would have been altered if Lee had not won the Battle of Gettysburg. Mr. Gladstone's threatened resignation from Lord Palmerton's Cabinet on the morrow of General Lee's pronouncement in favour of abolition, induced a political crisis in England of the most intense character. Old friendships were severed, old rancours died, and new connexions and resentments took their place. Lord Palmerston found himself at the parting of the ways. Having to choose between Mr. Gladstone and Lord John Russell, he did not hesitate. A Coalition Government was formed in which Lord Robert Cecil (afterwards the great Lord Salisbury) became Foreign Secretary, but of which Mr. Gladstone was henceforward the driving force. We remember how he had said at Newcastle on October 7, 1862, "We know quite well that the people of the Northern States have not yet drunk of the cup—they will try hard to hold it far from their lips—which all the rest of the world see they nevertheless must drink. We may have our own ideas about slavery; we may be for or against the South; but there is no doubt that Jefferson Davis and the other soldiers of the South have made an army; they are making, it appears, a navy; *and they have made what is more than either, they have made a nation.*" Now the slavery obstacle was out of the way; and under the ægis of his aged chief, Lord Palmerston, who in Mr. Gladstone's words "desired the severance (of North and South) as the diminution of a dangerous power," and aided by the tempered incisiveness of Lord Robert Cecil, Mr. Gladstone achieved not merely the recognition but an abiding alliance between Great Britain and the Southern States. But this carried him far. In the main the friends of the Confederacy in England belonged to the aristocratic well-to-do and Tory classes of the nation; the democracy, as yet almost entirely unenfranchised, and most of the Liberal elements sympathized with the North. Lord Palmerston's new Government, formed in September 1863, although nominally Coalition, almost entirely embodied the elements of Tory strength and inspiration. No one can say that Gladstone's reunion with the Tories would have been achieved apart from Gettysburg and Lee's declaration at Washington.

However, it was achieved, and henceforward the union of Mr. Gladstone and Lord Robert Cecil on all questions of Church, State, and Empire became an accomplished and fruitful fact. Once again the "rising hope of the stern and unbending Tories" had come back to his old friends, and the combination armed, as it was, with prodigious executive success, reigned for a decade irresistible.

It is strange, musing on Mr. Gladstone's career, how easily he might have drifted into radical and democratic courses. How easily he might have persuaded himself that he, a Tory and authoritarian to his finger-tips, was fitted to be the popular and even populist, leader of the working classes. There might in this event have stood to his credit nothing but sentimental pap, pusillanimous surrenders of British interests, and the easy and relaxing cosmopolitanism which would in practice have made him the friend of every country but his own. But the sabres of Jeb Stuart's cavalry and the bayonets of Pickett's division had, on the slopes of Gettsburg, embodied him for ever in a revivified Tory party. His career thus became a harmony instead of a discord; and he holds his place in the series of great builders to whom the larger synthesis of the world is due.

Precisely the reverse effect operated upon Mr. Disraeli. What had he to do with the Tory aristocracy? In his early days he was prejudiced in their eyes as a Jew by race. He had, indeed, only been saved from the stigma of exclusion from public life before the repeal of the Jewish disabilities by the fact of his having been baptized in infancy. He had stood originally for Parliament as a Radical. His natural place was with the left-out millions, with the dissenters, with the merchants of the North, with the voteless proletariat. He might never have found his place, if Lee had not won the Battle of Gettysburg. But for that he might have continued leading the Conservative Party, educating them against their will, dragging them into all sorts of social policies which they resented, making them serve as agents for extensions of the franchise. Always indispensable, always distrusted, but for Lee and Gettysburg he might well have ended his life in the House of Lords with the exclamation, "Power has come to me too late!"

But once he was united by the astonishing events of 1863 with the democratic and Radical forces of the nation, the real power of the man becomes apparent. He was in his native element. He had always espoused the cause of the North; and what he was pleased to describe as "the selfish and flagitious intrigue (of the Palmerston-Gladstone Government) to split the American Union and to rebuild out of the miseries of a valiant nation the vanished empire of George III," aroused passions in England strong enough to cast him once and for all from Tory circles. He went where his instinct and nature led him, to the Radical masses which were yearly gathering strength. It is to this we owe his immense contribution to our social services. If Disraeli had not been drawn out of the Conservative Party, the whole of those great schemes of social and industrial insurance which are for ever associated with his name, which followed so logically upon his speeches—"Health and the laws of health," "sanitas sanitatum omnia sanitas"—might never have been passed into law in the nineteenth century. They might no doubt well have come about in the twentieth. It might have been left to some sprout of the new democracy or some upstart from Scotland, Ireland, or even Wales, to give to England what her latest Socialist Prime Minister has described as "our incomparable social services." But "Dizzy" "the people's Dizzy," would never have set these merciful triumphs in his record.

We must return to the main theme. We may, however, note, by the way, that if Lee had not won the Battle of Gettysburg, Gladstone would not have become the greatest of Conservative Empire and Commonwealth builders, nor would Disraeli have been the idol of the toiling masses. Such is Fate.

But we cannot occupy ourselves too long upon the fortunes of individuals. During the whole of the rest of the nineteenth century the United States of America, as the truncated Union continued to style itself, grew in wealth and population. An iron determination seemed to have taken hold of the entire people. By the eighties they were already cleared of their war debt, and indeed all traces of the war, except in the hearts of men, were entirely eradicated. But the hearts of men are strange things, and the hearts of nations are still stranger. Never could the American Union endure the ghastly amputation which had been forced upon it. Just as France after 1870 nursed for more than forty years her dream of *revanche,* so did the multiplying peoples of the American Union concentrate their thoughts upon another trial of arms.

And to tell the truth, the behavior of the independent Confederacy helped but little in mitigating the ceaselessly fermenting wrath. The former Confederate States saw themselves possessed of a veteran army successful against numerous odds, and commanded by generals to whose military aptitude history has borne unquestioned tribute. To keep this army intact and—still more important—employed, became a high problem of state. To the south of the Confederacy lay Mexico, in perennial alternation between anarchy and dictatorship. Lee's early experiences in the former Mexican War had familiarized him with the military aspects of the country and its problems, and we must admit that it was natural that he should wish to turn the bayonets of the army of northern Virginia upon this sporadically defended Eldorado. In spite of the pious protests of Mr. Disraeli's Liberal and pacifist Government of 1884, the Confederate States after three years of sanguinary guerrilla fighting conquered, subdued, and reorganized the vast territories of Mexico. These proceedings involved a continuous accretion of Southern military forces. At the close of the Mexican War seven hundred thousand trained and well-tried soldiers were marshalled under what the North still called "the rebel flag." In the face of these potentially menacing armaments who can blame the Northern States for the precautions they took? Who can accuse them of provocation because they adopted the principle of compulsory military service? And when this was retorted by similar measures south of the Harper's Ferry Treaty line, can we be surprised that they increased the period of compulsory service from one year to two, and thereby turned their multitudinous militia into the cadres of an army "second to none." The Southern States, relying on their alliance with the supreme naval power of Britain, did not expend their money upon a salt-water navy. Their powerful ironclad fleet was designed solely for the Mississippi. Nevertheless, on land and water the process of armament and counter-armament proceeded ceaselessly over the whole expanse of the North American continent. Immense fortresses guarded the frontiers on either side and sought to canalize the lines of reciprocal invasion. The wealth of the Union States enabled them at enormous sacrifice at once to fortify their southern front and to maintain a strong fleet and heavy military garrison in the fortified harbours of the great lakes of the Canadian frontier. By the nineties North America bristled with armaments of every kind, and what with the ceaseless growth of the Confederate army—in which the reconciled negro population now formed a most important element—and the very large forces which England and Canada maintained in the North, it was computed that not less than two million armed men with trained reserves of six millions were required to preserve the uneasy peace of the North American continent. Such a process could not go on without a climax of tragedy or remedy.

The climax which came in 1905 was perhaps induced by the agitation of war excitement arising from the Russo-Japanese conflict. The roar of Asiatic cannon reverberated around the globe, and everywhere found immense military organizations in an actively receptive state. Never has the atmosphere of the world been so loaded with explosive forces. Europe and North America were armed camps, and a war of first magnitude was actually raging in Manchuria. At any moment, as the Dogger Bank incident had shown, the British Empire might be involved in war with Russia. Indeed, we had been within the ace on that occasion. And apart from such accidents the British Treaty obligations towards Japan might automatically have drawn us in. The President of the United States had been formally advised by the powerful and highly competent American General Staff that the entry of Great Britain into such a war would offer in every way a favourable opportunity for settling once and for all with the Southern Republic. This fact was also obvious to most people. Thus at the same time throughout Europe and America precautionary measures of all kinds by land and sea were actively taken; and everywhere fleets and armies were assembled and arsenals clanged and flared by night and day.

Now that these awful perils have been finally warded off it seems to us almost incomprehensible that they could have existed. Nevertheless, it is horrible even to reflect that scarcely a quarter of a century ago English-speaking people ranged on opposite sides, watched each other with ceaseless vigilance and drawn weapons. By the end of 1905 the tension was such that nothing could long avert a fratricidal struggle on a gigantic scale, except some great melting of hearts, some wave of inspiration which should lift the dull, deadly antagonisms of the hour to a level so high that—even as a mathematical quantity passing through infinity changes its sign—they would become actual unities.

We must not underrate the strength of the forces which on both sides of the Atlantic Ocean and on both sides of the American continental frontiers were labouring faithfully and dauntlessly to avert the hideous doom which kindred races seemed resolved to prepare for themselves. But these deep currents of sanity and goodwill would not have been effective unless the decisive moment had found simultaneously in England and the United States leaders great enough to dominate events and marvellously placed upon the summits of national power. In President [Theodore] Roosevelt and Mr. Arthur Balfour, the British Prime Minister, were present two diverse personalities which together embodied all the qualities necessary alike for profound negotiation and for supreme decision.

After all, when it happened it proved to be the easiest thing in the world. In fact, it seemed as if it could not help happening, and we who look back upon it take it so much for granted that we cannot understand how easily the most beneficent Covenant of which human records are witness might have been replaced by the most horrible conflict and world tragedy.

The Balfour-Roosevelt negotiations had advanced some distance before President Wilson, the enlightened Virginian chief of the Southern Republic, was involved in them. It must be remembered that, whatever may be thought of Mr. Gladstone's cold-blooded coup in 1863, the policy of successive British Governments had always been to assuage the antagonism between North and South. At every stage the British had sought to promote goodwill and close association between her Southern ally and the mighty Northern power with whom she had so much in common. For instance, we should remember how in the Spanish-American War of 1898 the influence of Great Britain was used to the utmost and grave risks were run in order to limit the quarrel and to free the United States from any foreign menace. The restraining counsels of England on this occasion had led the Southern Republic to adopt a neutrality not only benevolent, but actively helpful. Indeed, in this war several veteran generals of the Confederate army had actually served as volunteers with the Union forces. So that one must understand that, side by side with the piling up of armaments and the old antagonisms, there was an immense under-tide of mutual liking and respect. It is the glory of Balfour, Roosevelt, and Wilson—this august triumvirate—that they were able so to direct these tides that every opposing circumstance or element was swept before them.

On Christmas Day 1905 was signed the Covenant of the English-Speaking Association. The essence of this extraordinary measure was crystal clear. The doctrine of common citizenship for all the peoples involved in the agreement was proclaimed. There was not the slightest interference with the existing arrangements of any member. All that happened was that henceforward the peoples of the British Empire and of what were happily called in the language of the line "The Re-United States," deemed themselves to be members of one body and inheritors of one estate. The flexibility of the plan, which invaded no national privacy, which left all particularisms entirely unchallenged, which altered no institutions and required no elaborate machinery, was its salvation. It was, in fact, a moral and psychological rather than political reaction. Hundreds of millions of people suddenly adopted a new point of view. Without prejudice to their existing loyalties and sentiments, they gave birth in themselves to a new higher loyalty and a wider sentiment. The autumn of 1905 had seen the English-speaking world on the verge of catastrophe. The year did not die before they were associated by indissoluble ties for the maintenance of peace between themselves, for the prevention of war among outside powers, and for the economic development of their measureless resources and possessions.

The Association had not been in existence for a decade before it was called upon to face an emergency not less grave than that which had called it into being. Everyone remembers the European crisis of August 1914. The murder of the Archduke at Sarajevo, the disruption or decay of the Austrian and Turkish Empires, the old quarrel between Germany and France, and the increasing armaments of Russia—all taken together produced the most dangerous conjunction which Europe has ever known. Once the orders for Russian, Austrian, German, and French mobilization had been given and twelve million soldiers were gathering upon the frontiers of their respective countries, it seemed that nothing could avert a war which might well have become Armageddon itself.

What the course and consequences of such a war would have been are matters upon which we can only speculate. M. Bloch, in his thoughtful book published in 1909, indicated that such a war if fought with modern weapons would not be a short one. He predicted that field operations would quickly degenerate into long lines of fortifications, and that a devastating stalemate with siege warfare, or trench warfare, lasting for years might well ensue. We know his opinions are not accepted by the leading military experts of most countries. But, at any rate, we cannot doubt that a war in which four or five of the greatest European powers were engaged might well have led to the loss of many millions of lives, and to the destruction of capital that twenty years of toil, thrift, and privation could not have replaced. It is no exaggeration to say that, had the crisis of general mobilization of August 1914 been followed by war, we might today in this island see income tax at four or five shillings in the pound, and have two and a half million unemployed workmen on our hands. Even the United States far across the ocean might against all its traditions have been dragged into a purely European quarrel.

But in the nick of time friendly though resolute hands intervened to save Europe from what might well have been her ruin. It was inherent in the Covenant of the English-Speaking Association that the ideal of mutual disarmament to the lowest point compatible with their joint safety should be adopted by the signatory members.

It was also settled that every third year a Conference of the whole Association should be held in such places as might be found convenient. It happened that the third disarmament conference of the English-Speaking Association—the E.S.A. as it is called for short —was actually in session in July 1914. The Association had found itself hampered in its policy of disarmament by the immense military and naval establishments maintained in Europe. Their plenipotentiaries were actually assembled to consider this problem when the infinitely graver issue burst upon them. They acted as men accustomed to deal with the greatest events. They felt so sure of themselves that they were able to run risks for others. On August 1, when the German armies were already approaching the frontiers of Belgium, when the Austrian armies had actually begun the bombardment of Belgrade, and when all along the Russian and French frontiers desultory picket firing had broken out, the E.S.A. tendered its friendly offices to all the mobilized powers, counselling them to halt their armies within ten miles of their own frontiers, and to seek a solution of their differences by peaceful discussion. The memorable document added that "failing a peaceful outcome the Association must deem itself *ipso facto* at war with any power in either combination whose troops invaded the territory of its neighbour."

Although this suave yet menacing communication was received with indignation in many quarters, it in fact secured for Europe the breathing space which was so desperately required. The French had already forbidden their troops to approach within ten miles of the German frontier, and they replied in this sense. The Tsar eagerly embraced the opportunity offered to him. The secret wishes of the Kaiser and his emotions at this juncture have necessarily been much disputed. There are those who allege that, carried away by the excitement of mobilization and the clang and clatter of moving armies, he was not disposed to halt his troops already on the threshold of the Duchy of Luxembourg. Others avow that he received the message with a scream of joy and fell exhausted into a chair, exclaiming: "Saved! Saved! Saved! Whatever may have been the nature of the Imperial convulsion, all we know is that the acceptance of Germany was the last to reach the Association. With its arrival, although there yet remained many weeks of anxious negotiation, the danger of a European war may be said to have passed away.

Most of us have been so much absorbed by the immense increases of prosperity and wealth, or by the commercial activity and scientific and territorial development and exploitation which have been the history of the English-speaking world since 1905, that we have been inclined to allow European affairs to fall into a twilight of interest. Once the perils of 1914 had been successfully averted and the disarmament of Europe had been brought into harmony with that already effected by the E.S.A., the idea of "A United States of Europe" was bound to occur continually. The glittering spectacle of the great English-speaking combination, its assured safety, its boundless power, the rapidity with which wealth was created and widely distributed within its bounds, the sense of buoyancy and hope which seemed to pervade the entire populations; all this pointed to European eyes a moral which none but the dullest could ignore. Whether the Emperor Wilhelm II will be successful in carrying the project of European unity forward by another important stage at the forthcoming Pan-European Conference at Berlin in 1932, is still a matter of prophecy. Should he achieve his purpose he will have raised himself to a dazzling pinnacle of fame and honour, and no one will be more pleased than the members of the E.S.A. to witness the gradual formation of another great area of tranquillity and co-operation like that in which we ourselves have learned to dwell. If this prize should fall to his Imperial Majesty, he may perhaps reflect how easily his career might have been wrecked in 1914 by the outbreak of a war which might have cost him his throne, and have laid his country in the dust. If today he occupies in his old age the most splendid situation in Europe, let him not forget that he might well have found himself eating the bitter bread of exile, a dethroned sovereign and a broken man loaded with unutterable reproach. And this, we repeat, might well have been his fate, if Lee had not won the Battle of Gettysburg.

IF OR HISTORY REWRITTEN

VIKING - 1931

WINSTON CHURCHILL, JOURNALIST—

O𝒩

AMERICA

{ **"AMERICAN INTERVENTION IN CUBA"** }

THE SATURDAY REVIEW (LONDON)
MARCH 7, 1896

Three weeks ago in an article in this REVIEW I stated that the Cuban question was one of considerable difficulty. During the last few days its complications have become still "worse confounded" and have assumed a much more serious aspect. The recent action by the Senate and House of Representatives of the United States has raised the whole subject to one of the first importance, and Venezuela, the Transvaal, and Armenia have each and all been hustled into comparative obscurity to make room for the latest international sensation.

A double pressure has operated to induce Congress to adopt its present attitude. Firstly, the agitation of Americans at home, and, secondly, the influence exerted by those resident in Cuba. The people of the United States have long viewed the efforts which the Cubans are making to obtain independence with sympathy and approbation. Situated only three hundred miles from the coast of Florida, the island is much frequented as a winter and pleasure resort by all classes of Americans, and its troubles and disasters not unnaturally attract attention and excite interest throughout the States. The rebels have a powerful backing in New York and Washington. They make no secret of their desire to be included in the Union. Most of the wealthy Cubans are naturalized American citizens, and many daring spirits from the Southern and Eastern States are taking an active part in the rebellion. To these considerations add those of trade and commerce, and the interest with which the present struggle is regarded in America will be easily understood. Stimulated by organized agitation, that interest results directly in the resolutions passed by the Legislature of the United States, during the past week, in favour of according belligerent rights to the insurgents and of the ultimate independence of the island. Look, also, at the influence exerted by citizens resident in Cuba itself. Now that war and disease have driven away the tourists, there remain, broadly speaking, three classes of Americans in the island. First of all there is the planter, usually a native of Cuba who, out of dislike for the Spanish Government, has naturalized himself a citizen of the United States. This class is naturally eager for peace. They are over-taxed even at the best of times, and during the revolt are compelled to pay to both sides, as the insurgents extort money by threatening to burn their plantations. Secondly, there is the very complete consular service maintained in Cuba by the United States. These men—consuls and vice-consuls—are in entire sympathy with the rebels, and in many cases are actively intriguing on their behalf. Should the American administration follow their recommendations, there is little doubt as to what its action will be. Finally, there are the "filibusters"; active, daring men, who, drawn by love of adventure and hatred of the Spaniards into the insurgent ranks, are the real backbone of the rebellion. It will thus be seen that each class, though in a different way, exerts an influence in favour of some form of American intervention. And this brings us again to the resolutions of last week.

I have thus briefly discussed the causes which have led to the recent vote of Congress, by which the recognition of the insurgents was advocated. The motives are excellent and unassailable, but the action which those motives have produced is to be deprecated. The rebels have no claim to be called belligerents. They neither fight bravely nor do they use their weapons effectively. They cannot win a single battle or hold a single town. Their army, consisting to a large extent of coloured men, is an undisciplined rabble. Their President skulks in America. Their generals and bravest soldiers are aliens. Their supplies are obtained by plunder and blackmail, and their only formidable weapon is the torch of the incendiary. Besides all these facts, their success does not offer any prospect of better times or wiser government. Neither on the ground of their power nor of their courage do the insurgents deserve recognition or independence. It seems strange indeed that the very nation which denied autonomy to the Confederacy should advocate it in the case of the Cuban rebels.

Another argument which carried great weight with Congress was the alleged cruelty and barbarity of the Spaniards. Personally, I do not believe that there has been any unwarrantable exercise of severity during the present war. The Spanish Government have offered ample and sweeping reforms, and well-directed intervention might easily obtain adequate guarantees that they would be carried out. But Spain refuses, and rightly refuses, to treat with rebels in arms—a principle which is maintained by other civilized States. Nor, in the actual conduct of the war, has any departure from modern practices been permitted? Every rebel who cares to surrender himself becomes what is termed a "presentado" and is allowed to go to his home unquestioned and unharmed. Chiefs and leaders captured in the field are tried by court-martial and frequently shot, and the rank and file taken in arms are condemned to terms of penal servitude at Ceuta. But the numbers in both cases are but small, as Cuban patriots take no unnecessary chances. Certainly fewer have been shot as rebels by the Government than as so-called "traitors" by the insurgents.

When the sacrifices Spain is making to maintain an exasperating struggle are considered, it will be apparent that her moderation is extremely creditable. And if that may be said of the Government at home, with how much more force does it apply to the conduct of soldiers in the field who, though irritated by methods of warfare peculiarly trying and painful to European troops, have loyally carried out a temperate policy. Certainly when one recalls the methods of South American Republics in dealing with their frequent revolutions, and speculates on the terms which the administration of "Free Cuba" would offer to rebels, one cannot feel much indignation.

Finally, it is well to consider the aims and probable results of American intervention. If the United States is prepared to include Cuba in the Union, she could probably seize the island, though the undertaking would be a much bigger business than is sometimes imagined. Such a course would be manifestly unfair to Spain, and justifiable only by right of conquest; but it would be for the good of Cuba and of the world, and European nations would have no motive for interference. But if, as is probable, we are to be threatened with the establishment of another Republic, under the ægis of the Monroe Doctrine, or if Cuba is to be presented to Mexico—which comes to the same thing—then European protest will at least be justifiable.

In conclusion, it is by no means clear that active intervention by the United States would benefit the insurgents or immediately terminate the insurrection. The Spanish force in Cuba is very great, and it is impossible for 120,000 European soldiers to march and fight upwards of a year without acquiring endurance, composure under fire, and knowledge of the country to a considerable degree. When those troops begin by being as good material as are the Spanish infantry of to-day, they only require to be confronted with a tangible enemy to be formidable antagonists.

Three months at least would elapse before the American Government could place a sufficient number of regulars in Cuba to cope effectively with the Spanish army. By that time, restraint being removed by the declaration of war, there might, indeed, be some foundation for the charge of barbarity.

The matter is grave. It is a serious business for Cuba, for the United States, but most of all for Spain. Spaniards of all classes will find it to their advantage to adopt a calm and conciliatory demeanour, and so avert extremities. But should the Spanish people, hard pressed as they are already, be forced by the United States to further efforts to preserve their most treasured possession, they will not be without sympathizers among the nations of Europe, and perhaps may even find a friend.

 # "WILL AMERICA FAIL US?"

ILLUSTRATED SUNDAY HERALD (LONDON)
NOVEMBER 30, 1919

No one can understand what has happened in America about the Treaty of Peace and the League of Nations without remembering the history of party politics in the United States during the last few years. We can best illustrate this by taking an example from our own country. Suppose, for instance, Mr. Asquith, instead of being dependent from day to day upon the support of the House of Commons, had been in power on a fixed term of office which nothing could alter. Suppose during the war he had steadfastly refused to allow any Conservatives to join the Government, or even to serve under the Government in great situations of authority. Suppose he had said:

This is a Liberal war: I am a Liberal Prime Minister. The principles of party Government must be respected. I cannot take the step of allowing Conservative politicians to share in the responsibilities of Government and administration, either as Ministers or as organizers. Such a fusion would be contrary to the principles of party, in virtue of which I hold my great power at the head of the State.

THE UNFORGIVABLE THING

Suppose when by-elections occurred he had written letters and telegrams saying that Conservatives must on no account be returned—not even men who were giving their all to the war. Suppose, nevertheless, Conservatives had been returned by the electors until the Unionist Party possessed an actual majority in both Houses of Parliament and still Mr. Asquith had gone on conducting the war and making the peace without ever taking his opponents, either in the House of Commons or in the House of Lords, broadly and fully, into council or consideration.

And then suppose that at the end of it all he had come with his Treaty, on which he had worked so hard and for which he had striven so nobly, and presented it to these two hostile and slighted Houses of Parliament. Does it not seem highly probable that at this stage, when the fighting had stopped and when the actual danger was over, they would have had a good deal to say about it?

The one thing which people find it most difficult to forgive in public life is being shut out of their honourable and legitimate chance of taking part in a supreme national struggle. There is nothing which can make up for this. To wait during all those terrific months, and even years, eating out their hearts with desire to give their best to their country, and yet to feel themselves—rightly or wrongly—as—absolutely excluded from the public service as if they belonged to a foreign nation, is an experience which leaves an indelible mark upon men of light and leading.

OUR NATIONAL GOVERNMENT

How very different was the way in which we in this country conducted our affairs during the great war. Quite early in the struggle a National Government was formed representative of all great parties in the State: of Liberals, Conservatives and Labour men. It was not our fault that the Irish Nationalists were not included, too. When this Government, after two years of concerted action, changed its head, and a new Prime Minister succeeded to power, every effort was made to include representatives of all parties, and the most earnest appeals were addressed to the late Prime Minister and his friends to continue to share in bearing the burden. Even when the war was over, before an election was fought, attempts were renewed still further to widen the representation of the National Coalition. In fact it may be said that Great Britain fought the war without a thought of party; and so much was this the case that when at last the victory was won, those who had been working as comrades together found themselves so completely intermingled that they could hardly remember the old life-long quarrels which had divided them, and were able to recognise only all that great body of thought and action in which their hearts beat as one.

THE AMERICAN CONSTITUTION

The political system of the United States did not, however, lend itself to such arrangements. Ministers there are not the servants of the Legislature, capable of being dismissed from day to day by the mere exercise of a Parliamentary vote. They are the agents of a supreme and august authority which, once it has been derived from the electorate, continues majestically, whatever else may crash. In this respect we may perhaps claim that our ancient monarchy, proceeding as it does under forms which have come down to us from the Plantagenets and the Tudors, is a more flexible instrument of the national will than the republican constitution of the United States. There are, perhaps, some grave emergencies with which the American system of periodic autocracies can cope much better than ours. But for good or ill the conduct of the British Empire is based continuously upon public opinion and parliamentary agreement.

We never could have afforded thus circumstanced to go through the shocks and stresses of this obstinate and fearful war on a purely party basis. We had to trust all the people the whole of the time. We had to take all loyal and patriotic men into consultation. No Government less broad than the nation as a whole could possibly have contended with times of such extraordinary convulsion.

THE BRITISH WAY

What is true of the British people in these islands applies still more to the self-governing Dominions of the British Empire. The heads of these free Commonwealths, each of which had strong fighting armies in the field, had to be continually consulted. When Mr. Lloyd George went to Paris to negotiate the Peace Treaty, he took him with a British Empire Delegation which was in many respects an informal Senate. He was most careful not to take any action of importance without first of all obtaining their approval. It was, of course, a tremendously laborious business, but with incessant energy and general good-will all our affairs marched forward together. In consequence, whatever was done in the Peace Treaty in the name of the British Empire was done in the name and on the responsibility of the whole lot: every party in the State, every Dominion in the Empire, every leading responsible delegate was in it up to the neck. They all had, therefore, to put it through with their own people, and they all proved able to put it through with their own people. There may be great disadvantages in such a system. It may hamper the personal touch of an exceptional man working in full freedom. But, at any rate, the business thus settled goes through.

The immense services rendered by President Wilson to mankind, his stately ideals expressed in language which appealed to every heart, which encouraged the armies of every nation fighting in the good cause, and inspired the troops of the United States with the emotions of a veritable crusade, are an achievement which has rarely been surpassed by a single human being.

Nevertheless, the Republican Party, probably the strongest party numerically in the United States, possessing majorities in both branches of the Legislature, may well be pardoned if they feel a trifle sore, and if, when for the first time they have the effective power under their own constitution, they show a determination to use it.

All the same, people in England would make a great mistake if they supposed that the Republican Party in the United States is less friendly to this country, or less inclined to shoulder its obligations towards Europe, than the great Democratic Party with whom we have had such satisfactory relations.

PARTY CONSIDERATIONS

No doubt in America, as in Great Britain, a party which has been out of office for a long time, which fell out of power through a split, and which is hopefully expecting to present itself again to the electorate, would not be likely to throw away any kind of voting strength which it has a chance of rallying, or neglect any arguments which, rightly or wrongly, may tell against the Government of the day. But we know that the Republican Party, both by its composition and its history, is in fact the party least likely to be unduly influenced by Irish Sinn Fein tendencies or unregenerate German influence. It is extremely important, therefore, that at this time no harsh or impatient criticism should be passed by British statesmen and publicists upon the fierce workings of the party system in the United States.

For after all, in this struggle we have come to know the American people to the very bottom, and all that we have learned has increased our hope and confidence in the future.

There is no nation in the world which is less likely to put a grudging construction upon its honourable obligations; there is no people in the world who would feel more deeply any sense of reproach in regard to a matter of duty. They do not expect foreigners to tell them their duty. In that case they might argue about it; but left to themselves, in their own way and in their own time, the American democracy will make good to the extreme jot and tittle every honourable claim which may be made upon them.

THE CONSEQUENCES

It is impossible to exaggerate the gravity of the consequences which would arise from an American repudiation of the League of Nations or withdrawal from the general Peace Treaty. The League of Nations was an American plan, pressed upon the Powers at the Peace Conference with the influence and power of the United States. Months of precious time were consumed in its discussion, and with every day that passed the power of the Peace Conference to make the best arrangements for Europe and to have its decisions respected steadily declined. The whole shape and character of the peace settlement was determined by American influence.

The complete break up of the Austrian Empire and the establishment in its place of a system of small rival States was a world-shaking event due mainly to American initiative. As a consequence Central Europe is in grave disorder, and the great and famous city of Vienna is practically deprived of bread and fuel.

To carry such a policy half way and to carry it no further, to destroy the old organisation without attempting to supply the new, to sweep away the imperial system without setting in its place a League of Nations system, would indeed be an act from which America should recoil and which posterity would certainly condemn.

The whole Turkish Empire has remained in a suspended state of quasi-dissolution all these months waiting an American decision, and now perhaps for many months more all those millions of helpless human beings must remain sinking ever deeper into bankruptcy, famine and anarchy, without being able to make a single plan to save themselves.

THE VICTORY SQUANDERED!

It would only remain to leave France alone on the Rhine, confronted with Germany, and probably later on with Russia, to squander irretrievably the whole victory gained by French, British, and American exertions.

A more melancholy page in human history could hardly be conceived. We cannot believe that it will be written by American hands.

In these last few weeks the Prince of Wales* has been visiting the United States. He has, as it were, been inviting the new world to respect the venerable institutions of the old. The manner in which he has been received by all classes and parties in every city is the true gauge of the recent tide of Anglo-American sentiments and sympathy. There could scarcely be any more difficult adventure or delicate enterprise than that involved in the visit of a young Prince, Heir-Apparent to the British Throne, to the enormous keen-judging clairvoyant democracy of the American commonwealth. The brilliant result is as much a proof of the convictions and sympathies of the host as of the extraordinary personal qualities of the guest.

A SUPREME EVENT

From this and many other sets of circumstances it has become certain that the relationship of Great Britain and the United States has now definitely passed the critical turning point. When we look back upon the melancholy series of blunders and calamities, of hateful mutual injuries, of hopeless misunderstandings, embodied in the history of these two formidable kinsmen, the fact that they have at last advanced in battle side by side stands out as a supreme event in the story of civilisation. We have lived to see the most gigantic impossibilities overturned and swept from the path, we inherit to-day on both sides of the Atlantic a situation incomparably superior to any that has ever gone before. The Irish bias has dwindled in the general expansion of the population. The German imperialistic intrigue is patently exposed. Once again the two great branches of the English-speaking family are able to write their history in common. Once again their young men may study the tale of great things done and suffered together. Instead of the old and, thank God, now obsolete chronicles of past antagonisms, we have the gleaming memory that together we saved Europe from the hands of the spoiler, and the sure conviction that by acting together

* Edward VIII, later Duke of Windsor. [K.H.]

we can safeguard ourselves from every peril which the future may have in store.

"WHAT I SAW AND HEARD IN AMERICA"

LONDON DAILY TELEGRAPH
NOVEMBER 18, 1929

Words and phrases derive their importance from the atmosphere of opinion in which they are breathed. The finest sentiments expressed in the happiest terms will be inaudible without the sounding board of human consciousness. A broadcast message, however important, however powerfully launched, only agitates the ether idly, unless millions of individual instruments are attuned to receive it. The moments when nations can speak to one another occur only at irregular and infrequent intervals. Such moments are precious, but also fleeting. They must not be wasted.

Mr. Ramsay MacDonald's visit to the United States was fortunate in striking one of those periods when all the latent friendliness of the American people for the British Empire was awake and alert. A wave of good will welling from mysterious depths, has swept across the continent. A keen, intense, and self-surprising glance of recognition, of kinship, of comradeship, of identification, has flashed across the Atlantic to catch or kindle the answering light of other eyes.

BONDS BETWEEN TWO NATIONS

What manner of men are we, what language do we speak, what laws do we follow, what books do we read, what tests do we apply to the problems of daily life, what songs do we sing, what jokes do we laugh at, what sports do we pursue? And the answer, at once obvious and wonderful, "They are the same," grips, be it only with a momentary thrill, the hearts of vast communities. The sharp realization of all we have in common is the dominant factor of the hour, and is only more remarkable and pregnant because it springs from nothing new or previously unknown.

Many events and causes have contributed to produce this situation. First among them all are the associations of the Great War, where, for the first time after so many generations of severance, all the English-speaking peoples found themselves in a common fought battle. When on July 4, 1918 at Villers-Bretonneux, British, Australian and United States troops advanced together against the enemy and when, later in the year the Second American Army Corps played a noteworthy part in Haig's forcing of the Hindenburg Line, new martial episodes superimposed themselves upon the sombre records of the past, and for the first time for a hundred and fifty years the two kindred nations had history to write in common. Apart from association in the field, valuable new ties were established between individuals throughout the wide spheres of munition supply, war finance, and diplomacy.

DISCREDITED HATE-MAKERS

But of even greater practical force is the removal from American politics of the Irish question. The slow, virulent poison distilled against Great Britain for more than a century has suddenly exhausted itself. The great mass of Irishmen in the United States are strong supporters of the Irish Free State. They have accepted the Irish Treaty as a full and lasting settlement. They have gladly absorbed themselves in the general issues of American politics and in an expanding prosperity.

The professional hate-manufacturer is at a loss to find either the patrons or the materials for his wares. The politics of a hundred cities have been simultaneously freed from an element of jarring and extraneous bias. A purely American outlook has superseded and overridden this dismal particularism. The change has been widespread and swift and its consequences are unceasing.

The merging of the Anglo-Japanese Alliance in the wider Four-Power Pact governing the Pacific, removed a potential source of suspicion which, though unfounded in fact, was capable of being misunderstood by friends and misrepresented by ill-wishers.

Lastly, there is the settlement of the debt. Whatever we in England may feel about the broad equities of that transaction, and whatever controversies may have arisen upon it, it has certainly produced a profound impression in the United States, which has only been deepened by time and by contrast with the American settlements with France and Italy.

FROM LAFAYETTE TO—BALDWIN

The American visitor to England may be naïvely astonished at the comments and criticisms to which he is subjected when this subject is raised. He may even be distressed or offended by them, but the general opinion of the American nation, and particularly of its vast business elements, has crystallised. "England's word is her bond. She alone can be trusted, whatever her burdens, to discharge her obligations."

In a people so highly commercialised and accustomed, perhaps unduly, to judge men and things in ordinary life by money values, the British debt settlement has evoked widespread respect and, indeed admiration, only partially discounted by pained surprise that we do not seem to share their satisfaction.

Having very long considered these matters and frequently declared my opinion upon them, I must, nevertheless, record the decided view that if the burden is heavy the gains are also solid; and if one is long-lasting, so also will be the other. The rugged signature of Baldwin has, at any rate throughout wide circles, effaced the venerable fame of Lafayette.

It must be understood that all these events and causes have been working silently but ceaselessly beneath the uneven and often changing surface of American sentiment. They have had the effect of liberating, or rendering more powerful, strong elements—perhaps the strongest though not the most numerous in American life

—which are traditionally friendly to Great Britain, and look back across a vista of disasters to the origin and institutions of both peoples.

"ONLY ONE KING"

The most remarkable manifestations of the new sentiment towards Great Britain emerged during the illness of the King [George V]. Every phase of that long and grievous but triumphant struggle was attentively followed. Genuine sympathy and anxiety were felt. Churches and chapels sent up their prayers. British visitors and residents were everywhere interrogated as if they were the repositories of special information. The newspapers, responding to the public mood, assigned a continuous prominence to the bulletins far in excess of all other foreign news; and by an elision, the more significant because unstudied, and possibly unconscious, these bulletins were almost universally printed under the simple heading, "The King," as if there were only one in the world. All this was but the symptom and expression of a movement of public feeling which, though not dominant, has never been so strong, and is still growing.

The English traveller to-day is not only treated with a hospitality and politeness which have long been customary, but is received with unmistakable signs of pleasure and good will. Not only in the cities, but even in small country villages, there is a marked desire to help him and set him on his way. Powerful groups of newspapers, which twenty years ago indulged merrily and profitably in the pastime of "twisting the lion's tail," now advocate, month after month, the close cooperation of the English-speaking peoples to promote the peace of the world; and this same sentiment is enthusiastically hailed or expressed at every form of public gathering at which English visitors are present.

MR. MACDONALD'S RECEPTION

It was in these favourable circumstances that Mr. Ramsay MacDonald's visit was made. Speaking with the ease of a well-trained

Parliamentarian, with that complete command of agreeable and hopeful generalities in which he excels and guided at every footstep by extremely competent Foreign Office advice, the Prime Minister discharged his important and opportune mission with high distinction and complete success. Nothing was settled and nothing could be settled but understandings were established and an atmosphere created most favourable to the grave discussions which the New Year will inaugurate.

New York turned out in scores of thousands to receive its visitor. The English-Speaking Union revelled; Washington was delighted; and the Senate purred. Hosts and guests were equally pleased with one another. Only one doubt seems to have clouded American minds. Socialism in the United States is a very wicked thing. It is not allowed in any club or decent society or in any Legislature or public office. The newspapers hardly dare mention it. The workmen deride it. The police are after it with their batons. The Socialist candidates for the Presidency usually conduct their campaigns from gaol. In short, it is considered altogether un-American.

But Mr. Ramsay MacDonald! So dignified, so statesmanlike, so respectable! Such noble sentiments, such earnestness, such high ideals! "Tell me in confidence," I am anxiously asked, "is there any truth in the rumor that he has Socialistic leanings?"

FRANK INTERCHANGE OF VIEWS

The success of the MacDonald visit and the strong currents of good feeling now flowing across the Atlantic must not tempt us to underrate the obstinacy of the problem which lies before us. Naval parity and "the freedom of the seas" are the only outstanding topics in dispute between the two Governments. They are much more in dispute between the Governments, publicists, and navy groups than among the masses of the people.

Definite positions have, however, been assumed as the result of a lengthy series of events. Formulas have been framed and slogans uttered. The time has come for a frank and sincere interchange of views and for public discussion, in all friendliness and patience, of the large and difficult issues involved. We may embark upon it in the full confidence that if the leaders of each country will faithfully try to understand each other's point of view and clearly expose all the facts set in their proper proportion, to the judgment of their countrymen then no harm can come to Anglo-American friendship.

Let them therefore lay their difficulties soberly and amicably before each other. Let them not hesitate to state the causes of any soreness or complaint which may have arisen in the past. Let them meet as friends, and not as rivals, to make agreements which shall secure the strength and safety of each and the partnership of both in the maintenance of world peace.

※※※

"FEVER OF SPECULATION IN AMERICA"

LONDON DAILY TELEGRAPH
DECEMBER 9, 1929

"The dark, narrow, crooked lane leading to the river and the graveyard," to quote the local description of Wall Street, has been, during the last few years, the cynosure of American eyes. No social or political topic, no foreign or domestic event, not the Presidential election, not even Prohibition itself, has been a serious competitor.

Everybody dabbles in stocks. Earned increments are sweet, but those unearned are sweeter. . . . Millions of men and women are in the market, all eager to supplement the rewards of energetic toil by "easy money." From every part of its enormous territories the American public follows the game. Horseracing, baseball, football, every form of sport or gambling cedes its place to a casino whose amplitude and splendours make Monte Carlo the meanest midget in Lilliput.

No pages of the innumerable newspapers which cater to the public taste are more prominently or carefully printed, more eagerly and more earnestly studied, than those which record the daily operations of the stock markets. Brokers abound on every side. The more enterprising hotels have a complete apparatus of tape machine and telephone facilities, and provide entire suites where, amid the clack and rattle of tickers, expert clerks chalk up from minute to minute the latest quotations, not only from New York, but from other important exchanges.

NATION OF SPECULATORS

The housemaid who makes your bed is a stockholder on margin. Workmen of every class, brain or hand, the chauffeur, the tram conductor, the railwayman, the waiter, all have their open accounts, and so very often have their wives. Even the Transatlantic steamers have their floating migratory exchange; where seasick "bulls" and "bears" contend amid the heaves and lurches.

A speculative public, numbering in the United States alone many millions is, of course, utterly novel. Nothing approaching it has ever been seen or dreamed of since the world began. Nothing can stop these enormous multitudes when they come in full of ardour. Nothing can even delay them when, swept by panic, they stream out. Nevertheless, the physical structure of the New York Stock Exchange has rules and regulations which have been framed with such massive strength and strictness that the perils of the situation are less formidable than would appear to European eyes.

London has never attempted to handle such masses. Our people have not the wealth, nor is our machinery adapted to such strains. The British workman bets and gambles on the turf, and finds his bookmaker, legal or illegal, never far away. But the American public concentrates upon the stock markets, and it is as easy to buy shares, few or many on margin, as it is to buy a pound of tea, and far easier than to buy a motorcar or a gramophone upon the instalment system. The personal relation between broker and client, which is the staple of our old-world business, has been superseded in the United States by iron rules which, while they facilitate every form of speculation, have, nevertheless, enabled the brokers to weather, with scarcely a ship-wreck, the greatest financial hurricane that ever blew.

Before disparaging American methods, the English critic would do well to acquaint himself with the inherent probity and strength of the American speculative machine. It is not built to prevent crises, but to survive them.

The turbulent life-force of this community, its vast creative and productive effort and achievement, its sense of worlds to conquer, its unshakable faith in a golden future, lead it naturally, perhaps inevitably, certainly uncontrollably, to anticipate the good days which are surely coming. "What," they ask, "can stop the United States?" Has it not rather only just got on the move?

INHERENT STRENGTH

Vast enterprises, acquiring momentum every day, science and organisation smoothing and lighting the path, the very magnitude of every operation facilitating the next; a continent as raw material in the hands of industry, wealth abounding, and wealth diffused, millionaires multiplying, wages high and rising, seven million college students, motor-cars, also by millions, food plentiful, clean and cheap, room to live, room to breathe, room to grow, room to kick. Socialism a European delusion, politics an occasional pastime, the Constitution a rock—why should they fear? Forward! Headlong! All will be well.

Was it wonderful that a population thus circumstanced and thus inspired should outstrip advancing reality, should prefer speculation to thrift, should try to live a year or two ahead of time, should consume and cast away, and make again? A blunder! We can repair it. Hideous losses! We can make them good. Ruins! Watch us rebuild them.

To write thus of the solidity of the speculative apparatus, or of the buoyancy of the speculating public, must not lead to any underrating of the disappointment and suffering which the recent violent collapse of values has brought to millions of American homes. The steady inflation of prices has gone on so long, that ordinary people with busy lives and short views had readily and comfortably accepted its continuance as one of the regular conditions of life. The worker who had deposited his 35 per cent margin easily persuaded himself that he possessed one hundred units of capital. He felt himself doing business on a large scale like the great capitalists. Everyone round him was doing it too. It all seemed so good and sound; and behind it lay the broad United States.

A TRAGEDY IN FIFTH AVENUE

And then—suddenly, the earth trembled, the chimney stacks fell crashing into the streets, and many dead and wounded were carried away. Then, when it was assumed that all was over, came other shocks, heavier and heavier, and the fronts of buildings cracked or fell out, spreading havoc and panic in the crowded streets, and thousands of millions of capital value were annihilated in ten days; and all the small stockholders were ruthlessly sold out. And the women said to their husbands: "Sell out at all costs," "Let it all go," "You have your job or your salary," "Let's keep the home." And the great popular stores said: "Halve the orders to be given out for Christmas and the spring." And several million families decided to make the old car do for another year.

The consuming power was grievously weakened. In opulent Fifth-avenue fur coats, already half-accepted by clients, came back in scores and dozens because they did not fit. Under my very window a gentleman cast himself down fifteen storeys and was dashed to pieces, causing a wild commotion and the arrival of the fire brigade. Quite a number of persons seem to have over-balanced themselves by accident in the same sort of way. A workman smoking his pipe on the girder of an unfinished building 400 ft. above the ground blocked the traffic of the street below, through the crowd, who thought he was a ruined capitalist waiting in a respectful and prudently withdrawn crescent for the final act.

UNHEEDED WARNINGS

And then the bankers arrived upon the scene and lectured the unfortunates who had lost their money, and preached the virtues of thrift and the immorality of speculation, and picked up the securities that were lying about the streets in baskets, and even in wagons, and took them home for safety to their vaults. Grim!

Still, after all, no one can say the public was not warned. Many times have the Federal Reserve authorities denounced speculation and raised the rate to check it. Repeatedly Mr. Mellon declared the position unsafe, and counselled investments in bonds. The British Chancellor of the Exchequer, with the profound knowledge of the Treasury behind him, stigmatised the proceedings as "an orgy." A certain Mr. Babson, whose firm advises the American public about the markets in much the same way as "Hotspan" tells our betting crowd about the Turf, had the prescience and, what is more remarkable, the courage to predict an imminent fall of at least 60 points in values. But all these warnings fell upon ears deaf to unwelcome tidings. The American public have certainly been cleaned out, but they cannot say that they have been hoodwinked.

I happened to be walking down Wall Street at the worst moment of the panic, and a perfect stranger who recognized me invited me to enter the gallery of the Stock Exchange. I expected to see pandemonium; but the spectacle that met my eyes was one of surprising calm and orderliness. There are only 1,200 members of the New York Stock Exchange, each of whom has paid over £100,000 for his ticket. These gentlemen are precluded by the strictest rules from running or raising their voices unduly. So there they were, walking to and fro like a slow-motion picture of a disturbed ant heap, offering each other enormous blocks of securities at a third of their old prices and half their present value, and for many minutes together finding no one strong enough to pick up the sure fortunes they were compelled to offer.

"PASSING EPISODE"

It was refreshing to exchange this scene of sombre and, for the moment, almost helpless liquidation for a window high in a titanic building. The autumn afternoon was bright and clear, and the noble scene stretched to far horizons. Below lay the Hudson and the North Rivers, dotted with numerous tugs and shipping of all kinds, and traversed by the ocean streamers from all over the world moving in and out of the endless rows of docks. Beyond lay all the cities and workshops off the New Jersey shore, pouring out their clouds of smoke and steam. Around towered the mighty buildings of New York, with here and there glimpses far below of streets swarming with human life.

No one who gazed on such a scene could doubt that this financial disaster, huge as it is, cruel as it is to thousands, is only a passing episode in the march of a valiant and serviceable people who by fierce experiment are hewing new paths for man, and showing to all nations much that they should attempt and much that they should avoid.

LONDON DAILY TELEGRAPH
DECEMBER 9, 1929

"VASTNESS OF AMERICA'S INDUSTRY"

LONDON DAILY TELEGRAPH
JANUARY 27, 1930

The structure of American industry has qualities of magnificence not to be seen elsewhere and never seen before. In no other country has science so wide a field in which to range as in the vast territories of the United States. Nowhere else has production been attempted on so great a scale, nowhere else have the principles of method, management, and organisation been so boldly applied. A community of 120,000,000 in possession of what is almost a self-contained continent have walled themselves off from the outer world, and are in process of organising themselves as a single unit of production and distribution.

Within the tariff ramparts the keenest competition and the largest combinations have grown up together. Throughout an area nearly as large as Europe, and comprising almost every natural product and climate, utterly unrestricted, the freest interchange of goods and services prevails. The quality of their products may often fall below European level. Their cost frequently exceeds those of Old World industry. Their science is no greater nor the skill of their workmen higher than in European countries. Americans themselves often prefer the products of Europe to their own, and are not deterred by the highest tariff penalties from buying the foreign specialties they require.

But there is one outstanding characteristic of American industry, which lifts it above that of any other nation. Napoleon said, "I have always marched with the opinion of four or five millions of men." That is the spirit of American industry.

LIFE AND HABITS

Mass production of standardised articles of necessity or convenience for tens of millions and for scores of millions of consumers. Find out something that the average household requires, or would like, or might be tempted to buy. Choose some product or element in universal demand, and then make it the most perfect machinery and on the largest possible scale. There lies the secret of the mammoth fortunes, of standards of living, and of practical convenience for millions already beyond all compare.

The life and habits of the American people and the structure of their industries grow side by side, acting and reacting upon each other in intimate relation. People do not entirely live the life they choose, nor choose the things they buy. These are, to a remarkable extent, decided for them by the leaders of their industrial production.

The wants of scores of millions of households are comprehended and foreseen before they are expressed, and the individual purchaser adapts himself to the wholesale facilities offered and regulates his life accordingly. He clambers up, as it were, upon a scaffolding of standardised necessaries, comforts, conveniences, and luxuries, and finds, so long as his taste conforms to the rules, an incredibly efficient service. The hundred things he may require are offered him in cheap and excellent abundance. If he wants something different he must import it at enormous expense or do without it. He must march comfortably with the millions along the broad highway, or paddle about among the brambles and morasses by himself.

The connection between speculative finance and industry is omnipresent. The frenzies of speculation begin upon the buoyant platform of industry. All the standardised conveniences which the workshops offer to the American home, all the materials and money of the processes of production, are immediately caught into the quotations of the Stock Exchange and whirled about in furious speculation.

GAMBLING COUNTERS

The popular features of American life, the essentials of industrial production, are also the favourite gambling counters of the American people.

"Here is a bed. I sleep in a bed. All my neighbours sleep in beds. This is the best kind of bed for Americans to sleep in. Millions were bought last year; I will buy one for myself. I will buy it on the instalment principle. What's more, I will buy shares in the company. I will buy them also on margin. The shares will go up, I shall help to send them up by buying a bed. If I make a profit on the shares I shall get the bed for nothing. If I make a loss I will work all the harder and earn more wages." The producing, financing, and consuming powers are all seen striding forward, recklessly perhaps, but in intimate alliance and turbulent strength.

Nothing more repays British study than the mass mentality of American industry. The United States have largely passed the stage where businesses grow up by degrees, adding a little year by year to humble beginnings. Gigantic enterprises are planned from the outset, and lay-out plans, financing, advertising, distribution, are brought into being as by the stroke of a wand. Nothing like it has been known in England since the national shell and gun factories created under the Ministry of Munitions. The scale of American business and production is so large and the market so sure and fertile that the chiefs can plan and act with such comprehensive range, freedom, and power as have only been wielded in the European industrial field under conditions of war.

The results are surprising in many directions. Much of the old antagonism between the millions and the millionaire has become obsolete. There is a fairly widespread comprehension that multi-millionaires presiding over numerous businesses or trusts can give 120,000,000 people what they want far better than a multitude of small independent producers. The largest electorate in the world has, through universal suffrage, steadily supported the reduction of direct taxation upon the well-to-do, the rich, and the very rich. Even the most lamentable scandals have not alienated the masses from the dominant and ruling party.

ON THE RIGHT LINES

The conviction of growing prosperity and that in material things the country is on the right lines is deeply and widely spread. Moreover, every active, intelligent young American feels that he carries, like the soldiers of the French Revolution, the baton of a marshal in his knapsack. He does not want to pull down the millionaire. He wants to be one himself. And why not?

American industry and business cohesion, despite all its violent shocks, has brought the nation into grand position. The whole army is fighting hard; the soldiers know that they are winning the battle. They know they are conquering vast new territories from Nature. They know that they are supporting it by every resource of science. They believe that their organisation is more powerful and more well directed than any yet conceived. On, then, amid the explosions and pitfalls of the battlefield, over the bodies of the fallen, over the ruins of old-fashioned structures. Victory is certain! That there are prizes for the successful promotion for the many, and a good and improving livelihood for all! Such is the spirit which has been evoked by capitalist production competing and combining in the largest economic theatre ever freely opened to the enterprise of man.

THE NEW OUTLOOK

I must record the impression that these developments are only in their beginning, that they are only just getting into their stride, and that there are limits yet in sight to the material prosperity of the American democracy.

The new outlook of the American masses is matched by that of their leaders. American capitalists think on entirely different lines from those of Europe. They have during the present century freed their minds from the poverty complex, long hours, and low wage philosophies which reign in the Old World. The character of their mass production has unified the interests of capital and labour in a novel and impressive degree.

The capitalist, or industrial chief, knows that his fortune depends upon the consuming power of the broad masses. To preserve and extend that consuming power is the foundation of his policy. Thus, when the great market collapse occurred in October, and perhaps ten million pounds sterling of values evaporated in a month, a cry —odd to European ears—broke from the breasts of the millionaires: "At all costs keep up the wages." This was not so much the result of reasoning and study as an instinctive gesture. There was nothing particularly altruistic about it. That is the way they have learnt to think and act.

"Unless we can keep up their wages, they cannot buy our goods, and unless they buy our goods we are done for!" I thought it deeply impressive to hear in this crisis, from leading men on every side, this same doctrine, "So long as the wages are maintained nothing else matters, and everything will come right and go forward again."

OLD ANTAGONISMS HEALED

Whether they will succeed or not is not yet proved, and I have no instruments to measure the seismic shock which has been sustained. But it is their mentality and outlook which should rivet

European attention. It would seem that the mysterious gap between the producing and consuming powers has been more narrowed and that its inter-dependence is more effectively apparent in the United States than was ever known elsewhere. Mass production of standardised articles in a market sufficiently vast and an area sufficiently varied has begun to harmonize antagonisms of interest as old as the world. The capitalist advances under the banner of "High wages, enough leisure to spend them in and better times for all"; and the masses follow, confident that in one way or the other they will all win through.

Did I say all—well all but the unemployed and the unemployables. The American army, generals and rank-and-file alike, regard them as inevitable casualties and stragglers of a victorious battle. To them unemployment may be an episode, but is not a problem. They cannot understand our intense concentration upon this melancholy feature. They think we are working at the wrong end. "Look after the employed," they say, "and you will find in a very short time the unemployed will look after themselves."

Even though our respective situations are so different, it may be of interest to note the way they look at things.

⚎⚎⚎

"THE AMERICAN MIND AND OURS"

STRAND MAGAZINE
AUGUST, 1931

It is surely an elevated prospect which opens to those who are born into the English-speaking world. Spread wide around the globe and in possession of many of its fairest regions and main resources are more than one hundred and fifty millions of men and women speaking the same language, sprung in an overwhelming degree from a single origin, nursed by the same Common Law, and nourished and inspired by the same literature.

Such a vast community, abounding in wealth, power, and progress and enjoying liberal and democratic institutions and representative government, constitutes incomparably the largest and most harmonious grouping of the human race which has appeared since the zenith of the Roman Empire.

Although riven by the mischances of history and sundered into two branches, their joint inheritance of law and letters, the crimson thread of kinship, the similarity of their institutions, far outweigh the discordances and even antagonisms of politics, the rivalry of flags, the variants of climate, interest, and environment. Noble indeed is the opportunity of life offered to a citizen of this great common body. He moves with ease and very little sense of alienation across enormous distances, and, unpacking his suitcase at a thousand centres of industry and culture, finds himself very speedily almost at home. In dwelling, therefore, upon the differences which time, events, and climate have wrought in the mentality of the various branches of the English-speaking world, it is above all things important to remember that these divergences are far less in volume and importance than the ties of union, of homogeneity.

The social life of the United States is built around business. In Europe business is a newcomer in society. The numerous aristocrats, overthrown but still influential, the ancient landed families, the hierarchies of the Army, the Navy, Diplomacy, the Law, and the Church, frame and largely fill the old-world picture.

Successful business men in Europe find a society ready-made for them. They are welcomed to circles which, especially in England, existed many years before their fortunes were made or the processes and machinery which they direct were devised. In the United States, on the other hand, the struggle to subdue and utilize a continent has taken the place of dynastic, religious, and class controversies. It has absorbed the life of the American people. Everything else falls into a somewhat remote background; and business, commerce, money-making, in all their forms, occupy the centre of the stage. Business dominates the scene and itself gives the reception to which the leaders and members of the services and the professions are cordially invited.

By "society" I do not, of course, mean the gay world of fashion and amusement. In America, as in other countries, that is no more than an adjunct and a diversion. The society which guides and governs the United States is based not on play, but on an intense work which takes from its votaries a first charge on all their thought and energy. From the innumerable universities all their young men go into business as a matter of course. Business is to them the means of earning their living, of making money, of making a fortune; but it is much more than that: it is that career of interest, ambition, and possibly even glory, which in the older world is afforded by the learned professions and State services, military and civilian. A young American, wishing to play a worthy part in the control of affairs, directs himself instinctively towards the managing of factories, railroads, stores, banks, or any other of the thousand and one varieties of American business life.

Practically all the prizes of American life are to be gained in business. There, too, is the main path of useful service to the nation. Nearly all that is best and most active in the manhood and ability of the United States goes into business with the same sense of serving the country as a young Prussian before the War entered the Army, or as a son of a noble house in England in former times sought to represent a family borough in the House of Commons. The leading men of every State are all in business. Their businesses are interlaced; they compete, they collide, they overlap. A continued struggle proceeds, but under rules which, though unwritten, are getting stronger every year.

American industry is greatly the gainer from its power to attract practically all the vital elements of the nation. It is the gainer, also, in an increasing degree, from the intimate combination in every stage between business and social life.

For the leaders of business are also the leaders of society. They are gregarious; they band themselves together in groups, in clubs, in organizations. They do not only work together, they play together. They develop a strong corporate life, carrying with it a continual rising standard of discipline and behaviour. In every State and city they and their families are the nucleus of the local life; and in New York, where to a very large extent everything takes place on a super-scale, the leading business men are the leading figures of the whole nation. There has developed a confraternity the members of which help one another and stand together, and certainly have a far higher sense of comradeship and association than exists in business circles in England.

Very often it is at the golf club, or the country club, or across a private dinner table that the foundations of the largest transactions are laid. It is very important, therefore, in American business circles, to be a member of the club or to be a welcome guest at the dinner; to be popular, trusted, and thought a genial companion and a good sportsman.

Of course, no convention prevents anyone entering and succeeding in business, if he has the qualities and the luck for making a fortune. It is done every day. New figures armed with fiercely-gathered wealth advance resolutely. They require no aid. Liked or disliked, they can stand on their own feet and make their way. It is a free country, they need not bow the knee to any social clique. "No, *sir*." Yet it would be very nice to be elected to the golf club, and to be accepted into the social circles; and it would also be very helpful, and never more helpful than in times of crisis and trouble.

These subtle influences invest the business life of the United States with a quality of strength and order which it formerly lacked. They are healthy and far-reaching. They are creating a new standard of values among successful men. It is good to have a great fortune; but there is more distinction in having a fine business and in managing it well. Wealth ceases to be the aim; it becomes the means, agreeable, indispensable, but yet only the means. Freedom of action and a sense of close contact with the practical, the elating force of large propositions—all these are the elements of an interesting life. These colossal modern businesses offer a man in many ways more scope and power than he could find in a Cabinet office, or at the head of a squadron of the Fleet or a division of the Army.

The prospect is no less attractive because he may become a millionaire in the process.

In all concerned with production the American displays preeminent qualities. Conditions in America have favoured and fostered enterprises upon the largest scale. The American business mind turns naturally, instinctively, to bigness and boldness. In Europe, many of the important manufacturing firms have grown up over generations from small beginnings, and the works as they stand to-day represent the makeshift contributions of many years.

On the other hand, American development has had a clear field. To plan the "lay-out" of businesses upon a gigantic scale, to sweep away ruthlessly all encumbrances of the past, and to crush out all rivals or to merge with them are accepted as obvious ideals. The enormous plants make no compromise with the obsolete or the inefficient in any form.

Time—even in that land of hurry—is not grudged in preparation. Indeed, so vast were the preparations and establishments set on foot on both sides of the Atlantic for the maintenance and supply of the American Army, that the War was over before they had really begun to function, and, according to General Pershing, hardly a single American-made cannon fired an American shell at the enemy. Still, if the War had lasted into 1919, the results of these tremendous preparations would have been irresistible.

A most suggestive and illuminating book, "The American Omen," has extolled the industrial methods of the United States. In an amusing passage, pre-War Russian and American methods are contrasted. When a horse dies in Moscow, a single Russian arrives with a high, narrow cart and a long pole, and, by laying the cart on its side and using the wheel as a kind of windlass and the pole as a lever, single-handed, after long toil and with the utmost ingenuity, little by little manœuvres the carcass into the cart.

An American watching this performance would not, we are told, be at all impressed by this cleverness in overcoming difficulties. He would not accept the difficulties, but would seek to remove them in the first instance. He would not combat the fact that it is very hard for one man to move a heavy horse; he would change the fact. "Specifically, he thinks of a wagon built for the purpose, low-swung on bent axles with proper tackle attached. Having imagined the special wagon, he asks himself if it would pay. Perhaps not; such a wagon would not be right for general purposes also. Therefore, the special wagon called for an organized special activity. With two or three of them one might remove all the dead horses in Moscow. Then it would pay." This instance is typical, and illustrates an admirable mental characteristic.

But what business has gained, by this concentration of American ability and quality upon itself, has been very largely at the expense of politics, and of the professions and martial services. Except in times of war, the United States military or naval man occupies only a very modest position in the public eye or social world. Politics are frankly despised and lamentably neglected as a life-long vocation by the flower of American manhood.

In England, at any rate, the man of independent means and ability who devotes his whole life to Parliament and public affairs, forswearing the opportunities of gathering wealth and seeking only, by serving the State, to rule events, is still regarded as on a higher plane than the prosperous and successful founder of a great business. In the moral hierarchy of our society he is treated as a superior.

It is, or was until recently—for things are changing—quite the contrary in the United States. Politics, dominated by the machine, have produced a caste of professional politicians, beneath whose tough sway few illusions thrive. Aspiring, ardent youth is repulsed from political life, and the aristocracy of business finds ways of solving its political problems other than by personal participation. In the result, the foreigner sees little to admire in the political life of the United States, except its immense mechanical stability.

The Constitution grips the American people with a strong, unyielding hand. Public opinion, so powerful in England, plays but little part in the government of the United States. Presidents, senates, congresses, State legislatures, public officers of all kinds, sustained and erected by the party machine and working for fixed terms, are not to be influenced by the day-to-day emotions of democracy or its Press. At election time, the strong outbursts of popular feelings are all skillfully canalized and utilized. The forces are enormous; but the men in charge know how to bridle and guide them.

The average Englishman, indignant at some scandal or ill-usage, feels he can put the matter right. The average American feels quite sure that he cannot. Public opinion and the sensitive flexibility of our Parliamentary institutions will very quickly sweep away in England an unpopular law. The American resigns himself to put up with it or evade it.

The statute books (both Federal and State) are crowded with laws which have fallen into what is euphemistically called "innocuous desuetude." Politics are accepted like the weather: they go on; one must make the best of them; life has to be lived; work has to be done; and there are so many other more interesting, jolly, and profitable affairs to attend to.

A certain optimistic fatalism fortifies and consoles the American citizen. He feels his country is strong enough, and that its vital force is buoyant enough, to survive the worst that politics can do. It may be that in following democracy and universal suffrage the old controls of English politics will, in their turn, be destroyed. Politics will no longer be an essential part of the life of the country, merely a kind of continuous annoyance emanating from some detested organization which the intelligent or philosophical citizen learns by bitter experience how to mitigate or endure. Under the mask of democratic forms, great nations habituate themselves to arbitrary rule.

Having slipped into Prohibition unawares, America is unable to escape from its deadly embrace. The law cannot be altered, it appears. Therefore, it must be broken or evaded; and broken and evaded it has been on a scale without example in the history of self-respecting communities. But this great evil of almost universal law-breaking has bred still more deadly diseases. An inclined plane slopes unbrokenly from the senator or magnate sipping his glass of smuggled wine in Washington or New York, through layers of diminishing respectability, until the frontiers of murderous crime and blackest villainy are reached.

Here again the scale is gigantic. The worst types of European criminality find themselves banded together in formidable organizations and commanding enormous wealth. Back and up from this terrible underworld rise the ever-lengthening tentacles of graft and corruption. An attempt to interfere improperly with the rights and discretion of the citizen has carried the Legislature far beyond the bounds of public opinion, and the consequences, expanded and reacting from year to year, constitute a hideous disaster to American civilization. We simply cannot imagine either such a cause or such consequences arising in England.

But after all, the first characteristic of the American people is their happiness. The visitor feels himself in the presence of a race with a keen zest for life, a sure confidence in the future, and much enjoyment of things as they are. The American is more highly strung than the northern European; and in most cases this does not seem to lead to pessimism or a morbid condition. The impression of happiness is common to all classes: the people in the streets, in the shops, in the hotels; the liftmen, the bellhop, the telephone operator, all are gay.

No doubt there is a material basis for this. The purchasing power of the average wages of an American labourer is at least twice as much as that of his English equal, and the members of the other income strata are probably superior in the same proportions. A double income for a wage-earner means more than twice the amount of amenities and enjoyment. The necessities of life are a constant which has to be deducted in both cases. The resulting margin of the larger income offers possibilities, not twice, but probably many times as great.

The old orthodox tenet of European civilization that "money does not bring happiness," is probably only a modern adaptation of Æsop's fable of the "Fox and the Grapes." Vast wealth does not bring happiness; but that small margin of spare money after necessities have been provided for constitutes in America the structure of what is definitely a larger life.

In the United States this larger life—or, rather, larger share of life in its natural and rightful balance—is enjoyed by an incomparably greater number than in any other country in the world. "England," said Disraeli, speaking of the early years of the nineteenth century and of long centuries before it, "was for the few, and for the very few." Now we have broadened out. Millions of our people now participate in a wide and eventful form of existence.

In the United States the same classes are counted in scores of millions. Life there is organized not for the few, nor for the millions, but for the scores of millions. Culture, amusement, and reasonable ambitions are provided wholesale by mass production. Culture, indeed, is a standardized article; and the population is almost conscript for university education. Here is the great achievement and marvellous phenomenon of the Great Republic—namely, the vast numbers participating in the full life.

Because the overwhelming majority of Americans enjoy conditions which are not only incomparably fortunate according to European standards, opinion is hard upon failure in all its forms. The mortal sin in the American decalogue is failure; all others are venial. If a man is a failure, the American presumption is that he has himself to blame. There are no vast submerged classes in whose behalf it can be pleaded that they have never had a chance. The great majority of the United States citizens feel that those who have not been able to come up to the general standard have faults or weaknesses for which they deserve to suffer.

There is little place for pity in the schemes of the Great Republic for the failures, for the impoverished or the worn-out. A great chance was offered; it was fair and free; it was offered to all; and if these pitiful ones have not taken it, so much the worse for them. All this is the philosophy of an expanding prosperity and widely-diffused success.

But now, swiftly, suddenly, unexpectedly, though for only a spell, misfortune, contraction, disorganization, stagnation, unemployment have swept down upon the community which two years ago had reached the highest level of material well-being yet achieved by such great numbers of folk in this world. American optimism and complacency have been violently shaken. Millions of unemployed workpeople and clerks present themselves in the great cities. There are broad queues, there are riots, there are even what are called "Socialists," a terrible symptom! And in remote country districts, as well as in the back streets of stately cities, actual famine lays its bony hand upon individuals. This is, of course, only a passing phase from which the United States will emerge strengthened or more prosperous. It is on the rule and not the exception that we must dwell.

Next to happiness a marked heartiness characterizes the American people. This word, when used in its English meaning, is almost a term of opprobrium; but in America it means a genuine flow of friendly feeling. The traveller is welcomed with gusts of friendliness, expansive gestures, and every appearance of joy. Hospitality and every form of kindness are thrust upon him. To this the average British visitor makes but an inadequate return. He behaves with traditional reserve and frigidity, and too often seems to lack the technique for reciprocating the welcome he receives.

There is no doubt that the English people are chary of allowing the feeling of friendliness to take root quickly, and are diffident in its outward expression. They embody a complicated mass of sensitiveness and susceptibilities, acquired or inherited, which are due to a long succession of troubles and frustration. They are the children of a race for whom life has for many generations been less easy than the life of the last few generations in America. Since individual frustration and failure have been more common in his experience, the Englishman carries about scars and wounds which are liable to injury at the hands of another. In consequence, he is unwilling to come close to others in terms of friendliness until he has tried and tested them by various means, proved that they are unlikely to give offence in a thousand possible ways, and are capable of the many forms of give and take, self-restraint, and understanding, which friendship between such sensitive people must involve.

American susceptibilities are of a more childlike and superficial character. The American is more confident and free from the scars of many battles. He is less afraid of the stranger, and is capable of an immediate sensation of genuine friendliness. Affability and amiability come easier to all classes of Americans than to their corresponding types in England.

A third characteristic of the American is his earnestness. He dwells in an atmosphere of intense earnestness and seriousness about all matters of practical concern or general interest. The American prides himself on his sense of humour, but to a transatlantic visitor his earnestness is the predominating feature. We, with our experience that the goal, whatever it be, can only be attained by wary, roundabout, and imperfect methods, are reluctant to indulge in hopes of quick success. With us, the cautious and plodding attitude is appropriate. A super-intense or earnest Englishman always seems to have a flavour of hysteria or the ridiculous about him. Jests and irony run through our serious discussions, and even the gravest situation in England breeds its joke. Cynicism and ridicule have their part to play in the gamut of the human mind. Few are the public men in England who do not, from time to time, indulge such moods.

These attitudes do not represent an ultimate cynicism. They arise from a more just appreciation of the degree of enthusiasm which the situation allows. Since failure is more common in the Old World, its inhabitants have come to relish painful and cynical observations upon the difference between the ideal and the actual, or about the failure of our neighbours or ourselves to live up to our own standards.

Such an attitude is shocking to the average American. Any flavour of levity applied to the grave affairs of life is obnoxious to his mind. He feels it to be decadent and dangerous. He regards it in his visitor (although too polite to say so) as a sign of the corruption of the Old World.

These earnest enthusiasms and aspirations lead very readily to a habit of platitudinizing. A friend of mine who made prolonged travel with a learned delegation through the United States, far from the fashionable circles of New York, says: "They never seem to tire of enunciating the simplest truths with all the solemnity at their command. This may partly have been due to the belief that the platitudes were good for us; and to their habit of acting quickly on what they believe to be sound. Perceiving that we, in many of the matters which were discussed, had failed to give effect to the elementary principles of the subject, they assumed it was because we were ignorant of those principles. It was really because we knew that circumstances did not, indeed, allow the ideal solution, and that, therefore, old sentiments, prejudices, and tradition favouring less sound principles must not be too hastily discarded for the sake of unattainable ideals. Such an attitude was distressing to our American friends. Once they have decided upon the best way of doing something, they proceed to try to do it. They could not conceive that any failure to act on the best principles was due to anything except ignorance of those principles—or worse. Hence the well-meaning platitudes."

There is no doubt that the American love of platitude has a deeper root than this. It arises from their national situation. They have had great good fortune and success. They have a tremendous and obvious task to perform. Their mixture of many races—Poles, Italians, Serbs, and other southern European emigrants—has not yet been assimilated. The hundred-percent Americans have before them a serious problem of welding the nation together. For this the platitude is a powerful instrument. Everyone must be made to think the same things in certain important matters. Everyone must sing the chorus. Everyone must learn the slogans. Everyone must know the drill-book by heart. United sentiment must overcome diversity of racial origin. About certain important matters all must be taught to say the same thing, and to repeat it until it becomes tradition itself.

To sum up this brief examination of a tremendous subject, the Americans in their millions are a frailer race with a lighter structure than their British compeers. They are less indurated by disappointment; they have more hopes and more illusions; they swing more rapidly between the poles of joy and sorrow; and the poles are wider apart. They suffer more acutely both physical and moral pain. The texture of their national life is newly wrought; they have all the advantages and defects of newness and modernity. Their mighty finance, which two years ago soared so triumphantly to the skies, has now for the moment, with as little reason, crashed to the pavement.

These excesses both of elation and depression would have been avoided in England. Tough, buttoned-up, with much reserve and with many latent resources, the Englishman trudges forward, bearing his burden along the stony, uphill road, which we are taught will have no ending. He will not fail. Even if the first prizes of the future should fall to the United States, the Englishman will still remain a vast enduring force for virility, sanity, and goodwill. But it is in the combination across the Atlantic of these diversified minds, and in the union of these complementary virtues and resources, that the brightest promise of the future dwells.

❈❈❈

"MY NEW YORK MISADVENTURE"

THE DAILY MAIL
PART I–JANUARY 4, 1932
PART II–JANUARY 5, 1932

I

Some years ago there was a play at the Grand Guignol called "At the Telephone," which attracted much attention. A husband, called away to Paris, leaves his wife in their suburban home. Every precaution is taken again burglars. There is the maid who will stay in the kitchen; there is the door which is locked; there is the revolver in the drawer of the writing table; and lastly, of course, there is, if needed, the appeal for help by the telephone.

One by one the usefulness of all of these measures disappears. The servant is called away, she leaves the front door unlocked so that she can return. She takes with her the key of the drawer in which the revolver is kept. Darkness comes on, and in the final act the agonised husband hears over the telephone his wife's appeal for help while she is the victim of a murderous outrage. An impressive effect is given of doom marching forward step by step and of every human preventive slipping silently out of the path.

THE INVITATION

Something of this impression rests with me when I recall my experiences of the night of December 13.

I had finished dinner and was inclined to go to bed; but an old friend of mine rang up and suggested that I should go round to his house. He was Mr. Bernard Baruch, who was the head of the War Industries Board during the two years I was Minister of Munitions. We made friends over a long period of official cables on grave business, and have preserved these relations through the now lengthening years of peace. He said he had one or two mutual friends whom I was most anxious to meet, and as the hour was a little after half-past nine, I was readily enlisted in the project.

I descended by lift the thirty-nine storeys which separated my room from the street level. When I arrived at the bottom it occurred to me that I did not know the exact number in Fifth-avenue of my friend's house. I knew it was somewhere near 1,100. I knew the aspect of the house; I had been there by daylight on several occasions. It was a house of only five or six storeys standing with one or two others of similar construction amid large apartment buildings of more than double the height. I thought it probable I could pick it out from the windows of my waiting taxicab, so after a vain search in the telephone book—only Mr. Baruch's business address was there—I started.

A SEARCH IN THE NIGHT

Fifth-avenue is an immensely long thoroughfare, and the traffic upon it, as elsewhere in New York, is regulated by red and green lights. When the red light shows every vehicle must stop at the nearest crossroad. When after an interval of two minutes the lights turn green they all go on as hard as possible until the light changes into red. Thus we progressed by a series of jerks.

When I got near the eleven hundreds I peered out of the cab window and scanned the houses as we sped past, but could not see any like the one I was seeking. They all seemed to be tall buildings of fourteen or fifteen storeys. On the left lay the dark expanse of Central Park.

At length we reached the twelve hundreds and it was certain I had overshot my mark. I told the cabman to turn around and go back slowly so that I could scan every building in turn. Hitherto we had been moving up the right or centre of the thoroughfare and could at any moment have stopped opposite any house. Now we had turned around. We were on the Park, or far side, from the houses, with a stream of traffic between us and the pavement.

At length I saw a house smaller than the rest and told the cabman to turn in there to make inquiries. It occurred to me that as we must be within a hundred houses of Mr. Baruch's address, and that as he was so prominent a citizen, any of the porters of the big apartment houses would know which his house was. A London butler nearly always knows who lives in the three or four houses on the right or left.

The porter of the apartment house at which I inquired recognised me at once and said he had served in the South African War. He had no idea where Mr. Baruch lived, but eagerly produced the telephone book, which could, as I have stated, give no clue in my present quest.

IMPATIENCE

In order to stop opposite this house we had to wait until the light changed, then turn round on to the opposite course, draw up at the pavement, and thereafter make a second turn, again being very likely stopped by a change in the light. When this had happened three times and we were unlucky in missing the permissive green light, I began to be a little impatient.

It was now nearly half-past ten. My friends knew I had started an hour before. Ordinarily the journey should not have taken ten minutes. They might think some accident had happened to me or that I had changed my mind and was not coming at all. They would be waiting about for a tardy guest. I began to be worried about the situation at the house I was seeking. I thought I might have, after all, to go back to my hotel and go to bed.

We had now arrived, as I supposed, at about the nine hundreds, and here were certainly houses much smaller than the others. So instead of going through this long ritual of cab-turning on to the other side of the street with all the delays of the lights, and then returning again on to its general course, I told the cabman to stop where he was on the Central Park side of the avenue; I would walk across the road myself and inquire at the most likely house.

DEADLY HABIT

In England we frequently cross roads along which fast traffic is moving in both directions. I did not think the task I set myself now either difficult or rash. But at this moment habit played me a deadly trick. I no sooner got out of the cab somewhere about the middle of the road and told the driver to wait than I instinctively turned my eyes to the left. About 200 yards away were the yellow headlights of a swiftly approaching car. I thought I had just time to cross before it arrived; and I started to do so in the prepossession —wholly unwarranted—that my only dangers were from the left. The yellow-lighted car drew near and I increased my pace towards the pavement, perhaps twenty feet away.

Suddenly upon my right I was aware of something utterly unexpected and boding mortal peril. I turned my head sharply. Right upon me, scarcely its own length away, was what seemed a long dark car rushing forward at full speed.

There was one moment—I cannot measure it in time—of a world aglare, of a man aghast. I certainly thought quickly enough to achieve the idea *"I am going to be run down and probably killed."* Then came the blow.

I felt it on my forehead and across the thighs. But besides the blow there was an impact, a shock, a concussion indescribably violent.

Many years ago at "Plug-street," in Flanders, a 4.2 shell burst in a corner of the little room in which we were gathered for luncheon, reducing all to devastation. This shock was of the same order as the shell explosion. In my case it blotted out everything except thought.

THE DRIVER'S STORY

Mario Constasino, owner of a medium-sized automobile, was running between 30 and 35 miles an hour on roads which were wet and greasy. He was on his proper side of the road and perfectly entitled to make the best speed he could, when suddenly a dark figure appeared immediately in front of him. He applied all his brakes, and at the same moment, before they could act, he struck a heavy body. The car shuddered, and, after skidding somewhat under the brakes, came to rest in probably a few lengths. Three or four feet from the right-hand wheel lay a black, shapeless mass.

Mario had driven for eight or nine years and had never had an accident. He seems to have been overpoweringly agitated and distressed. He heard a loud cry, *"A man has been killed!"* The traffic banked up on either side. People came running from all directions. Constables appeared. One group clustered around Mario, another around the prostrate figure.

FORCE OF THE BLOW

A friend of mine of mathematical predilections has been kind enough to calculate the stresses involved in the collision. The car weighed some 2,400 pounds. With my evening coat on I could not have weighed much less than 200 pounds. Taking the rate of the car at 35 miles an hour—I think a moderate estimate—I had actually to absorb in my body 6,000 foot-pounds. It was the equivalent of falling 30 feet on to a pavement. The energy absorbed, *though not, of course, the application of destructive force,* was the equivalent of stopping 10 pounds of buckshot dropped 600 feet, or two charges of buckshot at point-blank range.

I do not understand why I was not broken like an egg-shell or squashed like a gooseberry. I have seen that the poor policeman who was killed on the Oxford road was hit by a vehicle travelling at very much the same speed and was completely shattered. I certainly must be very tough or very lucky, or both.

❊❊❊

"I WAS CONSCIOUS THROUGH IT ALL"

II

Meanwhile, I had not lost consciousness for an instant. Somewhere in the black bundle towards which the passers-by are running there is a small chamber or sanctum wherein all is orderly and undisturbed. There sits enthroned a mind intact and unshaken. Before it is a keyboard of letters or buttons directing the body. Above, a whole series of loudspeakers report the sensations and experiences of the empire controlled from this tiny headquarters. The mind is in possession of the following conclusion:

"I have been run over by a motor-car in America. All those worries about being late are now swept away. They do not matter any more. Here is a real catastrophe. Perhaps it is the end."

NO REGRET OR FEAR

The reader will observe from this authentic record that I experienced no emotion of regret or fear. I simply registered facts without, except for a general sense of disaster, the power to moralise upon them. But now all the loudspeakers began to blare together their information from the body. My mind was overpowered by the hideous noise they made from which no intelligible conclusion could be drawn. Wave upon wave of convulsive, painful sensations seemed to flood into this small room, preventing thought, paralysing action, but impossible to comprehend. I had, for instance, no knowledge of whether I was lying on my back or side or face.

How long this period lasted I cannot tell. I am told that from the time I was struck down to when I was lifted into a taxicab was perhaps five minutes, but, although I was in no way stunned, my physical sensations were so violent that I could not achieve any continuous mental process. I just had to endure them.

Presently, however, from my headquarter I see a swirl of figures assembling around me. I have an impression of traffic arrested and of dramatically gathered crowds. Friendly hands are laid upon me.

I suppose I ought now to have had some very pious and inspiring reflections. However, all that occurred to me was, *"I shall not be able to give my lecture to-morrow night in Brooklyn. Whatever will my poor agent do with it?"*

Then more definite impressions. A constable is bending over me. My head and shoulders are being raised towards him. He has a book, quite a big book, in his hand.

"What is your name?"

"Winston Churchill."

I protest I am no snob, but on this occasion I thought it lawful and prudent to add, "The Right Honourable Winston Churchill from England." I heard distinctly respectful "Oh, ohs" from the crowd.

"What is your age?" asked the officer, adhering to his routine.

"Fifty-seven," I replied, and at the same moment this odd thought intruded itself upon my mind, "How very old to be knocked down in the street by a motor-car. I shall have a very poor chance of getting over it."

DRIVER EXONERATED

The constable proceeded to demand particulars of the accident. My mind and speech apparatus worked apparently without hitch, and I could volubly have told him all that is set down here; but instead, to save trouble, I said:

"I am entirely to blame; it is all my own fault."

Later it seemed that another constable came with the question, "Do you make any charge against any person?" To which I replied, "I exonerate everyone."

At this the interrogation ceased abruptly, and Mario in the background (though I did not know this until afterwards) was released from captivity.

During all this time I was in what I suppose would be called great pain, though the sensations really presented themselves to me mainly as an overpowering of the mind. Gradually I began to be more aware of all that was going on around me.

It appears that an ambulance was passing, and the crowd stopped it and demanded that it should take me to the nearest hospital. The ambulance, which had a serious case on board, refused. Thereupon a taximan exclaimed in a voice which I could perfectly well hear, "Take him in my cab. There's the Lenox-hill Hospital on 76th Street."

Accordingly I was lifted by perhaps eight or ten persons to the floor of the taxicab. I now discovered that my overcoat had been half torn off me and trussed my arms back. I thought both shoulders were dislocated. My right shoulder dislocates chronically, and I asked repeatedly that care should be taken in lifting me by it. Eventually the constable and two others got into the cab and we all started, jammed up together.

Up till now nothing could have been more calm and clear than my interior thought, apart from the blaring of pain and discomfort which came through the loudspeakers. All was in order in my inner sanctum, but I had not ventured to touch the keyboard of action and had been content to remain an entirely inert mass.

I now saw, as I lay on the floor of the cab, both my hands, very white and covered with blood, lying across my breast. So I decided to give them an order to move their fingers and at the same time I pulled the levers which affect the toes. Neither hands nor feet took the slightest notice. They might as well have belonged to someone else for all the attention they paid to my will.

NEEDLESS ALARM

I now became, for the first time, seriously alarmed. I feared that in this bundle of dull pain which people were carting about, and which was my body, there might be some grave, serious injury to the spine. The impression "crippled for life" registered itself in the sanctum. Yet even then there was so much going on that one could not focus it very clearly or grieve about it much.

What a nice thing it would be to get to the hospital and have this overcoat cut off, to have my shoulders put back into their sockets, and, above all, to lie down straight upon a bed. My companions kept cheering me up. "We are very near now; only another block or two," and so on. So we rumbled on.

And then a most blessed thing happened. I began to experience violent pins and needles in both my upper arms. They hurt intensely; but I did not mind, because at the same time I found my fingers beginning to move in accordance with my will. Almost immediately afterwards the toes responded to my orders. Then swiftly, by waves of pins and needles almost agonising in their intensity, warmth, life and obedience began to flow back into the whole of my trunk.

By the time we pulled up at the hospital I had the assurance that, although I might have an arm or leg or two broken and was certainly bruised and shaken, the whole main structure of my body was sound. Blood continued to flow freely from my forehead and my nose; but I did not worry about that at all, because in my sanctum we had decided: *"There can be no brain injury, as we have never lost consciousness even for a second."*

At last we arrive at the hospital. A wheeled chair is brought. I am carried into it. I am wheeled up steps into a hall and a lift. By now I feel battered but perfectly competent. They said afterwards I was confused; but I did not feel so.

"Are you prepared to pay for a private room and doctor?" asked a clerk.

"Yes, bring all the best you have. . . . Take me to a private room. . . . Where is your telephone? . . . Give me the Waldorf

Astoria. . . . I will tell my wife myself that whatever has happened I am going to get quite well."

But after an interval they said, "She is already on the way here."

Not for one moment had I felt up to the present any sensation of faintness, but now I said, "Give me sal volatile, or something like that." A reviver was brought. A house surgeon stanched my wound.

"Let me," I asked, "get these clothes off and lie down. I can stand for a moment if you hold me up."

Soon I am on a bed. Presently come keen, comprehending eyes and deft, firm fingers.

"We shall have to dress that scalp wound at once. It is cut to the bone."

"Will it hurt?"

"Yes."

"I do not wish to be hurt any more. Give me chloroform or something."

"The anæsthetist is already on the way."

More lifting and wheeling. The operating room. White glaring lights. The mask of a nitrous-oxide inhaler. Whenever I have taken gas or chloroform I always follow this rule. I imagine myself sitting on a chair with my back to a lovely swimming bath into which I am to be tilted, and throw myself backwards; or, again, as if one were throwing one's self back after a tiring day into vast armchair. This helps the process of anæsthesia wonderfully. A few deep breaths, and one has no longer the power to speak to the world.

NO UNENDURABLE PAIN

With me the nitrous-oxide trance usually takes this form: the sanctum is occupied by alien powers. I see the absolute truth and and explanation of things, but something is left out which upsets the whole, so by a larger sweep of the mind I have to see a greater truth and a more complete explanation which comprises the erring element. Nevertheless, there is still something left out. So we have to take a still wider sweep. This almost breaks mortal comprehension. It is beyond anything the human mind was ever meant to master.

The process continued inexorably. Depth beyond depth of unendurable truth opens. I have, therefore, always regarded the nitrous-oxide trance as a mere substitution of mental for physical pain.

Pain it certainly is; but suddenly these poignant experiences end, and without a perceptible interval consciousness returns. Reassuring words are spoken. I see a beloved face. My wife is smiling. In the background there rises the grave, venerable countenance of Mr. Bernard Baruch. So I ask:

"Tell me, Baruch, when all is said and done, what *is* the number of your house?"

"1055."

"How near was I to it when I was smashed up?"

"Not within ten blocks." [Half a mile.]

Such, in short, were my experiences on the night of December 13; and the message I bring back from these dark places is one of encouragement.

I certainly suffered every pang, mental and physical, that a street accident or, I suppose, a shell wound can produce. None is unendurable. There is neither the time nor the strength for self-pity. There is no room for remorse or fears. If at any moment in this long series of sensations a grey veil deepening into blackness had descended upon the sanctum I should have felt or feared nothing additional.

Nature is merciful and does not try her children, man or beast, beyond their compass. It is only where the cruelty of man intervenes that hellish torments appear. For the rest—live dangerously; take things as they come; dread naught; all will be well.

I ought not to forget to add that I have since looked into my despatch-box and I have found that my far-seeing private secretary in England, Mrs. Pearman, had furnished me with a travelling address-book of people I might want to communicate with in the United States, and in this I read: "Baruch, 1055, Fifth Avenue," with the private telephone number duly set out.

All of which goes to show that even the best human precautions afford no definite guarantee of safety.

※※※※

"THE SHATTERED CAUSE OF TEMPERANCE"

COLLIER'S
AUGUST 13, 1932

As Chancellor of the Exchequer Winston Churchill was forced to grapple with the liquor problem in England. Now he brings to the American problem of prohibition a mind trained to the subject and experienced in the ways of government. Here he eloquently describes and interprets for you what he has seen and heard in this country.

I made two long journeys through the United States in 1929 and in 1932. I visited on each occasion many great cities and the Federal seat of government, and met, in all the confidence of friendly discussions, many leading Americans. When I am asked to state what is my prevailing impression, I must answer unhesitatingly: "The change in opinion about prohibition."

On the former occasion many championed it with vigor or at least defended it with conviction. The arguments about the well-being of the common people, all the improved efficiency of the working classes, of the importance of clear heads and steady hands in using high-speed machinery—all these, with which we have been familiar, were paraded with ceremony, if not with confidence.

But now, in 1932, I could find scarcely a voice raised in defense of such a system. Indeed, on every side in a score of states, among the dominant figures of American life, there was a fierce and universal chorus of disapproval and disdain for the principle of prohibition, and a general apologia for political institutions and party deadlocks which did not allow the impulse of the American nation to free itself from these absurd trammels and this oppressive incubus.

In the audiences which I addressed, comprising scores of thousands of American citizens from New York to Indiana and from Georgia to Maine, every critical or slighting allusion to prohibition which I ventured to make—with all the reserves of courtesy due from a foreigner—was received with immediate, spontaneous appreciation. Laughter and cheers from three fourth of every audience, even in the driest states, greeted the suggestion that it had failed, that it had not achieved any real advance toward true temperance and that it had brought novel and hideous evils in its train.

At the New York Economic Club, in the presence of over two thousand of the most influential active managers and public breadwinners in American affairs, I was actually permitted to ask, amid resounding applause, "Why don't you tax alcoholic liquor and strike a threefold blow at drunkenness, prohibition and crime?"

These conditions, to judge by my observation of the temper of the American people, justify one of those recurrences to first principles enjoyed by the founders of the American polity. Such questions are raised as these: What are the rights and duties of the government in relation to individuals? What is the nature of the implicit understanding between citizens and the organizations they combine to set up for themselves? Ought laws to be passed by a transient majority which, even in their heyday, affront enormous numbers of people in their intimate private lives? Is it not an undue intrusion by a government upon the discretion of the adult citizen to deny him such use of alcohol as has been sanctioned by the immemorial practice of almost every race in almost every age?

EVIL RETURNS—AT A GALLOP

Is it not indeed an act of positive aggression for one citizen to attempt to exercise this kind of petty control over the normal actions of his fellow? Does it not conflict with the fundamental doctrine of the United States Constitution that every citizen is entitled to "life, liberty and the pursuit of happiness"? Was not a great abuse perpetrated against the rights and liberties of individuals when laws were passed making criminal—or at least illegal—actions for committing which no man would withdraw friendship or respect from his neighbor?

When these great faults or errors in the march of a nation's affairs are committed they bring in their train most astonishing and often terrifying reactions. The French have said, "Drive away Nature and she returns at a gallop." But in this case it is not Nature that has returned at the gallop; it is monstrosity and social disease which have returned with the speed of the fastest automobile.

When I look out upon the broad, sunlit surface of the United States as from some great sky-scraping pinnacle, it seems no exaggeration to declare that three-fourths of the present grave evils and worries by which this vast mass of humanity is afflicted, take their origin and find their explanation in the attempt to enforce the prohibition of alcohol against the will, mood and habit, not only of the masses, but of their dominant elements.

First of all, a grievous injury has been inflicted upon the cause of temperance by those who wished most of all to serve it. It is possible that the dry, bracing, electrical atmosphere of North America makes the use of alcohol less necessary and more potent than does the humid climate of Britain. But the progress of Britain during the present century has been most remarkable.

Like the United States, we have had a mass of misery and poverty, of broken lives and ruined homes directly attributed to the abuse of strong drink. Like the United States, we have, especially under the impulsion of the war, attacked this evil with vigor. As in the United States, we have attacked it by direct interference with the liberty of the individual. But we have used different weapons. The two main weapons we have used are High Taxation and Strict Regulation. By high taxation I mean three or four hundred per cent upon the cost price of liquor. By strict regulation I mean regulations which are enforced and obeyed.

The results have been impressive: the British nation drinks today only half the beer, and less than a quarter the spirits, which, with a smaller and much less affluent population, it drank at the beginning of the century. In the year 1913, the last complete year before the war, there were 184,000 convictions for drunkenness in our island. In 1930, the last year for which the figures are yet available, these 184,000 convictions had fallen to 53,000, or considerably less than one third of the former figure. A similar decline can be shown in the crimes and diseases of drunkenness.

THE BENEFITS OF TEMPERANCE

A gratifying decline in the prison population has accompanied the general improvement in public habits. Several important convict prisons have been broken up, and none of the jails are crowded or even full. The British Temperance Party, once so active and powerful, has found its force evaporating in proportion as the evils against which it had warned begin to be increasingly and successfully controlled. The Royal Commission which recently reviewed the whole position found no single witness to appear before it who would advocate prohibition. Accordingly they did not even think it worth while to discuss such a proposal in their report.

Meanwhile the high taxation has of course yielded an immense revenue to the State. When I was Chancellor of the Exchequer I received between six and seven hundred million dollars per annum from the taxes on liquor. It is true that the yield of these taxes fell off year after year and in every one of my five budgets I had to write down my estimates by ten or twelve million dollars. This falling off was due to the decreasing use of alcohol in every form by all classes of the population, from the rich man's champagne to the poor man's glass of beer; and in every kind of spirits a similar and almost uniform reduction was evident.

But even in my last budget I still raised upward of six hundred million dollars from the severe taxation of this indulgence. I have seen it calculated that if taxation of the same rigor were imposed in the United States a yield of anything from a billion and a quarter to a billion and a half would inure to the Federal and state authorities.

I am well aware of the argument—we have heard it here—that the State must on no account profit from taxing anything so wicked as alcohol. We are told that a moral degradation would be involved from a pure-minded, high-souled State must guard itself no matter what the cost. It is vain to argue with bigots and fanatics. But sensible citizens must ask themselves where all this money goes now. There is no lack of liquor in the United States. There appears to be no difficulty in obtaining it almost anywhere. The recent conference of the leading bootleggers did not concern itself with the problem of smuggling the liquor or of manufacturing it illicitly in the United States. These problems have been solved. The praiseworthy concern of the bootleggers was an improvement in the quality and an abatement in the price.

American statistics show an enormous quantity of drinking, and of the worst kind of drinking, with large increases of drunkenness and all its attendant evils throughout the Union. Recently a new and surprising fact has become apparent. The United States, so far from being dry, is becoming an exporter of liquor upon a large scale. The Canadian authorities have become uneasy at a growing flow of smuggled liquor from the United States into Canada; thus affecting their lucrative government monopoly.

The empty cup has not merely been filled, is not merely being continually kept full, it is overflowing. And all the hundreds of millions of dollars which in Great Britain afford a welcome and indispensable relief to overburdened taxpayers, in the United States pour in far greater volume into the pockets not only of bootleggers but of that hideous underworld which thrives upon them. It is this frightful Frankenstein reaction which, even more than the injury to temperance or the loss of large potential revenue, has riveted and engrossed the attention of the American mind.

Prohibition has lent affluence to crime. Until its appearance the older type of ruffianly criminal was not only ignorant but poor. The profession of a bandit was at once precarious and illpaid. It was true to say that money could be much more easily made by honesty. But once an opportunity of manufacturing or importing liquor which could be sold to an almost limitless consuming public at three, four and five times the original cost presented itself, the underworld found itself in possession of revenues equal to those of great countries in the nineteenth century, or of considerable minor nations at the present time.

Here were funds to influence and even dominate municipal elections, to bribe policemen, custom-house officers and prohibition agents; to corrupt judges and juries, to tamper with legislators and political parties; to procure the finest apparatus of brigandage, to perfect the most elaborate organizations, and to command competent and reputable legal talent.

PROHIBITION'S GIFT TO THE NATION

A cold, insidious system of graft rose swiftly tier by tier in many of the great cities of the United States. Organized gangs competed against each other in this work, and fought out bloody and murderous vendettas; and every part of the foundation of this monstrous edifice, the like of which the civilized world has never before known, was well and truly laid. Whole series of new or half-forgotten crimes and tyrannies came into being. Highjackers preyed on bootleggers and the police preyed on both.

The prohibition agents, local and Federal, were exposed to all the temptations by which men have become wealthy. Crime propagated and pullulated; bootlegging was the first-born child of prohibition. Racketeering—that is to say, an organized blackmailing by threats and violence against persons carrying on lawful trades—was its second offspring. Kidnapping is its latest new-born baby, thriving and growing apace.

He must be a strange fellow, purblind, wrongheaded, nay, ruthless in heart, who, for the sake of his fads, wills obstinately that such a process shall continue. It is a repulsive mentality which is so squeamish, so fastidious, that it recoils with horror at the idea of the State "touching the evil thing" by taxing it, and yet consents in helpless fatalism to the indefinite continuance and aggravation of these awful, unforeseen and immeasureable consequences.

But not only has prohibition armed crime with gold; it has invested it with public sanction. Down from the very summit of American civilization falls the light of countenance and condonation upon the whole mass of weltering illegality and rapine. Everywhere, in every state, in every city, in every class, in every profession, in every public office, liquor is freely consumed and easily purchased. The highest in the land, many of its ablest men, many of its best citizens, have accustomed themselves to breaches of the law. They give their orders with a smile or a shrug, and their behests, passing down the tiers and stories of the social structure, are ultimately executed by agents as vile and ferocious as any who have ever shamed the world.

Worst of all is the effect upon the youth of both sexes, particularly well-educated, well-to-do youth. The natural unruliness of young people the world over here finds its stimulus in the lawless example of their parents. To get the better of irrational and unpopular law imparts to the ordinary indulgence of drinking the glitter of quite a special temptation. The young men and women of all the innumerable universities for which the United States is famous drink not merely for pleasure and diversion, but audaciously, out of bravado, to show that they are free and independent —or somberly, dully, just to get drunk.

WHAT YOUNG AMERICA DRINKS

The entire taste of the cultivated youth of America has been perverted by the unreasonable conditions in which they find themselves. They know nothing of the good light wines and wholescme beers which play so large a part in the life of Europe. The agreeable vintages of the Rhine and the Moselle, the clarets and champagnes of France, are unknown. The famous beers of Milwaukee are extinct, and Canadian ale is on the whole successfully excluded.

Of all these innocent amenities which add so much to the course and the variety of the life of the great white race all over the world, American youth tastes nothing. By an insult for which Bacchus will surely exact retribution, all these nymphs and fauns of the cellar are flung into the common category of "hooch." What an affront to

the whole history of mankind to have reduced them to that level!
Wine, that good gift of the gods, for the use of which there is so
much Scriptural warrant, is ranked with drug-taking—a foul thing
to be done furtively but resolutely by addicts in unpunished opposition to the law of the land.

And as all these innocent and, as I hold, improving beverages
are the form of alcohol most difficult for bootleggers to supply,
young America drinks gin and whisky in unnumbered variants of
the odious cocktail. At the hotel on the Canadian side of Niagara I
made particular inquiries. "Yes, sir, they come across continuously.
They acquire the qualifications to purchase liquor, necessary under
Canadian law, by taking a bedroom. They drink whisky or gin,
mostly straight, and they aim at getting drunk."

Anyone who has seen an American ship arrive in a "free" port
will recall the disgusting spectacle of intoxication of both old and
young American citizens so often paraded to the contempt of
foreigners.

DRY AND BOTHERED

No one who likes and admires the American people and has faith
in the grandeur of their destiny but has felt humiliated to see a
gathering of eminent and influential men shuffling about uneasily
from foot to foot at some officially dry party, forbidden as if they
were schoolboys from the whisky and soda which would have made
the entertainment easy and comfortable. Anyone who has seen a
great banquet where the guests smoke cigarettes with every spoonful
even of their soup, and flit out of the room at intervals to lap gin
and whisky in some privy apartment, will sympathize with the ill
usage to which all that is genial and all that is hospitable in Uncle
Sam is being subjected.

The traveler must not judge only from New York. There, everyone is in league against prohibition. Liquor flows in copious abundance, but through unwholesome channels. I must confess that on
one occasion I was taken to a speakeasy. I went, of course, in my
capacity of a Social Investigator. The den was but a few blocks

from my hotel. Some interchanges were made at the portals by my guides and companions, and we were admitted.

I was recognized and the two orchestras which had been alternating their performances played God Save the King. The room was fairly large, dark, stuffy and very overcrowded. The bulk of the company graciously stood up to the British national anthem, just as we do in England when The Star-Spangled Banner is played. I caught one or two comments, "We don't have to stand up; we are Americans." "Oh, well, we are all very friendly here."

DINING IN UPROAR

All the charm, grace, good will, courtesy of American life, but in what surroundings! What a place to eat a dinner! When *I* dine after a hard day's work, I like serenity, calm, good food, cold beverages. I like to see attractive female forms, elegantly attired, moving, parading to their places in the restaurant. I like the rhythm and murmur of distant music. I might even like a dance. But there I saw all that one would avoid at dinner-time—crowds, bad cooking, bad service, bawling jazz bands, funereal lighting, hustle and disturbance!

Yet this was one of the most fashionable dining places in New York. Why? Because there was liquor. Every kind of wine, all sorts of spirits (reputed safe) blazoned on the counter, could be purchased at prices not far ahead of those which rule in London now. And here was this large gathering of Americans putting up with all the discomfort, ugliness and craziness of their surroundings for the sake of being able to do what to every man and woman in Europe has never been denied.

The behavior of the company was most respectable and their demeanor dreary; but in their hearts they had the feeling of an awful joy. They were doing something which they ought not to do. They were doing something in defiance of a law which they hated and despised. All their insurgent impulses were enlisted in the enterprise. There were no hardships they would not face to get their rights and to get their way.

Meanwhile the magnificent hotel I had come from presented in its splendid dining-rooms an admirable cuisine, a wonderful orchestra, perfect attendance, everything that luxury could conceive —and it was absolutely deserted. No one would dine there. The hotel was too obvious a target, its interests were too large to break the law; so the dining-rooms were empty and the waiters stood kicking their heels in solitude.

As they dare not sell any drink, the hotels have to make their living out of the food. You are charged half a dollar for the juice of one orange such as you can buy for a halfpenny in the London streets. This is a world of topsy-turvydom.

But the same absurdities present themselves in the South and in the West. Always we used to be told how necessary it was to prevent the Negroes from obtaining liquor. They *make* all they want now. What is called "stumpjuice" is distilled in unlimited quantities over vast areas.

TOPSY-TURVY LAND

Twenty times the present police force would be required to prevent it, and probably half the present police force, out of good nature or improper interest, turns a blind eye. The acme was reached in the Middle West. Here, in bone-dry states, the law makes even the possession of liquor a crime. Yet the traveler experienced no difference in the hospitality which was proudly offered to him.

The responsible heads and magistrates of great cities uniformly denounced prohibition, and most of them observed a strict personal teetotalism in order to strengthen their position in attacking this evil. How different is their attitude from that of the shabby politician who spouts his dry peroration with a flask on his hip and refreshes himself after cooing to the electors by habitual and often excessive alcoholic indulgence!

In one hotel, which must be nameless, I was gravely informed that mineral water could not be served in public. "We are bound to regard the conjunction of mineral water, ice and a tumbler as a 'set-up' for drinking. It would only require the addition of whisky or gin to constitute a violation of the Eighteenth Amendment." Such risks could not be run. Temptation must be grappled with in its earliest and most insidious stages. Yet upstairs every kind of liquor could be consumed in the presence of the same waiters, and not only consumed if brought, but obtained on the spot by persons who desired it for themselves or for their guests.

For all the rest of the world except the United States the monetary question is the most clamant of our problems. It is also tremendously important to Americans. But the life-and-death issue in America is the cleansing of the land from the shams, shames, hypocrisies and diseases of prohibition.

Is there then no remedy? From this shattered cause of temperance, from these plundered American revenues, from these hideous cephalopods of crime springing at so many points into dominant life, from this misguided and irritated new generation, from these insulted laws of a great people—is there then no escape? The Constitution bars the way. Prohibition, carried while the first two million fighting men of the United States were overseas, carried in war hysteria and by the uncomprehending woman's vote, can never be reversed so long as thirteen states of the Union find partisans base enough to inflict this injury upon their country.

Ardent social reformers, earnest patriots, experienced able statesmen, senators and governors, recoiling disheartened from a mechanical deadlock, take refuge in cynicism.

In the highest quarters it is said, "Why worry? Those who like prohibition have got it, those who don't can get what they want." Or again, "The dry ticket is good for one more election." This is the philosophy of despair.

Meanwhile the great republic of the United States is in many ways, in most material ways, the leading nation of the world. In her successful surmounting of her own enormous difficulties, in her manifestations of her own inexhaustible strength, lies a large portion of the hopes and buoyancy of mankind. With the realization of their inherent strength, which imprints itself upon me the more I see of them, and of their future glory, which no man can doubt, I avow my confidence that, in one way or another and at no distant

date, the American democracy will shake itself free from these
mischievous follies, petty tyrannies and entanglements, and restore
law and liberty to the thrones from which they have so ignomini-
ously ejected each other.

"LAND OF CORN
AND LOBSTERS"

COLLIER'S
AUGUST 5, 1933

I feel shy about expressing my opinion about American food. I
was everywhere received with such charming hospitality that to
give any verdict of a critical character might seem churlish. However, as eating and drinking are matters in which the good taste of
different people and different countries naturally and legitimately
varies so widely, there may be no harm in my setting down a few
general impressions. Then there is the danger that one may be
thought greedy, and reproached for setting too much store by
creature comfort and dwelling unduly upon trivialities. But here I
fortify myself by Dr. Johnson's celebrated dictum: "I look upon it
that he who does not mind his belly will hardly mind anything else."

So I will start out boldly with the assertion that Americans of
every class live on lighter foods than their analogues in England.
Fruit, vegetables and cereals play a much larger part in their bills
of fare than with us, and they eat chicken much more often than
meat—by which of course I mean beef and mutton. All this is no
doubt very healthful, but personally I am a beef-eater, and I always expect my wife to provide me with butcher's meat once a day
when I am at home.

Moreover, the American chicken is a small bird compared with
the standard English fowl. Attractively served with rice and auxil-

iaries of all kinds, he makes an excellent dish. Still, I am on the side of the big chicken as regularly as Providence is on that of the big battalions. Indeed it seems strange in so large a country to find such small chickens. Conscious, perhaps, of their inferiority, the inhabitants call them "squabs." What an insulting title for a capon!

A dangerous, yet almost universal, habit of the American people is the drinking of immense quantities of iced water. This has become a ritual. If you go into a cafeteria or drug store and order a cup of coffee, a tumbler of iced water is immediately set before you. The bleak beverage is provided on every possible occasion; whatever you order, the man behind the counter will supply this apparently indispensable concomitant.

REVERSING THE OLD ORDER

American meals nearly always start with a large slice of melon or grapefruit accompanied by iced water. This is surely a somewhat austere welcome for a hungry man at the midday or evening meal. Dessert, in my view, should be eaten at the end of the meal, not at the beginning. The influence of American customs is now so all-pervading, that during the last few years I have noticed this habit creeping into England. It should be strongly repulsed.

The coffee in the United States is admirable, and a welcome contrast to the anemic or sticky liquid which judicious Americans rightly resent in English provincial towns. The American Blue Point is a serious undertaking. On the other hand, the American lobster is unrivaled anywhere in the world; he has a succulence and a flavor which I have found nowhere else. Shad roe and terrapin I have eaten only in the United States; I find them both entertaining. Soft-shell crabs and corn on the cob are by no means unpalatable, but should not be eaten too often.

A very general custom in American society is to have a little preliminary repast before the company sits down at table. The guests arrive any time within half an hour of the nominal dinner hour, and stand about conversing, smoking cigarettes, and drinking cocktails. There is, of course, the admirable tomato-juice cocktail.

But this is not the one most commonly used. It was explained to me that nothing in the laws of the United States forbids the convivial consumption in a private house of any stores of liquor which happened to be in the host's private cellars before prohibition became effective in 1920. Many people must have had very large and well-stocked cellars in those distant days, and these supplies have lasted extremely well. Indeed one might almost believe that, like the widow's cruse, they miracuously replenish themselves.

Alcoholic liquor could therefore, without any illegality, enter into the composition of many kinds of cocktails and these short, hard, wet drinks may be freely enjoyed without any presumption of illegality. I am no devotee of cocktails, still I must admit that this preliminary festival while the guests are arriving is most agreeable. The cocktails are supported by all sorts of dainty, tasty little dishes continually handed round upon trays or displayed upon tables. This custom is nothing more nor less than the old custom of Imperial Russia called "the zakouski."

I remember as a child, nearly fifty years ago, being taken by my mother on a visit to the Duke of Edinburgh, who had married a Russian princess. There I saw exactly the same ritual, with kümmel and vodka instead of the cocktails, and the same attractive, eatable kickshaws to keep them company. It was only after this was over that the regular dinner began. There is much to be said for this arrangement. No doubt it encourages unpunctuality, but on the other hand it protects those who have already arrived from starving helplessly till the late comers make their appearances.

TRAVEL-CONSCIOUS AMERICA

I expect the practice has come to stay. It makes for sociability and good mixing, both of the guests and their refreshments. Indeed I should not be surprised if some day the formal sit-down dinner were dropped altogether and an ethereal generation contented themselves with cocktails, cigarettes and caviar, and then went off and danced for glee. I should not approve of this; but we, live in a world of change, and who can control its oscillations?

The vast size of the United States and the imperative need of moving about have given the American an altogether different standard of distances from that which prevails in our small island. He thinks as little of a fourteen or fifteen hours' railway journey as we do of the hour and a half to Brighton or Oxford. He is no more balked by the prospect of traveling from New York to Palm Beach than we should be by going to Scotland. Even the mighty journey to California, from ocean to ocean, presents itself as quite an ordinary undertaking.

It is odd how quickly the visitor falls into this American order of ideas. A four- or six-hour journey by railway soon becomes a bagatelle. I have made three great journeys in the United States— the first separated from the two last (I am ashamed to say) by nearly thirty years. I dreaded the toil of traveling so much by railway, and it was a strong deterrent from undertaking a lecture tour. But I am bound to say that I did not find these long runs and this continuous traveling day after day, night after night, at all fatiguing on these later occasions. Indeed I started for a journey of nearly six weeks soon after I had been struck by a taxi, very weak and frail, and with much misgiving as to my capacity to fulfill my engagements; but in fact I throve on it.

RAILROAD TRAVEL DE LUXE

It was a fruitful convalescence, and I was much stronger at the end than at the beginning. The truth is that the trains are extremely comfortable: the enormous rolling stock, the weight of the metals and the steady pace maintained—even when interrupted occasionally by formidable bangs and jolts—give a sense of repose which I do not feel on our quick, tremulous, and comparatively light railways. In England, indeed, except for long journeys of four or five hours, I almost always go by motor car. In America one resigns oneself easily to many hours of train, and tranquilly settles down to work or reading without any feeling of impatience.

When in 1929 I traversed Canada from east to west and came back across the United States from California through Chicago to New York, and then down to the battlefields of the South, I had the wonderful experience of being transported (through the magnificent kindness of Canadian and American friends) entirely in a private car. This rare and costly luxury gave a really joyous feeling. It was a home from home. And what a sense of power and choice, to be able to stop where you would and for as long as you would, and to sleep on till you wished to get up, and to hook onto any train when satiated with the wonders of the Yosemite Valley, or the Grand Canyon, or the roar of Niagara, or the clack and clutter of the Chicago stockyards! It was like marching and camping in war time in enormous lands. Indeed, I meditated hiring a private car for my lecture tour. Alas, the cost! Twenty-four tickets were more than my business would bear.

Many English people do not like the long sleeping-cars in which strangers of both sexes are separated from one another only by curtains, and where the temperature is often tropical till you open the window, and arctic when you do. Still, they are very practical once you are used to them. No one could require better accommodation than a drawing-room compartment all to oneself. Our sleeping-berths are nearly always at right angles to the train, and the beds are so narrow that one can hardly turn over in them. Moreover, the sheets and blankets are also on the narrow side, and at the slightest movement come untucked. The United States railway bed is a splendid, soft, broad affair. It lies lengthwise with the train, and I slept in one, night after night, as soundly as I should in any house.

Nowhere in the world have I seen such gargantuan meals as are provided upon American trains. Every plate would feed at least two people. I have always been amazed at the immense variety of foodstuffs which are carried in the dining-cars, and the skill and delicacy with which they are cooked even upon the longest journey through the very heart of the continent.

The darky attendants with their soft voices and delightful drawl and courteous, docile, agreeable ways were an unfailing source not only of comfort but of perpetual amusement to me. In view of the results of the late presidential election, I may perhaps confess that, armed with a medical certificate, I somewhat anticipated the verdict of the American nation upon the Eighteenth Amendment. But these discreet attendants never seemed to let their eyes stray upon any vessels or containers not officially brought to their notice. Indeed one would have thought that where liquids were concerned they were entirely color-blind. One of them, however, shrouding with a napkin a gold-topped bottle which might well have contained ginger ale, when I returned to the compartment after a few moments' absence, made this memorable remark: "Yo' ought to be very careful with this, sah. Men will steal this who would not steal di'monds." It is pleasant to reflect that such a temptation will soon be forever removed from the weaker members of American society.

On one occasion only was there cause for alarm. A friend of mine when I left California in 1929 sent as a parting gift a good-sized suitcase, unlabeled, which at the last minute was thrust unostentatiously into my compartment. Unluckily something seemed to have gone wrong with its contents, and a very curious trickle had left its trail all along the station platform. However, no one said a word; and fortunately, on examination, the damage was found to be confined to only one of the articles which this mysterious, anonymous package contained.

Whenever I come to a new city I always make haste to climb the tallest building in it and examine the whole scene from this eagle's nest. They are wonderful, these bird's-eye views; each one gives an impression of its own which lies in the memory like a well-known picture. I have heard the opinion expressed that all American cities are alike. I do not agree with this shortsighted view. The hotels are the same in their excellence and comfort, in their routine and service; but anyone who will not only perch himself on a pinnacle, but thread and circumnavigate the streets in a motor car, will soon perceive that each city has a panorama and a personality all its own.

THE LAND OF FAIR CITIES

Nothing of course can equal the world-famous silhouette of New York from the sea. It is a spectacle the magnificence of which is perhaps unsurpassed in the whole world and, though each building taken separately may have its failings, the entire mass of these vast structures is potent with grandeur and beauty. But San Francisco, earthquake-defying, makes a fine counterpart as it gazes on the Pacific. Nothing could be more different from San Francisco than Los Angeles, the one towering up under its cloud canopy, its buildings crowded together on the narrow promontory; the other spreading its garden villas over an enormous expanse, a system of rural townships basking in the sunlight.

From west to south! What lovely country surrounds the city of Atlanta! Its rich red soils, the cotton-quilted hills and uplands, the rushing, turgid rivers, are all alive with tragic memories of the Civil War. And who would miss Chattanooga, lying in its cup between the Blue Ridge and Lookout Mountain? The scenery itself is exhilarating, but to it all is added the intense significance of history. All these rugged heights and peaks have their meaning in military topography: a short drive to the battlefield of Chickamauga, kept like a beautiful park, with many of the field batteries standing in the very positions where they fought, is enough to reward the visitor.

In Minneapolis amid its rolling plains my small party had its most affectionate welcome. Cincinnati, I thought, was the most beautiful of the inland cities of the Union. From the tower of its unsurpassed hotel the city spreads far and wide its pageant of crimson, purple, and gold, laced by silver streams that are great rivers. There is a splendor in Chicago and a life-thrust that is all its own.

AMERICANS KNOW HOW TO LISTEN

To me, Rochester makes a personal appeal. Here it was that my grandfather and his brother, having married two sisters, built two small, old-fashioned houses in what was then the best quarter of the town, and linked them by a bridge. Here they founded the newspaper which is still the leading daily.

It would be easy to illustrate this theme further and recall the kind impressions of Boston, Cleveland, Pittsburgh, Philadelphia and a dozen others; but these examples suffice to convey the sense of variety and character which the great cities of America present to a sympathetic and inquiring eye.

For more than thirty years I have been accustomed to address the largest public audiences on all sorts of topics. A lecture tour as such, therefore, had no serious terrors for me. Still, to a stranger in a foreign land, it must always be something of an ordeal to come into the close, direct relationship of speaker and listener night after night, with thousands of men and women whose outlook and traditions are sundered from his own.

But American audiences yield to none in the interest, attention and good nature with which they follow a lengthy considered statement.

These large assemblies always seemed to take particular pleasures in asking questions after my address was over. At every place I encouraged this, and sheaves of written questions were speedily composed and handed up, covering a discursive range of topics. The audiences appeared delighted when some sort of an answer was given immediately to each. Any fair retort, however controversial, was received with the greatest good humor. I remember, for instance, that I was asked: "What do you think of the dole?" I affected to misunderstand the question, and replied: "I presume you are referring to the Veterans' bonus." This gained an immediate success.

The most critical of my audiences was, of course, at Washington. Here one met the leading men of the Union, and the keen society of the political capital, with all its currents of organized, responsible opinion. But the most interesting, and in some ways the most testing, of all my experiences was not on the public platform.

A Washington hostess, in the center of the political world, invited the British Ambassador [Sir Ronald Lindsay] and me to a dinner of some forty or fifty persons. There were gathered many of the most important men and some of the most influential women in the United States. After the dinner was over, the whole company formed a half-circle around me, and then began one of the frankest and most direct political interrogations to which I have ever been subjected. The unspoken, but perfectly well-comprehended condition was that any question, however awkward, might be asked, and that any answer, however pointed, would be taken in good part.

For two hours we wrestled strenuously, unsparingly, but in the best of tempers, with one another, and when I was tired of defending Great Britain on all her misdeeds, I counter-attacked with a series of pretty direct questions of my own. Nothing was shirked on either side—debts, disarmament, naval parity, liquor legislation, the gold standard and the dole were all tackled on the dead level.

Nowhere else in the world, only between our two people, could such a discussion have proceeded. The priceless gift of a common language, and the pervading atmosphere of good sense and fellow feeling, enabled us to rap all the most delicate topics without the slightest offense given or received. It was to me a memorable evening, unique in my experience, and it left in my mind enormous hopes of what will some day happen in the world when, no doubt, after most of us are dead and gone, the English-speaking peoples will really understand each other.

✖✖✖

"WHILE THE WORLD WATCHES PRESIDENT FRANKLIN D. ROOSEVELT"

COLLIER'S
DECEMBER 29, 1934

The life and well-being of every country are influenced by the economic and financial policy of the United States. From the cotton spinners of Lancashire to the ryots of India; from the peasantry of China to the pawnbrokers of Amsterdam; from the millionaire financier watching the ticker tape to the sturdy blacksmith swinging his hammer in the forge; from the monetary philosopher or student to the hard-headed business man or sentimental social reformer—all are consciously or unconsciously affected.

For in truth Roosevelt is an explorer who has embarked on a voyage as uncertain as that of Columbus, and upon a quest which might conceivably be as important as the discovery of the New World. In those old days it was the gulf of oceans with their unknown perils and vicissitudes. Now in the modern world, just as mysterious and forbidding as the stormy waters of the Atlantic, is the gulf between the producer with the limitless powers of science at his command, and the consumer with legitimate appetites which need never be satiated.

Plenty has become a curse. Bountiful harvests are viewed with a dread which in the old times accompanied a barren season. The gift of well-organized leisure which machines should have given to men has only emerged in the hateful spectacle of scores of millions of able and willing workers kicking their heels by closed factories and subsisting upon charity or, as in England, upon systematized relief. Always the peoples are asking themselves: "Why should these things be? Why should not the new powers man has wrested from nature open the portals of a broader life to men and women all over the world?" And with increasing vehemence they demand that the thinkers and pioneers of humanity should answer the riddle and open these new possibilities to their enjoyment.

A single man whom accident, destiny, or Providence has placed at the head of one hundred and twenty millions of active, educated, excitable and harassed people, has set out upon this momentous expedition. Many doubt he will succeed. Some hope he will fail. Although the policies of President Roosevelt are conceived in many respects from a narrow view of American self-interest, the courage, the power and the scale of his effort must enlist the ardent sympathy of every country, and his success could not fail to lift the whole world forward into the sunlight of an easier and more genial age.

There is, therefore, a widespread desire to look at this man in the midst of his adventure. Trained to public affairs, connected with the modern history of the United States by a famous name, at forty-two he was struck down with infantile paralysis. His lower limbs refused their office. Crutches or assistance was needed for the smallest movement from place to place. To ninety-nine men out of a hundred, such an affliction would have terminated all forms of public activity except those of the mind.

He refused to accept this sentence. He fought against it with that same rebellion against commonly adopted conventions which we now see in his policy. He contested elections; he harangued the multitude; he faced the hurly-burly of American politics in a decade when they were exceptionally darkened by all the hideous crimes and corruption of gangsterdom which followed upon prohibition; he beat down opponents in this rough arena; he sought, gained and discharged offices of the utmost labor and of the highest consequence.

THE MAN OF THE HOUR EMERGES

As governor of New York State his administration, whatever its shortcomings, revealed a competent, purposeful personality. He stooped to conquer. He adapted himself to the special conditions and to the humiliations which had long obstructed entry of the best of American manhood into the unsavory world of politics. He subscribed to the Democratic ticket and made himself the mouthpiece of party aims without losing hold upon the larger objectives of American public life.

World events began to move. The Hoover administration could only gape upon the unheard-of problems of depression through glut. The long ascendancy of the Republican régime was clearly drawing to its close. The presidency of the United States awaited a Democratic candidate. Five or six outstanding figures presented themselves, in busy, scheming rivalry.

In the general opinion of many of the shrewdest leaders of his party, Roosevelt was the weakest of these contestants. And there are still those who consider that in hard common sense and genuine statecraft Roosevelt's former leader, Governor Al Smith, was unquestionably the strongest. But Roosevelt pulled his wires and played his cards in such a way that Fortune could befriend him.

Fortune came along, not only as a friend or even as a lover, but as an idolater. There was one moment when his nomination turned upon as little as the spin of a coin. But when it fell there was no doubt whose head was stamped upon it.

He arrived at the summit of the greatest economic community in the world at the moment of its greatest embarrassment. Everybody had lost faith in everything. Credit was frozen. Millions of unemployed without provision filled the streets or wandered despairing about the vast spaces of America. The rotten foundations of the banks were simultaneously undermined and exposed. A universal deadlock gripped the United States. The richest man could not cash the smallest check. People possessing enormous intrinsic assets in every kind of valuable security found themselves for some days without the means to pay a hotel bill or even a taxi fare. We must never forget that this was the basis from which he started: Supreme power in the ruler and a clutching anxiety of scores of millions who demanded and awaited orders.

Since then there has been no lack of orders. Although the dictatorship is veiled by constitutional forms, it is none the less effective. Great things have been done, and greater attempted. To compare Roosevelt's effort with that of Hitler is to insult, not Roosevelt, but civilization. The petty persecutions and Old World assertions of brutality in which the German idol has indulged only show their smallness and squalor compared to the renaissance of creative effort with which the name of Roosevelt will always be associated.

The President's second momentous experiment is an attempt to reduce unemployment by shortening the hours of labor of those who are employed and spreading the labor more evenly through the wage-earning masses. Who can doubt that this is one of the paths which will soon be trodden throughout the world? If it is not to be so, we may well ask what is the use to the working masses of invention and science? Are great discoveries of organization or processes only to mean that fewer laborers will produce more than is required during the same long hours, while an even larger proportion of their mates are flung redundant upon the labor market?

OUR MOST IMPORTANT PROBLEM

If that were so, surely the poor English Luddites of a hundred years ago were right in attempting to break up the new machines. Through the establishment of shorter hours alone the wage-earners can enjoy the blessings of modern mass production; and indeed without shorter hours these blessings are but a curse.

Thus the Roosevelt adventure claims sympathy and admiration from all of those in England and no doubt in foreign countries who are convinced that the fixing of a universal measure of value not based upon the rarity or abundance of any commodity but conforming to the advancing powers of mankind, is the supreme achievement which at this time lies before the intellect of man. But very considerable misgivings must necessarily arise when an expedition to attack the monetary problem becomes intermingled with, and hampered by, the elaborate processes of social reform and the struggles of class warfare.

In Great Britain we know a lot about trade unions. It is now nearly a century since they began to play a part in our life. It is half a century since Lord Beaconsfield, a Conservative Prime Minister at the head of an aristocratic and bourgeois Parliament, accorded them exceptional favor before the law and protected them from being sued in their corporate capacity. We have dwelt with British trade unionism ever since. It has been a keenly felt impediment upon our productive and competitive power. It has become the main foundation of a socialist political party which has ruled the state greatly to its disadvantage, and will assuredly do so again. It reached a climax in a general strike, which, if it had been successful, would have subverted the Parliamentary constitution of our island.

But when all is said and done, there are very few well-informed persons in Great Britain, and not many employers of labor on a large scale, who would not sooner have to deal with the British trade unions as we know them, than with the wild vagaries of communist-agitated and totally unorganized labor discontent.

THE RESPONSIBILITY OF UNIONISM

The trade unions have been a stable force in the industrial development of Britain in the last fifty years. They have brought steadily to the front the point of view of the toiler and the urgent requirements of his cottage home, and have made these vital matters imprint themselves upon the laws and the customs of our country. They have been a steadying force which has counterbalanced and corrected the reckless extravagances of the Red intelligentsia. Over and over again in thirty years, we have heard employers say: "We might easily go further than the trade union leaders and fare a good deal worse"; and in the Great War, the sturdy patriotism of the trade unionist and the masculine common sense of their officials gave us an invaluable and, as it proved, unbreakable basis upon which to carry forward the struggle for national self-preservation.

But when one sees an attempt made within the space of a few months to lift American trade unionism by great heaves and bounds to the position so slowly grown up—and even then with much pain and loss—in Great Britain, we cannot help feeling grave doubts. One wonders whether the struggle of American industrial life, its richness and fertility, its vivid possibilities to brains and brawn, to handicraft and industry—the whole spread over so vast a continent with such sharp contrasts in conditions and climate—may not result in a very general crippling of that enterprise and flexibility upon which not only the wealth but the happiness of modern communities depends.

One wonders whether the rigid and hitherto comparatively modest structure of American trade unionism will be capable of bearing the immense responsibilities for national well-being and for the production of necessaries of all kinds for the people of the United States which the power now given to them implies. If anything like a beer racket or any other racket broke in upon the responsible leaders of American trade unions, the American democracy might easily wander in a very uncomfortable wilderness for ten or twenty years.

Our trade unions have grown to manhood and power amid an

enormous company of counterchecks and consequential corrections. But to raise American trade unionism from its previous condition to industrial sovereignty by a few sweeping decrees may easily confront both the trade unions and the United States with problems which for the time being will be at once paralyzing and unsolvable.

A second danger to President Roosevelt's valiant and heroic experiments seems to arise from the mood to hunt down rich men as if they were noxious beasts. It is a very attractive sport, and once it gets started quite a lot of people everywhere are found ready to join in the chase. Moreover, the quarry is at once swift and crafty and, therefore, elusive. The pursuit is long and exciting and everyone's blood is roused by its ardor. The question arises whether the general well-being of the masses of the community will be advanced by an excessive indulgence in this amusement.

THE VALUE OF MILLIONAIRES

The millionaire or multi-millionaire is a highly economical animal. He sucks up with sponge-like efficiency money from all quarters. In this process, far from depriving ordinary people of their earnings, he launches enterprise and carries it through—raises values and expands that credit without which on a vast scale no fuller economic life can be opened to the millions. To hunt wealth is not to capture commonwealth.

This money-gathering, credit-producing animal can not only walk—he can run. And when frightened he can fly. If his wings are clipped, he can dive or crawl. When in the end he is hunted down, what is left but a very ordinary individual apologizing volubly for his mistakes, and particularly for not having been able to get away?

But meanwhile, great propositions have crumbled to the ground. Confidence is shaken and enterprises chilled and the unemployed queue up at the soup-kitchens or march out upon the public works with ever-growing expense to the taxpayer and nothing more appetizing to take home to their families than the leg or the wing of what was once a millionaire.

One quite sees that people who have got interested in this fight will not accept such arguments against their sport. What they will have to accept is the consequences of ignoring such arguments. It is indispensable to the wealth of nations and to the wage and life standards of labor that capital and credit should be honored and cherished partners in the economic system.

If this is rejected there is always, of course, the Russian alternative. But no one can suppose that the self-reliant population of the United States which cut down the forests and plowed up the soil and laced the continent with railroads and carried wealth-getting and wealth-diffusing to a higher point than has ever before been reached by mankind, would be content for a week with the dull, brutish servitude of Russia.

PROFITS ARE ESSENTIAL

It was a prudent instinct that led Mr. Roosevelt to discard those attempts at legal price-fixing which have so often been made in Old World countries and have always, except in time of war or in very circumscribed localities, broken down in practice. Such measures are appropriate to break monopolies or rings, but can never be accepted as a humdrum foundation for economic life. There can never be good wages or good employment for any length of time without good profits, and the sooner this is recognized, the sooner the corner will be turned.

Writing as a former Chancellor of the British Exchequer for nearly five years, I find myself very much astonished by a law recently passed in the United States that all returns of income for the purposes of taxation may be made public.

Such a rule would seem highly obstructive to commercial revival as well as being—though this is minor—objectionable in the sphere of personal relations. In Great Britain we plume ourselves on collecting effectually the largest possible revenues from wealth upon as high a scheme of graduated taxation as will not defeat its own purpose. Our income and super-tax payers have frequently been paid tributes by foreign observers for the thoroughness and punctuality with which they meet their dues. Even our own Socialist ministers have testified to this. But it has always been accepted that the relations of the taxpayer, rich or poor, are with the state and the state alone, and that neither his employees nor his trade rivals, neither his neighbor nor his creditors, neither his enemies nor his friends, should know what has passed between him and the Treasury.

To ask a trader or manufacturer engaged in productive enterprise, with all the hazards attendant thereupon, to reveal not only to the collectors of the public revenue but to all and sundry his income for the year, must be an impediment to national business almost measureless in its irritation and in its mischief. It seems to me to be only another variant of that hideous folly of prohibition.

LEAKY BOAT OR NEW RAFT

No one could write in this way without at the same time feeling the justification there is for the anger of the American public against many of their great leaders of finance. The revelations and exposures which have flowed in a widening stream, and even flood, during the last four years, have laid many prominent persons open to prejudice and public censure, apart altogther from the law. The passionate desire of the struggling wage-earner with a family at home and many applicants for his job is for clean hands in the higher ranks and for a square deal even if it be only a raw deal.

A thousand speeches could be made on this. The important question is whether American democracy can clear up scandals and punish improprieties without losing its head, and without injuring the vital impulses of economic enterprise and organization. It is no use marching up against ordinary private business men, working on small margins, as if they were the officials of government departments, who so long as they have attended at their offices from ten to four in a respectable condition have done their job. There are elements of contrivance, of housekeeping, and of taking risks which are essential to all profitable activity. If these are destroyed the capitalist system fails, and some other system must be substituted.

No doubt the capitalist system is replete with abuses and errors and inequities, like everything else in our imperfect human life; but it was under it that only a few years ago the United States produced the greatest prosperity for the greatest numbers that has ever been experienced in human record. It is not illogical to say: "Rather than condone these faults and these abuses we will sweep this system away, no matter what it costs in our material well-being. We will replace it by the only other system which enables large organizations and developments to be undertaken—namely, nationalization of all the means of production, distribution, credit and exchange." It is, however, irrational to tear down or cripple the capitalist system without having the fortitude of spirit and ruthlessness of action to create a new Communist system.

There, it seems to foreign observers, lies the big choice of the United States at the present time. If the capitalist system is to continue with its rights of private property, with its pillars of rents, interest and profit, and the sanctity of contracts recognized and enforced by the state, then it must be given a fair chance. It is the same for us in the Old World. If we are to continue in the old leaky lifeboat amid these stormy seas, we must do our best to keep it bailed, to keep it afloat and to steer for port. If we decide to take to the rafts of a new system, there, also, we are vociferously assured there is a chance of making land. But the Siberian coast is rugged and bleak, and there are long, cruel frosts in the Arctic Ocean.

It is a very open question, which any household may argue to the small hours, whether it is better to have equality at the price of poverty, or well-being at the price of inequality. Life will be pretty rough anyhow. Whether we are ruled by tyrannical bureaucrats or self-seeking capitalists, the ordinary man who has to earn his living, and tries to make provision for old age and for his dear ones when his powers are exhausted, will have a hard pilgrimage through this dusty world. The United States was built upon property, liberty and enterprise, and certainly it has afforded the most spacious and ample life to the scores of millions that has ever yet been witnessed. To make an irrevocable departure into Asiatic conceptions would be a serious step, and should be measured with fearless eye at the outset.

PROPHECY IS CHEAP

We must then hope that neither the tangles of the NRA nor the vague, ethereal illusions of sentimentalists or doctrinaires will prevent President Roosevelt from testing and plumbing the secrets of the monetary problem. If he succeeds, all the world will be his debtor; if he fails, he will at any rate have made an experiment for mankind on a scale which only the immense strength of the United States could sustain. It would be a thousand pities if this tremendous effort by the richest nation in the world to expand consciously and swiftly the bounds of the consuming power should be vitiated by being mixed up with an ordinary radical program and a commonplace class fight. If failure there be, which God forfend, it will be taken for a generation as proof positive that all efforts to procure prosperity by currency and credit inflation are doomed to failure.

But the President has need to be on his guard. To a foreign eye it seems that forces are getting under his shield which at a certain stage may thrust him into the background and take the lead themselves. If that misfortune were to occur, we should see the not unfamiliar spectacle of a leader running after his followers to pull them back. It is to be hoped, and indeed believed, that the strong common sense, the sturdy individualism and the cold, disillusioned intelligence of the American people will protect their leader from such inglorious experiences.

Will he succeed or will he fail? That is not the question we set ourselves, and to prophesy is cheap. But succeed or fail, his impulse is one which makes toward the fuller life of the masses of the people in every land, and which as it glows the brighter, may well eclipse both the lurid flames of German Nordic national self-assertion and the baleful unnatural lights which are diffused from Soviet Russia.

❊❊❊

"WHAT GOOD'S A CONSTITUTION?"

COLLIER'S
AUGUST 22, 1936

No one can think clearly or sensibly about this vast and burning topic without in the first instance making up his mind upon the fundamental issue. Does he value the State above the citizen, or the citizen above the State? Does a government exist for the individual, or do individuals exist for the government? One must recognize that the world today is deeply divided upon this. Some of the most powerful nations and races have definitely chosen to subordinate the citizen or subject to the life of the State. In Russia, Germany and Italy we have this somber, tremendous decision, expressed in varying forms. All nations agree that in time of war, where the life and independence of the country are at stake, every man and woman must be ready to work and, if need be, die in defense of these supreme objects; and that the government must be empowered to call upon them to any extent.

But what we are now considering is the existence of this principle in times of peace and its erection into a permanent system to which the life of great communities must be made to conform. The argument is used that economic crises are only another form of war, and as they are always with us, or can always be alleged to be with with us, it is claimed that we must live our lives in a perpetual state of war, only without actual shooting, bayoneting or cannonading.

This is, of course, the Socialist view. As long as Socialists present themselves in an international guise as creators of a new world order, like the beehive or the ant heap, with a new human heart to fit these novel conceptions, they could easily be beaten, and have been very effectively beaten both by argument and by nature. But when new forms of socialism arose which were grafted not upon world ideas but upon the strongest forms of nationalism, their success was remarkable.

In Germany, for instance, the alliance between national patriotism, tradition and pride on the one hand, and discontent about the inequalities of wealth on the other, made the Weimar Constitution "a scrap of paper." Either of these two fierce, turbulent torrents separately might have been kept within bounds. Joined together in a fierce confluence, they proved irresistible.

Once the rulers of a country can create a war atmosphere in time of peace, can allege that the State is in danger and appeal to all the noblest national instincts, as well as all the basest, it is only in very solidly established countries that the rights of the citizens can be preserved. In Germany these rights vanished almost overnight. Today no one may criticize the dictatorship, either in speech or writing. Voters still go to the polls—in fact, are herded to the polls like sheep—but the method of election has become a fantastic travesty of popular government. A German can vote for the regime, but not against it. If he attempts to indicate disapproval, his ballot paper is reckoned as "spoiled."

The tyranny of the ruling junta extends into every department of life. Friends may not greet each other without invoking the name of Hitler. At least on certain days, the very meals that a family eats in the privacy of its home are regulated by decree. The shadow of an all-powerful State falls between parent and child, husband and wife. Love itself is fettered and confined. No marriage, no love relation of any kind is permitted which offends against a narrow and arbitrary code based upon virulent race prejudice.

Nor is this all. Even in the sphere of religion the State must intervene. It comes between the priest and his penitent, between the worshiper and the God to whom he prays. And this last, by one of the curious ironies of history, in the land of Luther.

To rivet this intolerable yoke upon the necks of the German people, all the resources of propaganda have been utilized to magnify the sense of a crisis and to exhibit sometimes France, sometimes Poland, sometimes Lithuania, always the Soviets and the Jews as antagonists at whom the patriotic Teuton must grind his teeth.

Much the same thing has happened in Russia. The powerful aid of national sentiment and imperialist aspirations has been invoked to buttress a decaying Communism.

TESTS FOR CIVILIZATION

In the United States, also, economic crisis has led to an extension of the activities of the Executive and to the pillorying, by irresponsible agitators, of certain groups and sections of the population as enemies of the rest. There have been efforts to exalt the power of the central government and to limit the rights of individuals. It has been sought to mobilize behind this reversal of the American tradition, at once the selfishness of the pensioners, or would-be pensioners, of Washington, and the patriotism of all who wish to see their country prosperous once more.

It is when passions and cupidities are thus unleashed and, at the same time, the sense of public duty rides high in the hearts of all men and women of good will, that the handcuffs can be slipped upon the citizens and they can be brought into entire subjugation to the executive government. Then they are led to believe that, if they will only yield themselves, body, mind and soul, to the State, and obey unquestioningly its injunctions, some dazzling future of riches and power will open to them, either—as in Italy—by the conquest of the territories of others, or—as in America—by a further liberation and exploitation of the national resources.

I take the opposite view. I hold that governments are meant to be, and must remain, the servants of the citizens; that states and federations only come into existence and can only be justified by preserving the "life, liberty and the pursuit of happiness" in the homes and families of individuals. The true right and power rest in the individual. He gives of his right and power to the State, expecting and requiring thereby in return to receive certain advantages and guarantees. I do not admit that an economic crisis can ever truly be compared with the kind of struggle for existence by races constantly under primordial conditions. I do not think that modern nations in time of peace ought to regard themselves as if they were the inhabitants of besieged cities, liable to be put to the sword or led into slavery if they cannot make good their defense.

One of the greatest reasons for avoiding war is that it is destructive to liberty. But we must not be led into adopting for ourselves the evils of war in time of peace upon any pretext whatever. The word "civilization" means not only peace by the nonregimentation of the people such as is required in war. Civilization means that officials and authorities, whether uniformed or not, whether armed or not, are made to realize that they are servants and not masters.

Socialism or overweening State life, whether in peace or war, is only sharing miseries and not blessings. Every self-respecting citizen in every country must be on his guard lest the rulers demand of him in time of peace sacrifices only tolerable in a period of war for national self-preservation.

I judge the civilization of any community by simple tests. What is the degree of freedom possessed by the citizen or subject? Can he think, speak and act freely under well-established, well-known laws? Can he criticize the executive government? Can he sue the State if it has infringed his rights? Are there also great processes for changing the law to meet new conditions?

Judging by these standards, Great Britain and the United States can claim to be in the forefront of civilized communities. But we owe this only in part to the good sense and watchfulness of our citizens. In both our countries the character of the judiciary is a vital factor in the maintenance of the rights and liberties of the individual citizen.

Our judges extend impartially to all men protection, not only against wrongs committed by private persons, but also against the arbitrary acts of public authority. The independence of the courts is, to all of us, the guarantee of freedom and the equal rule of law.

It must, therefore, be the first concern of the citizens of a free country to preserve and maintain the independence of the courts of justice, however inconvenient that independence may be, on occasion, to the government of the day.

But all this implies peace conditions, an atmosphere of civilization rather than militarization or officialization. It implies a balance and equipoise of society which can be altered only gradually. It is so hard to build the structure of a vast economic community, and so easy to upset it and throw it into confusion. The onus must lie always upon those who propose a change, and the process of change is hardly ever beneficial unless it considers what is due to the past as well as what is claimed for the future.

BULWARK OR FETTER?

It is for these reasons among many others that the founders of the American Republic in their Declaration of Independence inculcate as a duty binding upon all worthy sons of America "a frequent recurrence to first principles." Do not let us too readily brush aside the grand simple affirmations of the past. All wisdom is not new wisdom. Let us never forget that the glory of the nineteenth century was founded upon what seemed to be the successful putting down of those twin curses, anarchy and tyranny.

The question we are discussing is whether a fixed constitution is a bulwark or a fetter. From what I have written it is plain that I incline to the side of those who would regard it as a bulwark, and that I rank the citizen higher than the State, and regard the State as useful only in so far as it preserves his inherent rights. All forms of tyranny are odious. It makes very little difference to the citizen, father of a family, head of a household, whether tyranny comes from a royal or imperial despot, or from a Pope or Inquisitor, or from a military caste, or from an aristocratic or plutocratic oligarchy, or from a ring of employers, or a trade union, or a party caucus—or worst of all, from a terrified and infuriated mob. "A man's a man for a' that." The whole point is, whether he can make head against oppression in any of its Protean shapes, and defend the island of his home, his life and soul. And here is the point at which we may consider and contrast the constitutions of our respective countries.

It is very difficult for us in England to realize the kind of deadlock which has been reached in the United States. Imagine, for instance, the gigantic India Bill, passed through Parliament and for two or three years in active operation throughout the whole of India, suddenly being declared illegal by the law lords sitting as a tribunal. Imagine—to take an instance nearer home—some gigantic measure of insurance as big as our widows' pensions, health and employment insurance rolled together, which had deeply interwoven itself in the whole life of the people, upon which every kind of contract and business arrangement had been based, being declared to have no validity by a court of law. We simply cannot conceive it. Yet something very like that has occurred on your side of the Atlantic.

A FAITH JUSTIFIED

In our country an act of Parliament which, upon the advice of the ministers responsible for it, has received the royal assent is the law of the land. Its authority cannot be questioned by any court. There is no limit to the powers of Crown and Parliament. Even the gravest changes in our Constitution can in theory be carried out by simple majority votes in both Houses and the consequential assent of the Crown.

But we now watch the workings of a written Constitution enforced by a Supreme Court according to the letter of the law, under which anyone may bring a test case challenging not merely the interpretation of a law, but the law itself, and if the Court decides for the appellant, be he only an owner of a few chickens, the whole action of the Legislature and the Executive becomes to that extent null and void. We know that to modify the Constitution even in the smallest particular requires a two-thirds majority of the sovereign states forming the American Union. And this has been achieved, after prodigious struggles, on only a score of occasions during the whole history of the United States.

American citizens or jurists, in their turn, gaze with wonder at our great British democracy expressing itself with plenary powers through a Government and a Parliament controlled only by the fluctuating currents of public opinion. British Governments live from day to day only upon the approval of the House of Commons. There is no divorce between the Executive and the Legislature. The ministers, new or old, must be chosen from men and parties which in the aggregate will command a majority in the House of Commons. Parliament can, if it chooses, even prolong its own life beyond the statutory limit. Ministers may at any time advise the King to a sudden dissolution. Yet all classes and all parties have a deep, underlying conviction that these vast, flexible powers will not be abused, that the spirit of our unwritten Constitution will be respected at every stage.

To understand how this faith is justified, how the British people are able to enjoy a real stability of government without a written Constitution, it is necessary to consider the beginnings of party politics in Britain. Whigs and Tories were almost equally concerned to assert the authority of Parliament as a check upon the Executive. With the Whigs this was a matter of fundamental principle; with the Tories it was a question of expediency. James II was a Catholic and his efforts to further the cause of his co-religionists alienated the great bulk of the Tory party, who were loyal to the Church of England. Then, from the advent of William of Orange to the accession of George III with a brief interval in the reign of Queen Anne, the Crown could do nothing without the Whigs and the government of the country was predominantly or exclusively in the hands of that party.

The Tories were thus vitally interested in preserving and extending the rights of the parliamentary opposition. In this way a jealous care for constitutional rights came to mark both the great parties of the State. And as to all men the Constitution represented security and freedom, none would consent willingly to any breach of it, even to gain a temporary advantage.

Modern times offer respect for law and constitutional usage. Nothing contributed so much to the collapse of the general strike ten years ago as the declaration by great lawyers that it was illegal. And the right of freedom of speech and publication is extended, under the Constitution, to those who in theory seek to overthrow established institutions by force of arms so long as they do not commit any illegal act.

CAN IT HAPPEN HERE?

Another factor making for stability is our permanent civil service. Governments come and go; parliamentary majorities fluctuate; but the civil servants remain. To new and inexperienced ministers they are "guides, philosophers and friends." Themselves untouched by the vicissitudes of party fortunes, they impart to the business of administration a real continuity.

On the whole, too, popular opinion acts as a guardian of the unwritten Constitution. Public chastisement would speedily overtake any minister, however powerful, who fell below the accepted standards of fair play or who descended to trickwork or dodgery.

When one considers the immense size of the United States and the extraordinary contrasts of climate and character which differentiate the forty-eight sovereign states of the American Union, as well as the inevitable conflict of interests between North and South and between East and West, it would seem that the participants of so vast a federation have the right to effectual guarantees upon the fundamental laws, and that these should not be easily changed to suit a particular emergency or fraction of the country.

The founders of the Union, although its corpus was then so much smaller, realized this with profound conviction. They did not think it possible to entrust legislation for so diverse a community and enormous an area to a simple majority. They were as well acquainted with the follies and intolerance of parliaments as with the oppression of princes. "To control the powers and conduct of the legislature," said a leading member of the Convention of 1787, "by an overruling constitution was an improvement in the science and practice of government reserved to the American States."

All the great names of American history can be invoked behind this principle. Why should it be considered obsolete? If today we are framing that constitution for a "United States of Europe" for which so many thinkers on this side of the ocean aspire, fixed and almost unalterable guarantees would be required by the acceding nations.

It may well be that this very quality of rigidity, which is today thought to be so galling, has been a prime factor in founding the greatness of the United States. In the shelter of the Constitution nature has been conquered, a mighty continent has been brought under the sway of man, and an economic entity established, unrivaled in the whole history of the globe.

In this small island of Britain we make laws for ourselves. But if we had again attempted to apply this flexibility and freedom to the British Empire, and to frame an Imperial Constitution to make laws for the whole body, it would have been broken to pieces. Although we have a free, flexible Constitution at the center and for the center of the Empire, nothing is more rigid than the established practice—namely, that we claim no powers to interfere with the affairs of its self-governing component parts. No supreme court is needed to enforce this rule. We have learned the lessons of the past too well.

And here we must note a dangerous misuse of terminology. "Taking the rigidity out of the American Constitution" means, and is intended to mean, new gigantic accessions of power to the dominating center of government and giving it the means to make new fundamental laws enforceable upon all American citizens.

Such a departure in the British Empire by a chance parliamentary majority, or even by aggregate Dominion parliamentary majorities, would shatter it to bits. The so-called "rigidity" of the American Constitution is in fact the guarantee of freedom to its widespread component parts. That a set of persons, however eminent, carried into office upon some populist heave should have the power to make the will of a bare majority effective over the whole of the United States might cause disasters upon the greatest scale from which recovery would not be swift or easy.

I was reading the other day a recent American novel by Sinclair Lewis—*It Can't Happen Here*. Such books render a public service to the English-speaking world. When we see what has happened in

Germany, Italy and Russia we cannot neglect their warning. This is an age in which the citizen requires more, and not less, legal protection in the exercise of his rights and liberties.

THE CONSTITUTION MUST WORK

That is doubtless why, after all the complaints against the rigidity of the United States Constitution and the threats of a presidential election on this issue, none of the suggested constitutional amendments has so far been adopted by the Administration. This may explain why the "Nine Old Men" of the Supreme Court have not been more seriously challenged. But the challenge may come at a later date, though it would perhaps be wiser to dissociate it from any question of the age of the judges, lest it be the liberal element in the court which is weakened.

Now, at the end of these reflections, I must strike a minor and different note. The rigidity of the Constitution of the United States is the shield of the common man. But that rigidity ought not to be interpreted by pedants. In England we continually give new interpretation to the archaic language of our fundamental institutions, and this is no new thing in the United States. The judiciary have obligations which go beyond expounding the mere letter of the law. The Constitution must be made to work.

A true interpretation, however, of the British or the American Constitution is certainly not a chop-logic or pedantic interpretation. So august a body as the Supreme Court in dealing with law must also deal with the life of the United States, and words, however solemn, are only true when they preserve their vital relationship to facts. It would certainly be a great disaster, not only to the American Republic but to the whole world, if a violent collision should take place between the large majority of the American people and the great instrument of government which has so long presided over their expanding fortunes.

"THE UNION OF THE ENGLISH-SPEAKING PEOPLES"

NEWS OF THE WORLD
MAY 15, 1938

It is a relief to turn from the quarrels and jealousies of distracted Europe to contemplate the majestic edifice of Anglo-American friendship.

But let us not deceive ourselves. Look more closely. In places the facing stone has been eaten away by acids in the atmosphere. There are cracks in the pillars that support the mighty dome.

Pierce to the foundations. Beneath a crust that sometimes seems all too thin are bitter waters of suspicion, a marsh of misunderstanding.

No one is really afraid that the building will collapse. Something stronger than any masonry holds it together—a cement of the spirit.

But it would be well to strengthen the foundations; to grout and bind and buttress till the great structure is indeed secure.

We can best serve the cause of Anglo-American friendship if we understand clearly the factors that threaten and diminish it.

And to do that we much examine the past as well as the present. As a nation, we have short memories. We fight and forget. But others remember.

The founders of America fled from Britain to escape persecution. Tyranny—or what can be more disastrous than tyranny, a purblind, pettifogging legalism—pursued them across the Atlantic.

Taxed by men they had never seen, sitting in a Parliament in whose deliberations they had no voice, the descendants of the Pilgrim Fathers and the Virginian Cavaliers raised, together, the standard of revolt.

But we forget—and America remembers—that the first shots

in the War of Independence were fired by British troops—"unmolested and unprovoked," says the contemporary Massachusetts "Spy"—on men who offered no resistance.

The long war, in which German mercenaries were lavishly, if unsuccessfully, employed, was ended by a grudging peace. Suspicion and bitterness remained.

France beheaded a King—and crowned an Emperor whose armies trampled the map of Europe. At death-grips with Napoleon, Britain blockaded the coast of the United States, seized American ships, and pressed American sailors into service on her men-o'-war.

The resulting war of 1814 to 1815 was to Britain only a vexatious diversion.

But it was a life-and-death struggle to the United States, and its incidents left an indelible impress on the American mind.

Indian tribes, fighting as allies of England, killed and ravaged. Fort Dearborn, on the site where Chicago now stands, was stormed by painted savages and the entire garrison massacred. Women and children were murdered.

A British fleet sailed up the Potomac to Washington, burned the Capitol and the Government offices and the President's house.

NEARLY BLUNDERED INTO CONFLICT

It is doubtful if one in ten thousand of our population has ever heard of that raid of reprisals.

But we should remember—vividly—for centuries after the event, if London were, even for a day, in the hands of an American force that destroyed Buckingham Palace, the Houses of Parliament, Whitehall and Downing-street.

True, we should also remember the strong ties of blood and race that bound the Americans and ourselves. But might not these make the injury all the worse?

In the American Civil War, again, it seemed to the North that we thought more of cotton than of principles.

A majority of Englishmen, including Mr. Gladsone, believed that it was impossible to maintain the Union by force of arms, and were prepared—at any rate at one point in the struggle—to recognise the Confederate States.

There was a moment when Britain and America almost blundered into war which would inevitably have established the independence of the South and perpetuated the shame of slavery.

From Past to Present
FORGET THE HISTORY STAINED WITH BLOOD

During the early stages of the Great War, many awkward incidents arose from differing interpretations of neutral rights. But for the U-boat campaign and its atrocities, the blockade of Germany might have led to a grave crisis in Anglo-American relations.

In the long series of quarrels and disputes, Britain was not always in the wrong, nor America always in the right. Usually, at the root of our differences there was the clash of incompatible rights, or sheer misunderstanding.

We have done terrible things to each other through misunderstanding. Odious chapters of our common history are stained with blood and the hatreds that are fed by blood.

Wrongs, revenges, insults, calumnies, battles and executions crowd the pages, with noble, suffering, or conquering figures silhouetted against the dull red haze.

To us, however, these conflicts have, as a rule, been side issues. That has helped us to forget. And sometimes we have wanted to forget because we were ashamed.

But America was concerned more vitally, and some of the most glorious episodes of her history are bound up with these tragic happenings. So Americans have a double reason to remember.

The cheers of vanished armies, the rumbling of long-silenced cannonades, still come down to them to-day.

Turn from those old unhappy events to our present situation.

Although the ideals of the two countries are similar, their interests in some respects diverge. Their industries are competitive in the world market.

Every instinct of America is to keep out of European affairs; Britain cannot do so even if she wished.

THAT PERPLEXING WAR DEBT

The question of the War Debt rankles. In the eyes of the great bulk of the American people, war debts are on exactly the same footing as private or commercial indebtedness.

They cannot understand the difficulties in the way of payment, or the strain which it would put on the delicate machinery of international exchange.

To them, given the ability and the willingness to meet an obligation, there is no difference between payment across the exchange and across the ocean, and payment across the counter.

They have no doubt about our ability to pay. Why should they? They contrast our balanced Budget with the chaos of their own national finances.

So they brand Britain as a defaulter—a dishonest debtor.

Yet the fact is that, apart from shipments of gold (which is not available in sufficient quantity and, in any case, is not wanted), there are only two ways in which we can discharge our debt.

One is by selling more goods and services to the United States.

But America cannot receive these without injury to her own nationals. That method, therefore, is ruled out by the Americans' decision.

The second way is to reduce our purchases from the United States and to tax such commodities—cotton, for instance—as we must buy and America must sell, to create dollar credits from which debt payments might be made.

Such a process would be equally injurious to both countries, and it could not fail to raise an increasing friction between them.

Yet while this ugly and irritating business of the War Debt remains in suspense it is a real barrier to Anglo-American friendship.

A COUNTRY OF COSMOPOLITANS

We must also remember that for over a century America has attracted immigrants not only from Britain, but from all Europe.

There is a great German population in the Middle West. Swedes and Italians are to be found everywhere. Of every hundred American citizens nine are negroes. Practically every nation on earth has contributed its quota to this vast melting-pot.

These foreign elements may learn to speak English, but will they think English thoughts?

Though those of European stock may be fused into the nation of their adoption and become "hundred per cent. Americans," it can only be by processes which tend to separate the American mind from ours.

Another factor—though, happily, fading—must be taken into account: the powerful and highly organised Irish-American community.

They have taken with them across the ocean a burning and deep-rooted hatred of the English name. They are irreconcilable enemies of the British Empire.

When we talk of collaboration between the two great branches of the English-speaking peoples and of Anglo-American friendship, these are facts which we must face.

Otherwise we shall merely be repeating our wishes in the form of platitudes.

Yet, when all has been urged and weighed, it still remains true that the conceptions which unite us are incomparably stronger than those that divide; that they are vital, not morbid; that they embrace the future rather than the past.

The mischances of history have riven and sundered us, but our roots lie deep in the same rich soil.

The great Republic of the West, no less than the British Empire, sprang from the loins of Shakespeare's England.

The beginnings of American history are to be found, not across the Atlantic, but where the Thames flows between green lawns and woodlands down to a grey sea.

Britain and America are joint sharers in a great inheritance of law and letters. Our political institutions, under the mask of outward difference, bear the marks of a common origin and a common aim.

We are both democracies—and to-day our countries are, with

France, the last great strongholds of Parliamentary government and individual liberty.

It is the English-speaking nations who, almost alone, keep alight the torch of Freedom.

These things are a powerful incentive to collaboration.

With nations, as with individuals, if you care deeply for the same things, and these things are threatened, it is natural to work together to preserve them.

This Is Our Bond
WORDS CANNOT BE EFFACED BY TIME.

The greatest tie of all is *language*. There is nothing like that.

Ancient alliances, solemn treaties, faithful services given and re-paid, important mutual interests—not all these taken together are equal, or nearly equal, to the bond of a common tongue.

Words are the only things that last for ever.

The most tremendous monuments or prodigies of engineering crumble under the hand of Time.

The Pyramids moulder, the bridges rust, the canals fill up, grass covers the railway track; but words spoken two or three thousand years ago remain with us now, not as mere relics of the past, but with all their pristine vital force.

Leaping across the gulf of Time, they light the world for us to-day.

It is this power of words—words written in the past; words spoken at this moment; words printed in the newspapers; words sent speeding through the ether in a Transatlantic broadcast; the flashing interchange of thought—that is our principal agency of union.

Its work must continue indefinitely—will continue, indeed, on an ever larger scale.

With every new school that is opened, with every book that is printed, with every improvement in travel, with every film, with every record, identity of language gathers greater power and ap-plies its processes more often to more people.

COMMON OUTLOOK AND PURPOSE

Of course, there is the other side. There is always the other side. A common language may become a vehicle of quarrel.

I remember that sometimes trouble arose in France between British and American soldiers that would not have arisen had one party been French or Italian.

But such troubles blow over. They are, no doubt, to be expected after so many generations of misunderstanding.

But as British and American troops stood in the line together, shoulder to shoulder in a common cause, the bitterness gradually melted away.

So far as these men were concerned the sponge was drawn across the scores of the past.

It is for us to see that this great level of a common language is rightly used. We must employ it to explore and, so far as possible, compose the differences between us, and to bring to the surface our underlying identity of outlook and purpose.

Above all, we must use it to understand each other.

We, on this side of the Atlantic, know too little of American history. Not only are we ignorant of the full extent of our past quarrels with the United States, but we have only the most superficial comprehension of that great Westward drive which carried civilisation across a Continent.

We have heard of Buffalo Bill. Thanks to "The Plainsman" we have now been introduced to Wild Bill Hickock. But we see the story through a reducing-glass.

The Odyssey of a people has been an individual adventure; the epic has been dwarfed to the proportions of a fairy-tale.

We talk glibly of the Monroe Doctrine. How many of us understand it?

How many of us realise when we criticise America as selfishly holding aloof from the League of Nations, that for over a hundred years the United States has been the guarantor of the whole of the Western Hemisphere against aggression from without?

Such is the practical effect of the Monroe Doctrine.

LET THE CHILDREN BE TOLD

I should like to see American history taught in our schools concurrently with our own Island story. It might help to correct the popular idea of the United States as a land of money-grubbers and multiple divorces.

But that conception should also be assailed directly. No doubt there is a certain excuse for it. It is easier to secure a divorce in certain American States than it is here.

But the American divorce law is merely the logical development of ideas held nearly 400 years ago by the first Protestant Archbishop of Canterbury and, in the 17th century, by the English Puritans.

Divorce, however, may be available for those who desire it without affecting the permanence of marriage.

For the vast majority of Americans, as for the vast majority of British people, marriage is a contract for life, a partnership which only death dissolves.

The charge of money-grubbing arises directly from the needs and circumstances of a dynamically expanding society. The great tasks which Americans have set themselves for a century have been in the economic field.

Washington, Hamilton, Jefferson, Jackson, Adams, and Marshall—these men, soldiers, statesmen, lawyers, made a nation. They fashioned the instruments of government and established the broad lines on which American politics were to develop.

But when they leave the stage, the searchlight of history wheels —save for the years of the Civil War—to the struggle to subdue and utilise a Continent.

BUSINESS BEFORE POLITICS

That struggle has necessarily and rightly taken the first place in the life of the American people.

So business to the American is more than the means of earning a living or making a fortune; it is that career of interest, ambition, possibly even glory, which in the older world is afforded by the learned professions and State services, military and civilian.

A young American, wishing to play a worthy part in the control of affairs, directs himself instinctively towards the managing of factories, railroads, banks, stores, or some other of the thousand-and-one varieties of industrial or commercial enterprise.

Practically all the prizes of American life are to be gained in business.

There, too, is the main path of useful service to the nation.

Nearly all that is best and most active in the manhood and ability of the United States goes into business with the same sense of serving the country as a son of an old family in England might enter Parliament.

It is this concentration of American talent on business that has gained for the United States the title, *The Land of the Dollar.*

But for the best type of Americans, dollars have been a by-product in business activity rather than its main aim.

On the other hand, dollars have played too great a part in American politics, left, as they have been, very largely to men of inferior moral and intellectual calibre.

It is as a result of this that to-day, when the phase of intensive economic expansion is over, the flower of American manhood still regards the political scene with suspicion and distaste.

We, in this country, must try to understand these things, just as we must seek to correct American misconceptions of England.

Some of these, however, are already being corrected by pressures arising from the slump. Americans have learned by bitter experience that to provide for the casualties of civilisation by means of social insurance is not necessarily the sign of an effete society.

Politics and Business
WE HAVE SOMETHING TO LEARN FROM EACH OTHER.

They are being forced in this matter to follow the pathways we have opened. There are, indeed, many ways in which both countries might, with advantage, learn from each other.

For instance, Americans ought to pay more attention to their politics and we to our business.

The process has begun. There is a new sense of reality in American politics. And in current political controversies there are frequent appeals to English examples.

We, on our side, are studying American business organisation. And the conception of business as a form of public service is taking root strongly among us.

It is encouraging also that so many American books are being read in England and so many English books in America. The literature of a nation is the best interpreter of its spirit.

Reading each other's books, we come to appreciate more clearly our fundamental kinship, and to see our differences in truer perspective.

The best British and American films carry this work of mutual illumination a stage farther.

BY LECTURE AND TRAVEL

But direct personal contact is still of the first importance. We cannot dispense with it.

British lecture tours in America have been of immense value in this respect. They have taken a number of people from this side of the Atlantic—myself among them—over a considerable part of the the American Continent, and enabled them to meet large numbers of American citizens of varying types.

These Americans have thus learned something of England; the lecturers have brought home with them a new and truer picture of America.

The lecture habit has not been developed in English as in American life, but there are great provincial cities in which, every winter, men and women of national reputation may be heard on the lecture platform.

It would be an excellent thing if the societies which arrange these matters would include American speakers in their programmes more frequently.

Private visits also play their part. Every year thousands of Americans come to this country. As yet we do not return these visits to a sufficient extent.

But increasing numbers of our people are learning the delights of travel, and its field widens every year.

I look forward to the day when British holidaymakers who now spend a fortnight or three weeks on the Continent will be able to visit America with equal ease.

I can conceive of nothing better calculated to remove prejudices.

The friendliness of Americans to the traveller from Britain, their unfailing kindliness, their generous hospitality, are something to marvel at. I am afraid that we do not always extend the same welcome to American visitors to our shores.

Yet, in spite of "British reserve," some of us manage to make friends. Ties are formed strong enough to defy time and distance. We cherish pleasant memories of American homes, and they of ours.

Such friendships make a notable contribution to the cause of Anglo-American understanding. It is in the homes, not the hotels, of a nation that we each can learn the truth about our people.

Here I might make an appeal to those British business men who have dealings with the United States.

When Americans call upon you over here, don't be content with purely business contacts. Ask them to your homes and your clubs, so that they may see something of the real England.

The social life of America is built mainly around business. When an Englishman crosses the Atlantic on a commercial mission, his business card opens to him a whole world of American social life. Let us respond in kind.

In these various ways the two great divisons of the English-speaking race may be drawn closer together.

Private contacts and friendships between individuals, by increasing the area of understanding and good will, pave the way for a closer understanding between the two nations and their Governments, with all that this would mean to the peace of the world.

IF WAR CAME TO BRITAIN

Britain and America both desire peace. God knows we have had enough of war!

And though we are both arming to-day, we are arming only for defence. We have all we want in territory. We seek no aggrandisement; we have no old scores to wipe out.

We know we have more to lose by war than any two human organisations that have ever existed.

We have learned that our security and honour are most surely to be found in reconciling and identifying our several national interests with the general interests of the world.

We believe that the prosperity of others makes for our prosperity; that their peace is our safety, that their progress smooths our path.

Ought we not, then, to take counsel with one another? Ought we not, when necessary, to be prepared to act together?

One great stumbling-block is the determination of the American people to keep clear of European entanglements and to many Americans Britain is primarily a European Power.

We cannot, indeed, cut ourselves adrift from Europe. But we are primarily not a European, but a World Power.

Our commerce is carried on all the oceans; great lands in every continent are proud to be parts of the British Empire.

That Empire, indeed, unites the Old World with the New. Its existence makes it difficult, if not impossible, for America to maintain a rigidly isolationist attitude.

In any great war of the future in which the British Empire was engaged is it conceivable that the mandatory embargo of the Neutrality Act would be, or could be, enforced against Canada?

And suppose that Canada were invaded or attacked, would there be no appeal to the spirit of the Monroe Doctrine?

Apart from any sentiment of friendship towards England, here are powerful forces which, in any such situation, would tend to modify American neutrality policy in favour of the British Empire.

IF WE UNITE IN SPIRIT

But need such a situation arise? If Britain and the United States were agreed to act together the risk would be slight.

These two great kindred Powers in collaboration could prevent— or at least localise and limit—almost any quarrel that might break out among men.

They could do this, almost certainly, without any resort to force themselves, by moral, economic, and financial power, provided that in reserve there were armaments of sufficient strength to ensure that moral, economic, and financial powers were not violently ruptured and suspended.

Collaboration of this kind does not imply any formal union of the English-speaking peoples. It is a union of spirit, not of forms, that we seek.

There need not even be an alliance.

All that is necessary is a willingness to consult together, an understanding that Britain and America shall pursue, side by side, their mutual good and the good of the whole world.

There would be nothing in such an understanding that need arouse fears elsewhere. Collaboration of the English-speaking peoples threatens no one. It might safeguard all.

Here, then, is the goal towards which we should work and the spirit in which we should pursue it.

And hopeful signs are not wanting.

In spite of all impediments, Britain and America have never been closer in aim and purpose than now, or nearer to full mutual understanding.

Our ways have diverged in the past. I believe that, increasingly, they will lie together in the future.

We shall certainly follow the path of our joint destiny more prosperously, and far more safely, if we treat it together like good companions.

※※※

INDEX